The Yankee Yorkshireman

STUDIES OF WORLD MIGRATIONS

Donna R. Gabaccia
and Leslie Page Moch, editors

*A list of books in the series
appears at the end of the book.*

Hedley Smith, c. 1974. Courtesy of Gordon Rowley, Duncan Smith, and Portia Thompson.

The Yankee Yorkshireman

Migration Lived and Imagined

MARY H. BLEWETT

UNIVERSITY OF ILLINOIS PRESS

Urbana and Chicago

Library of Congress Cataloging-in-Publication Data
Blewett, Mary H.
The Yankee Yorkshireman: migration lived and imagined /
Mary H. Blewett.
   p.   cm. — (Studies of world migrations)
"Hedley Smith's published and unpublished works": p.
Includes bibliographical references and index.
ISBN 978-0-252-03405-3 (cloth: alk. paper) —
ISBN 978-0-252-07613-8 (pbk.: alk. paper)
1. Smith, Hedley, 1909–1994. 2. Immigrants—Rhode Island—
Biography. 3. Emigration and immigration—Psychological
aspects. 4. Place (Philosophy) 5. Rhode Island—Biography.
6. Yorkshire (England)—Biography. 7. Authors, American—
20th century—Biography. 8. Woolen and worsted manufacture—
England—West Yorkshire—History. 9. Woolen and worsted
manufacture—New England—History. 10. Yorkshire
(England)—In literature.
I. Title.
CT275.S5434B54   2009
974.5′043092—dc22   [B] 2008038365

To Portia and Duncan,
the devoted children of Hedley Smith,
who enabled me to give their father
and his writing their place in history

Contents

Preface   xi

Introduction   1

1. A Region of Movement and Change, 1650–1923   17

2. Migrations of Capital, Industry, and People, 1891–1922   51

3. Working, Writing, Loving, Enduring, 1923–1994   97

4. Transatlantic Perspectives, Strong Women, and Sexual Politics in Fiction   126

   Conclusion: The Inner World of Emigration and Migration   153

   Notes   161

   Hedley Smith's Published and Unpublished Works   191

   Index   193

Preface

I have been, it seems, more familiar with the experience of migration than I had thought. As a resident since 1965 of Lowell, Massachusetts, a former cotton textile center that attracted thousands of immigrants, I am still a "blow-in": a newcomer. As a new Ph.D. from the Midwest where I was born and educated, I migrated to my first job in New England, not knowing if I would stay. I had a different accent and overly conservative politics but loved the industrial landscape and the mix of people. My ethnic background is Dutch on my maternal side: Dykemans and Drinkards who in family stories came down the Ohio River on flatboats to Missouri. They were poor farmers and railroad workers. My paternal family members were Protestant Scots Irish via Pennsylvania: Hedges and MacReynolds. They became prosperous farmers in Nebraska.

I was born in St. Louis, Missouri, in 1938 and lived in Omaha, Nebraska, from where my father worked as an expeditor of war production during World War II. In 1944 my family moved to Hoyne Avenue in South Chicago, an ethnically mixed but still all-white neighborhood. My parents did not feel at home there, and my father bought a house in the western suburbs as soon as possible. But I remember an exciting street crowded with houses, families, and many children into which I could easily disappear. Their games were new and wild: glorious, end-of-the-season, rotten tomato fights from the huge neighborhood Victory Garden. Another of my memories is of Irene in the first grade at Sutherland School. She was called a "D.P." or "Displaced Person" from Romania. At the age of six, I visited her family and was presented to her aged, black-gowned, invalid grandmother. Irene and I were quite different:

she, a thin child with olive skin, limpid brown eyes, an intense little face, and black hair, and I, a smiling and well-nourished little girl with blonde curls. She had seen something of the world; I knew three houses in the Midwest. I remember her and that neighborhood as my most exciting childhood place. New England in 1965 where I got my first academic job was emphatically not the suburban Midwest. No wonder I stayed.

I met and married in 1968 my second husband, Peter Blewett, a deeply reluctant emigrant from working-class East London who had arrived in New York in 1949 at the age of eleven. We worked in the same Department of History. Fifty years later in 1999, he became an American citizen. His mother, aunt, and uncle also emigrated and lived in Massachusetts. The attractions of New England, our academic jobs, and my scholarly interests held us in Lowell, but I still identify myself as a Midwesterner. I respond to people who describe themselves as such as if they were kin. Outside the United States, I am a New Englander and an American.

My husband, Peter, thinks of himself as an "immigrant," and I once had trouble understanding his "English" English. As I considered the issues involved in this book, I realized that the complex experience of emigration and my involvement with the culture and ambivalent emotions of English immigrant families is something I have come to understand well. There are two English immigrants of whom I have deep emotional knowledge: the dearest, my husband, and through him his uncle Dennis Vinsun. Their experiences as reluctant emigrants, involuntary exiles of the mid-twentieth century, confirm the feelings of Hedley Smith, the subject of this book.

Peter continued to travel on a green card and a British passport for fifty years. Julius Isaac's *British Postwar Migration* (Cambridge University Press, 1954) shows Peter as one of 23,400 emigrants from Great Britain in 1949 and Dennis Vinsun as one of 17,200 in 1950. As an outsider who married into the Vinsun family, I have felt the condescension of the English-born, whatever their class or experience. Dennis Vinsun's privately printed memoirs, "An Interrupted Life: From Boy to Man" (2001), expressed profound disappointment and bitterness upon his arrival from London in 1950 to join his two sisters. His military service owed to Great Britain was fulfilled as a draftee in the U.S. Marine Corps during the Korean War. There his bonds with his fellows Marines in a 155mm howitzer unit provided such intense comradeship under terrible fire in 1953 that he stayed in the United States. As one of the 398 survivors from his Marine draft of 3600, he signed his reminiscences "Sergeant Dennis Vinsun 1311107 United States Marine Corps, An Englishman." Arriving on the West Coast with his back pay, he considered a return to his homeland, but stayed on the East Coast. As a Korean War veteran, he quickly became an American citizen in 1954, but carried both passports. With the breakup of each of his two marriages, he considered for a time returning to London. But he half-joked to me in October 2006 at his Hyannis home that he thought about returning to England every day.

I have also migrated internally in my discipline. Finishing my dissertation in 1965 on the Roosevelt/Truman presidential transition in 1944–46, I left behind as I traveled east many of my sources and interests. My primary training in political history and foreign policy did not prepare me for the social upheavals of the 1960s or the protracted war in Vietnam. New England seems to offer a dazzling array of research possibilities. The industrial remains lay about me; the students I taught sprang from millworker families. Retraining myself in social and labor history, I specialized in New England light industry in the nineteenth and twentieth centuries. My shoe workers in *Men, Women and Work* (1988) and textile workers in cotton and woolen mills were both internal migrants and immigrants. One of my books, *The Last Generation* (1990), relied on oral histories of immigrant textile workers. Although I saw myself as a historian of gender and class, there was no escaping the multicultural nature of this early twentieth-century industrial workforce. My most recent book, *Constant Turmoil* (2000), on nineteenth-century Lancashire migrants and immigrants to the southeastern New England cotton textile industry, was my first real step into transatlantic connections. During the research I came across the published short stories of Hedley Smith. I found them fascinating. While I was researching and writing this book, I was also gathering data and dreaming about a book on the New England granite industry. Hedley Smith won.

Eleanor Guy of the North Scituate Public Library, R.I., provided information on the whereabouts of Hedley Smith's children. When I contacted them in 1996, Portia Smith Thompson and Duncan Smith, I found a goldmine. Both worked tirelessly alongside of me. With the skills of an archivist, Portia organized her father's papers. Duncan answered countless questions. They both inspired me to write this book, not only through their painstaking attention to my years of inquiries (thank heavens for email) but with an imaginative and generous willingness to reconsider their family situation. Portia repeatedly answered my call to search for "lost" items and to decipher her father's handwriting. Portia and Duncan insisted that their father knew that one day he would be famous and that I was the person to make him famous. It is a heavy responsibility. I trust I have not disappointed them. My greatest debt of thanks is to them. Portia is in turn indebted to the late Stanley Bradbury of Wilsden, Bradford, for the detailed genealogy of her Yorkshire ancestors.

So what did I have? A reconstructed life based on various documents and the memories of his two children. Those memories came from one taped oral interview in 1997 and hundreds of subsequent emails as I wrote the chapters. The emails that I received will be preserved in the Hedley Smith Collection at the University of Rhode Island at Kingston. But what about all those other emails sent between brother and sister, only one of which was inadvertently sent to me, probably discussing among many other things what to "tell her"? I only hope that they were printed out and saved, not deleted. They are prime documents on the historical process. There were clearly topics not to be discussed, as I found out to my embarrassment when I blundered and hurt feelings. I did not read all of Hedley Smith's fiction. Some of the handwritten manuscripts were not found or are not decipherable. I have chosen to analyze what I considered the best for this book. I suspect that one novella was kept from me. I just hope that the manuscript was not destroyed. Those texts that I read are now available to be analyzed from other viewpoints.

Many others helped in various ways in the bookmaking process. My thanks to Suzy Sinke for an initial boost and a decided push. Donna Gabaccia's support for interdisciplinary work captivated a social historian who had found some interesting evidence in literature and biography. As an editor, she has been the finest: amazingly responsive, helpful, patient, arranging for exceedingly helpful readers, and giving me all the time I needed to get it "right," by my own lights. My thanks also to editor Leslie Moch and for her very useful work on European migrations. For valuable suggestions, helpful comments, and general encouragement, I thank Joanna Bornat, Paul Buhle, John Cumbler, Joe Doyle, Wendy Gamber, Susan Hartmann, Pat Hudson, Angel Kolwek-Folland, Carolyn Merithew, Carol Morgan, Craig Phelan, Peter Stearns, Deborah Valenze, an unidentified but extremely insightful second reader, and first-reader Dirk Hoerder. Felicity Harrison of Leeds, Yorkshire, provided invaluable help both as a skilled researcher and as a keen and knowledgeable critic. Clare Sheridan of the American Textile History Museum was always helpful no matter how busy. At a very low point, with gentle calmness and energetic technical expertise, Janet Pohl dealt with the 1910 and 1920 census and put me back on the right path. The talents and delightful companionship of librarians Debby Friedman and Rose Paton cheered me on my way. The skills and good fellowship of Paul Coppens made mapmaking fun. Bruce Lepore did important photographic work with speed and ease. Steve Adlestein kept me in focus. Andy Gill helped to understand Hedley Smith's dilemmas. Therese Boyd provided superb copyediting.

And many thanks to Hedley Smith, whose tastes in literature led me to reread or to read for the first time the works of Thomas Hardy, Ivan Turgenev, Honoré Balzac, Patrick MacGill, Phyllis Bentley, and J. B. Priestley. For this empiricist, it was indeed a delight. I suspect that the writer of the Yankee Yorkshireman stories would have greatly enjoyed both Gish Jen's comic spirit in her depiction of the Chang family in *Typical American* (Plume, 1992) and her riffs on the "Chang-kees."

And a final thanks to my husband, Peter, who served as a walking dictionary, computer fixer, travel buddy, inspired cook, constant source of support and patience, and an eager critic of style, language, and concepts. I have learned more from him than I could ever acknowledge.

The Yankee Yorkshireman

Introduction

This is the story of an early twentieth-century English migrant who called himself "an involuntary exile at an early age," a "Yankee Yorkshireman," a transplant.[1] He wrote a short story about his parents titled "Uprooted." Hedley Smith (1909–94) became a naturalized American citizen who lived in a multicultural area of Rhode Island. He was a big man with a large build and well-developed legs as a result of his preference for walking everywhere. He had light hair, fair skin, blue eyes, and tapering fingers on well-shaped hands. As an accountant and business manager, Smith habitually wore white shirts, ties, and good worsted suits. He married a Yankee schoolteacher and enjoyed the life of a middle-class family man in late twentieth-century Rhode Island. They had two children and eight grandchildren. All were successful, and he was proud of them. Smith appeared to be an integrated, even "invisible," immigrant of English birth, but all this was armor for an alienated self.[2]

His outward behaviors and descriptions of himself and his family include all of the classic categories created by immigration historians: uprooted, transplanted, bicultural, and in some ways integrated.[3] But in his private world of feeling and emotion, his life was a misfortune, his marriage suffocating, and his talents and desires unfulfilled. Although he was outwardly cheerful and stoical as he became a Yorkshireman, his inner being was filled with grief and rage. He wished he had never left Yorkshire. Emigration was the transformatory moment of his life.

The private and emotional experiences composing individual identity, such as those of Hedley Smith, enrich the knowledge of ethnic life and provide a deeper understanding of the impact of emigration.[4] Emigration has been studied as process and state policy but also involves physical movement and states of mind and emotion that cannot be inferred from mobility or behavior.[5] Emigration can be a lifelong, incomplete project that need not involve a physical return to the homeland.

Hedley Smith's fiction attests to his long-term endurance of profound loss. As a self-identified alien, he returned to his homeland only through his writing. Smith appeared to be uprooted, but he remained rooted in another place. He chose not to belong.[6] Like the letter writers in Oscar Handlin's *The Uprooted,* Smith's sheets of typing paper for his manuscripts on fictional "Briardale" were "the symbol of the ties that continued to bind."[7] Letter writers ultimately become weary; Smith's literary endeavors strengthened as he matured. Using his imagination, he refused to become a "separated" man.[8] John Bodnar's sensitivity to the complexities of the immigration process provides an approximate definition for Hedley Smith. To paraphrase Bodnar's words: some immigrants just did not care about what was occurring around them in American society. Their decisions were incomplete or imprecise. They, as Smith did, valued other things not evident to those who look only at the obvious arguments and debates of their times.[9] The question is why?

Hedley Smith left rich sources on his life and on his creative imagination. His works include three privately published volumes: two collections of short stories, *The Yankee Yorkshireman* and *More Yankee Yorkshiremen,* and a short novel, *Yankee Yorkshirewomen.* He also wrote short stories for an additional collection, three novels for a "Briardale Trilogy," eight other unpublished novels, and six novellas, "all with a Yankee Yorkshire theme" or Rhode Island background.[10] In them, Smith fiercely defended Yorkshire culture against its dilution and disintegration by asserting its superiority to, its distance from, and its defiance of Yankee society.

When I interviewed Smith's adult children in 1997, Portia and Duncan proved eager to talk about their father and his work. This three-hour taped conversation was followed by a long trail of contacts and email between 2000 and 2007. They had carefully preserved and generously loaned originals and copies of Smith's correspondence with his friends, legal documents, family photographs, and everything that had survived of their father's writings, including his diary of a trip to the Isle of Man in 1922. Both had journeyed to Bradford, Yorkshire, where they visited old family connections and haunts. Convinced of his literary talents, they also understood much about family life and its dilemmas. I employed Felicity Harrison, Ph.D., of Leeds, Yorkshire, familiar with the area libraries, to undertake extensive research in the Bradford area.

Taking advantage of all these resources, using empirical data on Rhode Island and on Bradford, Yorkshire, and focusing on the background and emigration of Hedley Smith, his brother, and his parents is a venture in microhistory.[11] Classic studies in social history in the qualitative sense can explore ordinary lives "from the bottom up" only if one is lucky enough to find the rare rich trove of evidence. Once located, these surviving treasures exercise their own fascinating grip on the researcher. They spoke to me in special ways (see Preface). While the analysis of social networks gives meaning to empirical data, the personal information on the Smith family and the fiction reveal a highly textured tale of individual experiences so valued by historians to test social network theory.[12]

All microhistory has of necessity a framework or a metanarrative. Mine, simply put, is Dirk Hoerder's *Cultures in Contact*.[13] That multilayered, sweeping work on global migration seemed almost paralyzing at first, but on subsequent readings of the introduction and relevant chapters, it issues a seductive call to contribute. Hoerder, for example, argues that the twentieth century was one of refugees. But migrants from traditional countries of origin continued their journeys to the United States and other destinations. Among them were English immigrants like the Smith family who came to Boston in 1923. And Hedley Smith offers rare evidence on the intensity of his individual responses to that migration.

The nature of the material on Smith and his fiction provides examples for Hoerder's holistic material-emotional approach to understanding migration.[14] This approach includes the elusive memories, words, and images about feelings, intimate relationships, and aspirations of individuals. Smith's own experiences and his fictional treatment of three generations of Yorkshire migrants and the dynamics of their family lives illuminate Hoerder's "non-measureable emotional and spiritual factors."[15] Hoerder argued for a three-level analysis for global migration: first, an exploration of the macrolevel of transoceanic migration streams and economic patterns, and second, an analysis of the mesolevel, defined as segmented labor markets in the culture of origin and consideration of the impact of family economies and networks on the timing of departure. Both are essential to understand the complex factors surrounding the lives of migrants.[16] This study includes macrolevel and mesolevel of structure and context and also provides a detailed third level of microanalysis of the individual, familial, and generational experiences of migration and its imaginative expression in fiction.

Transnational/Translocal

Ongoing interest among historians in the centrality of assimilation or of cultural distinctiveness and transnationalism to the experience of migration is intense. Many of these exchanges have focused on the "new immigration" at the turn of the twentieth century and concern the shifting interrelations of immigration/migration, race, ethnicity, class, and gender.[17] Donna Gabaccia advocated a transnational perspective to end the "tyranny" of the national in the immigration paradigm. Others find the transregional less dependent on nation-state definitions and truer to cultural distinctions. In contrast with the more intense, urgent, and active involvement of the contemporary transnational migrant, other historians view translocal behaviors and attitudes as moderate, periodic, limited, and casual contacts with the homelands. The translocal appears to be a place along the road to assimilation but can also contain less visible long-term longings, great heartache, and openly expressed, deep-felt emotional ties to the homeland.[18]

Loretta Baldassar's *Visits Home* suggested that the translocal is less an occasion for measurable activity and more an appropriate description of the deeply emotional connective identities and geographies between migrants from their villages in Italy and their residential neighborhoods in Perth, Australia.[19] Baldassar wrote about the expressions of "agony of distance, the painful longing for home—like unresolved grief" among Italian migrants in mid-twentieth-century Australia. The translocal in this sense carries a heavy weight of memory, imagery, sensory experiences, and imagination. As in the case of Hedley Smith's fiction, the geographic locale becomes important in defining personal recollection and recognition and conveying homeland culture. Another contribution of Hedley Smith's distinct experience and his fiction is to strengthen the translocal as an analytic frame for cultural contact and family ties.

Hedley Smith's sense of loss and anger was hardly unique, and his outpouring of literary production suggests an intense intellectual activity that might be labeled transnational.[20] But in a geographic sense, even the category of the transregional, in this case southeastern New England or even the tiny state of Rhode Island, is too wide to apply to Smith's scenarios of life and prose. His locale of fictional "Briardale" is more like Baldassar's villages in northern Italy. In Yorkshire, the city of Bradford plus its surrounding towns, villages, and moors was only one industrial center in the West Riding. This textile center provided a translocal match with the city of Providence, the mill villages in the town of North Providence, and the adjacent towns circling Providence. These locales did not represent all of Hedley Smith's lived experience in New England, but they did constitute the major landscape of his imagination.[21]

Transnational and transregional comparisons provide other ways to step outside the category of the nation.[22] Jose Moya offered his 1998 study, *Cousins and Strangers,* of Spanish immigrants between 1850 and 1930 to the Iberian postcolonial culture of Buenos Aires, Argentina, as a comparative model for English immigrants to the United States. Both immigrant groups encountered dual problems of identity and integration. Spanish immigrants largely from small villages and nonindustrial towns confronted a mixed ethnic population in Buenos Aires from other European nations. Among them were some skilled Spanish workers from industrial Mataró comparable, he argued, to skilled textile workers from the English Midlands to the United States.[23] Moya found the global/local approach most revealing for identifying patterns of emigration in nineteenth- and twentieth-century world migration. The nation-state, Moya concluded, offers the best arena to analyze policy but not the "actual process of emigration and immigration."[24]

Matthew Frye Jacobson identifies the corporation as one primary transnational player to be pursued by migration historians, while calling for more analysis of "trans" and less of "nation."[25] Indeed in 1903 the worsted manufacturer Joseph Benn Ltd. of Great Horton, Bradford, Yorkshire, established a branch operation in North Providence, Rhode Island, which provided the mill village setting and attracted the Yorkshire people who later became the characters in Hedley Smith's fiction. The Rhode Island worsted industry was an integral part of Frank Thistlewaite's Atlantic economy of European investment and labor migration, more culturally complicated than many European worsted centers.[26]

Marcel van der Linden advocated a transnational perspective to reshape American labor history.[27] Placing Smith's life and fiction in the empirical context of early twentieth-century Rhode Island's labor struggles by textile workers provides new evidence on working-class Yorkshire migrants. Refused customary standards and work rules, they adopted a multiethnic or transcultural labor politics, even as they cherished and defended their homeland culture and transnational traditions of labor protest. Probing the connections between ethnic loyalties and multicultural class coalitions can also deepen an understanding of the relationship between transregional culture and transcultural class action.

Recent debates over the divided categories of migration history suggest that refugees and migrants, the economically coerced and voluntary labor, differed little in their actual journeys.[28] But members of such families experienced migration differently. Degrees of opportunity or freedom of action among siblings vary. Hedley's brother Sam, who found a promising apprenticeship, felt differently about the family's emigration than Hedley, who lost his chance to finish high school. Furthermore, the state could intervene to cancel the offer of well-paid, skilled work for men like Hedley's father, Ernest

Smith, and ruin their prospects and those of their families. Comparative work on migrations "then" and "now" rarely offer material on immigration from Western and Northern Europe, but supposedly privileged groups, such as English emigrants, did not always benefit from expected advantages.

The past history of migrants, including this study, which examines multicultural labor protest in early twentieth-century Rhode Island and Massachusetts, can inform new research on late twentieth- and early twenty-first-century migration. Human capital, a main ingredient in contemporary assimilation theory, needs to be balanced by past experience. Human capital possessed by Smith's family, such as educational aspiration, mechanical training, and skilled hands that wove fine worsteds and fashioned specialty brushes, can be rejected or blocked by industrial change, misfortune, and the state even to the most privileged immigrants. Yorkshireman Hedley Smith would have been astonished to find himself in agreement with Carlos Morales's dislike of America, its customs, and its climate. Morales, a man who had also emigrated in the 1920s from Mexico, fervently wished to take his son home.[29] Movement has unforeseen perils for groups from all nations.

Hedley Smith's fictional world captures a late nineteenth- and early twentieth-century forced migration of mill "fowk" from Yorkshire industrial centers based on specific economic circumstances.[30] Sociologist Robin Cohen redefined the classic catastrophic/racial diaspora to include contemporary movements of peoples prompted by trade, imperial, labor, and cultural considerations. Although his work focuses on immigration during the 1990s, he explicitly questions whether the nation-state was ever historically able to contain "the wider socialities" it sought to represent. For Cohen, diaspora includes those "whose movements are primarily dictated by circumstances in their home countries rather than a desire to establish a new life" and "by an acceptance of an inescapable link with their past migration history and a sense of co-ethnicity with others of a similar background." The old country" becomes a "notion often buried deep in language, religion, custom or folklore."[31] Cohen's analysis applies to the culture of the labor migration of Yorkshire people as portrayed in Smith's tales. Increasingly diaspora is being applied to contemporary forced labor migrations and debated as similar to past migrations.

The English as Visible Migrants

Historians know much about seventeenth- and eighteenth-century English immigrants and their cultural impact on the colonies before and after the

American Revolution.[32] Smith's assertions about early twentieth-century Yorkshire migrants contradict much existing scholarship, notably by Charlotte Erickson on the relatively "invisible" assimilation of English immigrants into American society. Rowland T. Berthoff explored a wide range of skilled English industrial and craft workers who contributed to the nineteenth- and early twentieth-century American economic development and formed conservative trade unions.[33] Berthoff did not, however, analyze any particular industry in depth. Based on the work of Erickson and Berthoff, English immigrants have become defined as a culturally invisible and predominately conservative people who adjusted easily to American society.[34]

Alejandro Portes and Rubén Rumbaut reiterated the invisible English immigrant view in *Immigrant American: A Portrait* by classifying "British" emigration and labor as "apolitical," driven by economic concerns and uninvolved in changing either the homeland or the American political system.[35]

William Van Vugt recently confirmed the view of invisibility in his summary of British (English, Welsh, Scots, Scotch-Irish) immigrants in a 1999 survey of the multicultural heritage of the United States. His images of an enterprising, educated English people, primarily from the North Country and the Thames Valley who shaped the American economic system and set the cultural "tone," ignore class friction or aloof disdain for Yankee ways. Apparently these invisible immigrants felt no need for ethnic organizations.[36]

Celebrations of late twentieth-century ethnic groups by Rhode Island's Heritage Commission treat the English as invisible.[37] Still, Paul Spickard's *Almost All Aliens* in 2007 declared late nineteenth-century "British" immigrants as both slighted and erased: awaiting their historian.[38]

This concept of invisibility remains the major view of English immigrants within much ethnic literature, but this stereotype is changing.[39] In David Gerber's study of nineteenth-century British immigrant correspondents, four letter-writers defined their lives and personalities vividly. Two of them, including Mary Ann Wodrow Archbald, wished they had never emigrated from their homelands. British immigrants, Gerber argued, possessed group consciousness, "what has come to be called *ethnicity*," and, as "trenchant critics," distanced themselves by calling all Americans "Yankees."[40] Certainly the experiences of the strike-prone, union-building Lancashire-born cotton textile workers of nineteenth-century New England, many of whom were literate and articulate with class-based political agendas, and of Scottish and Welsh coal miners among many other working-class British immigrants indicate a highly visible, annoying presence in many industrial centers.[41] R. W. Widdis studied the migration of early twentieth-century English Canadians across the U.S. border to small and large cities in northern New York State and explored their resistance to assimilation. Despite a common language, as Canadians they brought with them different conceptions of politics, of their cultural heritage, and of economic values than their American neighbors. They did not become American citizens, married within their own community, and in smaller communities remained in unskilled and semi-skilled positions. Widdis described them as "new immigrants" who definitely made "ripples."[42] Throughout Canada, English-accented immigrants were at the least an "audible" minority.[43]

Yorkshire migrants in the culturally rich stories set in fictional "Briardale" also did not seek a new life, having been forcibly dispersed by regional economic change. Rather, they maintained Robin Cohen's "inescapable link" with their cultural past and possessed "a sense of co-ethnicity" with others. Smith makes them memorably visible and treats them as migrants, not immigrants. Immigrants came to destinations with the clearly expressed intention of remaining. In Briardale, most wished to return when the time was right. Or they went on to other parts of the British Empire as "overseas settlers," following other migrants who had preceded them.[44] The self-styled "Yankee Yorkshireman," Hedley Smith based his privately published and unpublished fiction on personal observations made and stories overheard in Bradford, Yorkshire, and North Providence.[45] Smith's short stories and novellas about a fictional "Briardale" depict a tightly knit mill village between 1890 and 1930. Scorned for their aloof distinctiveness by the dominant Yankee culture, the characters in Smith's fiction demonstrate the resilient imprint of the culture, language, and politics of Yorkshire life in Rhode Island textile villages. In fact, Rhode Islanders coined a special ethnic insult for Yorkshire working-class folk: "jickey," meaning dialect-speaking, uneducated vulgarians (see chap. 2). The hostility was mutual.

Donna Gabaccia called for new perspectives on the sexuality of female migrants and agreed with Dirk Hoerder that the concept of kin has been idealized by ethnic historians to the exclusion of "massive friction and conflict."[46] *Family Connections,* Judith E. Smith's 1985 study of Italian and Jewish immigrants living in Providence, Rhode Island, in the early twentieth century, provides a partial comparative perspective for Yorkshire immigrants, using empirical evidence on the family.[47] Hedley Smith's Yorkshire relatives, in-laws, and fictional folk include both connected families and *dis*connected families. Family dynamics, culture clashes, the flourishing of Yorkshire dialect, values, social customs, and a persisting interest in transatlantic politics shaped society and culture in Smith's fictional Briardale. In addition, Smith's fiction creates opportunities to explore the gendered meanings of manhood and womanhood as a historic and social relationship in terms of sexuality and physicality, family and work roles, and the patterns of village life.[48]

Outwardly, this Yankee Yorkshireman Hedley Smith lived and worked in a multicultural society. Privately, he immersed himself in nineteenth-century literature, cultivated Yorkshire habits, and from childhood wrote intensively. When he retired in 1971 at age sixty-two to concentrate on his Briardale fiction, Smith bitterly lamented the physical ruin of the "Briardale" villages and regarded late twentieth-century real estate development in northern Rhode Island as creating an "unlovely urban pustule," obliterating Yorkshire "ways of living and thinking . . . to which emigrant textile workers" had held fast for so long in a "new and alien country."[49] Smith's literary and personal expressions of Yorkshire disdain and superiority displace American society in his lifelong project.

For Hedley Smith, "Briardale" people conducted no dialectic of accommodation and resistance with American culture, only a fundamental affirmation of Yorkshire life. The first generation of Yorkshire migrants to North Providence in the 1890s—whether middle class or working class—never thought of themselves as ethnic Americans. Smith recalled in a 1973 interview that

> [m]any of the English, I am afraid, came with a chip on their shoulder. . . . "Here am I,—a skilled tradesman with great knowledge and ability, but through no fault of my own but through the workings of damned politicians, I am being robbed of my liv[e]lihood. I am coming here to get even. . . ." They were the last of the ethnic groups to assimilate and merge in with the mainstream of American culture. Perhaps it was a reflection of their indoctrination in Kiplingesque Empire . . . [,] but they didn't look upon themselves as aliens privileged to have a new start in a new country. They looked upon themselves as people who knew more than the people they were coming among.[50]

For Smith, Yorkshire identity was a historical and cultural heritage interrupted by economic necessity, neither socially constructed nor contested.[51] But as Gerber argued, English migrants had a sense of ethnicity, and so did Hedley Smith, despite his denials. He struggled throughout his life and in his writings to remain distinct from New England society. Such is the classic dilemma of ethnicity.

Rudolph J. Vecoli pointed out a neglect of language, religion, and social class in understanding ethnic culture and "ethnicity," which he defined as an empirically *lived* as well as *imagined* culture.[52] His words inspired part of this book's title. Smith's fiction blurs the edges between the lived experiences in

Bradford and North Providence and the imagined world of Briardale. As a writer, Smith recreated a distinct culture—nondominant but resistant—that he ardently wished to preserve.

The uses of literature and autobiographies to explore and specify the diverse, distinctive experiences of immigrants are staples in textbooks on ethnic studies.[53] In this literature, however, it is hard to find any experiences of late nineteenth- and early twentieth-century English immigrants, largely I suspect because of that persistent notion of invisibility. The Yankee Yorkshireman's stories and novellas offer to fill this gap. Aside from his own experiences, Smith insisted that his stories represented a composite portrait of many similar immigrants living and working in various Rhode Island mill villages. Indeed, so familiar were the situations, dilemmas, and expressions in Smith's work based on the North Providence mill villages that Yorkshire-born readers of his stories in other Rhode Island towns, such as Cranston and Pontiac, south of Providence, and Westerly at the southwestern edge of Rhode Island, believed that he had written specifically about their own mill villages.[54] Beyond that he made no claims.

As a writer Smith regarded himself as a traditionalist, even a "sentimentalist," in the best sense, in portraying Yorkshire values and culture as stubbornly refusing assimilation. Yet, his own life and the titles of his short-story collections suggest a man caught between the two cultures of the West Riding and Rhode Island. Fictional Briardale and its people lived in a cultural isolation that he could not. He never found the opportunity or the money to return to Yorkshire. The absence of a visit home, in the context of Loretta Baldassar's analysis, implies a further refusal by Smith to reconcile with the act of emigration.[55] He remained a lifelong involuntary exile. After his death, his children returned his ashes to the places and the moors around Bradford that he had loved as a child.

The Yankee Yorkshireman and Assimilation Theory

Where can Hedley Smith find a place in immigration and ethnic historiography? In a 2003 critique of assimilation theory, Richard Alba and Victor Nee examine Milton Gordon's 1964 model of assimilation in American life, rejecting his requirement that ethnic and racial groups "unlearn" their culture and wholly adopt the "majority culture." Gordon defined this English-derived host culture as having an "Anglo Saxon core," unchanged from the colonial era. Hegemonic and superior with a Western European cultural basis, it was characterized by whiteness, Protestant religion, and middle-class values.[56]

According to Alba and Nee, the "final fatal flaw" of this "canonical" theory is the failure to grant any ethnic or racial group a contribution to the culture in which that group lives. Their own model of assimilation includes contributions by ethnic and racial groups to the mainstream culture and sustaining, advantageous cultures of their own.[57] Smith's fiction and the oppositional cultures of nineteenth- and twentieth-century Lancashire and Yorkshire working-class immigrants and migrants support their conclusions.

But there was a *first* fatal flaw in the old assimilation model: the concept of a vague, ahistorical, static mainstream culture with an "Anglo Saxon" core. My research on Lancashire and Yorkshire working-class immigrants and migrants draws my attention to this issue. In much of the current assimilation literature either the "Anglo" or the "Anglo-Saxon" label is used or rejected outright but rarely critiqued. The simplistic ideological assumptions about "Anglo-Saxon roots" linger.

The use of a static Anglo-Saxon core does not reflect the changing nature of nineteenth- and twentieth-century English culture and regional identities. Moreover, one of David Fischer's main points in *Albion's Seed* was that British cultural heritage even in the seventeenth and eighteenth centuries was deeply divided by region over concepts of religion, social rank, historic generation, and imperial politics and was also in conflict with other colonial cultures. In one of Hedley Smith's novels, "Sinners Corner: A Romance of King's Province," he creates a seventeenth-century Rhode Island colonial village founded by Yorkshire immigrants speaking in dialect who had been farmers and clothiers in Clayton, West Riding, Yorkshire. David Fischer would expect emigrants from the seventeenth-century West Riding to arrive as Quakers in Delaware. Only a few from East Yorkshire settled in Massachusetts. Indeed, Hedley Smith's Yorkshire settlement in colonial Rhode Island sits uneasily in a Puritan-dominated New England. They are in rebellion in 1688 against the royal governor Sir Edmund Andros in Boston appointed by James II to rule the dominion of New England. By Hedley Smith's lights, the "Anglo Saxon" contribution to the American mainstream contained a regional Yorkshire component to add historic complexity to its supposedly homogeneous character.[58] This novel is Smith's singular expression of anti-English colonial patriotism.

Historians and sociologists agree that the upheavals of the 1960s shook the established social order and destroyed the old Anglo-American prototype mainstream core culture. But what was destroyed? Did it exist as a cultural hegemony and if so when and where? Rudolph Vecoli vigorously ridiculed the concept, but before such an entrenched idea can be discarded, it needs historicizing.[59] How did Hedley Smith and other "Anglo-Saxon" migrants view this "Anglo-American mainstream" core culture to which they were supposed to assimilate? English workers in the nineteenth- and twentieth-century cotton and worsted centers of Fall River, New Bedford, Lawrence, and the many mill villages of Rhode Island saw the American mainstream culture as dominated by New England Yankee industrial capitalists, merchants, and landlords. These working-class immigrants/migrants rejected the workings of the industrial system in the United States as corruptly defective and the political system untrue to the proclaimed ideals of America.[60]

Smith's experience was admittedly of southeastern New England with its own history and peculiarities. But even the middle-class English and Scots immigrants in early nineteenth-century Buffalo, New York, according to David Gerber, turned their local ethnic societies, organized around celebrations of St. George and St. Andrew, into uproarious expressions of transnational political and emotional loyalties at variance with local Yankee culture, sometimes colliding in the process.[61] There seemed to be no dominant Anglo-Saxon core culture in Buffalo. The concept of mainstream culture needs to be specified and historically grounded for nineteenth- and twentieth-century immigrants and for contemporary migrants, as sketched out in the coauthored 1990 essay, "The Invention of Ethnicity: A Perspective from the USA."[62]

What elements of American economic development had created the twentieth-century middle-class out of that nineteenth-century industrialized society? There is no better champion of this approach than John Bodnar in *The Transplanted* or a more precise definition of the American mainstream than his: the single-minded culture of power, wealth, and personal gain associated with the middle class.[63] Oscar Handlin's *Boston's Immigrants, 1790–1880* provides an excellent example of historical grounding of Boston's mainstream culture in the early nineteenth century. The first chapter is a comprehensive and rigorous analysis of the complex economic changes that constructed the context of wealth and power in the city before the arrival of Irish immigrants. Brahmin Boston as a social and cultural order was built on a foundation of canny economic investments in industries outside of the city. But Boston is hardly mainstream America. Neither is Providence, its industrialists, engineers, and investors, and its Yankee aristocracy, among whom are the *Anglo-phobic* relatives with whom Smith's Yorkshire characters contend in his novel "The Lion and the Eagle" (see chap. 4).

The continued use of the terms "British roots" and "Anglo-Americans" suggests that the memory of that Anglo-Saxon heritage *survives*. The collectively authored "Invention of Ethnicity" decisively shrugs off the Anglo-Saxon, but accepts the English immigrant as "invisible." As a group, the authors insist on collective, interactive behavior and group negotiation between immigrant groups and the dominant "ethnoculture" to define a distinctively American culture. Hedley Smith as an individual writer of stories on Briardale will, I suppose, face dismissal.[64] Still, his transatlantic stories both reject American society with his disdain for phony "Anglo-Saxon" or American mainstream values and pointedly ignore American identity as inapplicable to many migrants. Eric Hobsbawn's insights into the invention of tradition and Benedict Anderson's *Imagined Communities* suggest that the formation of modern nations who in Hobsbawn's words "generally claim to be the opposite of novel, namely rooted in the remotest antiquity, and the opposite of constructed, namely human communities so 'natural' as to require no definition other than self-assertion."[65] Perhaps this provides a plausible explanation for those tenacious "Anglo-Saxon" roots.

Yet some insist that the English immigrants must be different. Elliott Barkan's 1995 model of the process toward assimilation is dynamic, flexible, and inclusive with multiple alternative outcomes.[66] Refusal and isolation, however, is not an imaginable choice. Furthermore, immigrants, such as the English and English Canadians (especially the more urban, educated, and professional trained), are seen as rapidly proceeding, in some cases leaping over stages, toward accommodation and assimilation, presumably without any distaste for American culture. Reflecting policy debates on immigration, Elliott Barkan included in his 2006 model the term "incorporation" as a flexible process, which can involve various levels of transnational contacts and can be influenced by international crises or upheaval in the homelands.[67]

Can these models contain the Smiths: an immigrant family from a traditionally privileged group with long-term urban/industrial experience and human capital who met with downward social and economic mobility and collapsed expectations? Can it contain an underage member of that family who rejected the emigration although he was made a citizen along with his family? That young man's personal response involved emotional, literary, and imaginative rejection of New England/American society. His literature expressed disdain for the American mainstream culture as falling short of what was deeply valued in his homeland. Can it also include his American-born children who were assimilated yet became devoted to the homeland culture? If Hedley Smith could have voted with his "heart" as Barkan put it, he would have been back with his friends in Bradford.[68] As he never made it back, must he be classified as an integrated immigrant? Models need to become even more flexible to include the Hedley Smiths.

Yet in some important ways, the English immigrant is different. Thirty-four relatively privileged "English" residents of the American Northeast in 1995 talked to sociologist Katharine Jones, who probed how their identities were socially constructed and contested in an Anglophilic society. The structure of her study suggested that by the late twentieth century regional cultures no longer influenced identity for most English people. Only one of the interviewees objected, insisting that his regional identity as a Yorkshireman and his political identity as a Marxist far outweighed his Englishness.[69] The focus of Jones's questions remained the nation, whether defined as England or in some cases "British," one of the most discussed issues along with the use and quality of accent. Still, Jones explored a major theme that all these late twentieth-century English migrants could agree upon: the sense of English cultural and national superiority to American values and practices.[70] So could Hedley Smith.

Refusing to Settle-In

Migration historians, more interested in the context, direction, and consequences of movement, replace integration with settling-in, a process of insertion into the host/receiving society. This process involves community building and identity formation for groups and individuals over time. Adaptation, the shedding of old country habits or the creation of cushioning enclaves, marks the insertion process.[71] The example of Hedley Smith demonstrates that the process of insertion can be refused, and that throughout a lifetime old habits and values can be cherished as decidedly superior. As a mature man he fought changes to his identity through silence, stubbornness, and his fiction. Whatever the residents of Greystone village in North Providence, Rhode Island, actually felt about their lives, we know what the Briardale characters and Hedley Smith felt.

Immigrant and migrant textile workers to Greystone in the early twentieth century remained culturally rooted in Yorkshire and on the move among New England mill towns. They left fish-and-chip shops all over the area. Some became internal migrants, most to other worsted centers. The process of settling-in was more protracted. If they departed the United States, they probably either returned to Yorkshire or went on to other locations within the British Empire. They had become Yankee Yorkshire im/migrants: a New England ethnic group defined by where they worked and their connections with their homeland region.

Karen Majewski and Werner Sollors argue that ethnicity as invented is "the foe" of assimilation and that literature can actively contribute to shaping community and identity.[72] The Yorkshire people he knew and imagined, Smith insisted, did not think of themselves as ethnic Americans. They were, he stated, the last of the ethnic groups to assimilate and merge with the mainstream of American culture.[73] Perhaps Smith had read a book or two about ethnicity. Yet those first-generation immigrants who left Greystone, Rhode Island, but stayed in New England must have integrated and assimilated to some degree or other. Those who ended up as American citizens in the worsted trades of Sanford, Maine; Smithfield, Rhode Island; and Philadelphia, Pennsylvania, found other Yorkshire people to associate with. Those who left textile work behind, such as weavers who became motormen or warpers who ran country stores, might lose contact with Yorkshire-born people. In their new work, they would find their identities changed and perhaps contested. Their stories are unknown to me.

Stubborn and pervasive resistance to acculturation and settling-in, an abiding transatlantic perspective, and a fierce loyalty to a Yorkshire cultural identity defined life in fictional Briardale. The Great War in 1914 shifted their loyalties to a form of "Englishness." This shift to a larger sense of nationalism was shared by other migrant groups.[74] Many young men from North Providence mill villages and from fictional Briardale returned to England to serve and die in World War I, while those who stayed behind added outbursts of patriotism to their energetic material support. In the 1920s, when times got hard in New England textiles, the skilled worsted workers of Briardale returned to Yorkshire with their savings. Widows took their children home to Yorkshire, while other migrants relocated to New Zealand or English Canada. Thus many of these Yorkshire people resemble "new immigrants," forced to relocate abroad and determined to return with their earnings to their homeland.[75]

Here then in Hedley Smith's life and his imagination are English immigrants and migrants: some as naturalized citizens out of cynical convenience, not any sort of commitment. They came from a region used to both internal and external migrations into their developing urban/industrial economy. As such, they were seasoned city people, used to factory routines or artisan work cultures. Capitalism had entered their world long ago, unlike many of the immigrants in John Bodnar's *The Transplanted*.[76] As a first generation, they were culturally rooted elsewhere, not uprooted. Not transplants but—to follow the botanical metaphors—living potted in their own soil or as bulbs and seeds ready to grow when transported back to the homeland or on to other places within the British Empire. Jon Gjerde, the master of botanical metaphors, encourages new shoots from the old vines of immigration and ethnic history.[77] Hedley Smith was also something of a gardener. Gjerde values contingency and historic context and relishes irony and paradox in historical change. The transatlantic perspective of Smith's fiction, the decentering of national boundaries for his beloved Yorkshire, and the thorny brambles in and around the little village of Briardale fit this agenda of new growth.

Exploring the World of Hedley Smith

The interconnections between Hedley Smith's ancestors, relatives, and immediate family and the industrialization of the worsted industry in the West Riding of Yorkshire, 1650–1923, are closely intertwined and are explored in chapter 1. Next examined is the historic movement of capital investment in the worsted industry from Germany, France, Belgian, and Yorkshire to the American Northeast beginning in the 1890s, which connected Rhode Island cities and towns more firmly to the Atlantic economy. Complex multicultural interactions in this new industry transformed social life and labor politics, reaching into the smallest New England mill villages. In 1923 the Smiths immigrated to Boston and ended up in a mill village near Providence, Rhode Island, hoping to find work in the New England worsted industry. Hedley, at thirteen, seemed almost immediately to face a dismal future in an industrially declining region and refused to accept the emigration. He struggled throughout his long life (1923–1994), explored in chapter 3, to find meaningful work while he continued to write, married, and raised his family. He wrote even more intensely after his retirement in 1971, which proved to be his most productive years. The best of the Briardale fiction analyzed in depth in chapter 4 expressed his hopes and illusions about the persistence and preservation of the values of his homeland culture in a new society. This book seeks to probe the meanings of his life course as a self-conceived migrant and his fiction as a window into the inner alienations of the emigrant.

1

A Region of Movement and Change, 1650–1923

The old provincial capital of York with its huge Minster—a cathedral second only to Canterbury—its prosperous markets, and its situation on the River Ouse, which flowed eastward to the seaport of Hull, dominated Yorkshire and the whole North of England in the sixteenth and seventeenth centuries. But growth and change in eighteenth-century London and in rising "new towns," such as the worsted textile city of Norwich in East Anglia, left other provincial areas stalled economically and politically. These new towns included the woolen centers of the West Riding of Yorkshire that drew internal migrants to expanding employment.[1] Cloth sellers called "clothiers" depended on the clip from local sheep grazing on the Yorkshire moors and abundant waterpower from the "becks" or streams to market coarse woven cloth from Hull.

Eighteenth-century Yorkshire towns began to challenge Norwich in the making of worsted cloth. Worsted yarns made with a tighter twist produced cloth with a finer, flatter surface preferred for men's wear. By the early nineteenth century, the mills of the West Riding dominated English worsted production. The forebears of Hedley Smith lived, married, and died in the villages and towns surrounding Bradford Parish in West Yorkshire during these centuries of economic and social change. When Hedley Smith's parents immigrated to the United States in 1923 with their two sons, Yorkshire's history, dialect, and culture came with them.

Beginnings of Yorkshire Worsted Industrialization

Mobility and migration usually associated with nineteenth-century industrialization preceded industrial growth in Yorkshire, as was the case in many other areas of Western Europe.[2] Preindustrial migration, often temporary and seasonal, moved rural families short distances. But in some agricultural parishes, such as Methley, West Yorkshire, which became increasingly attached economically to the nearby woolen city of Leeds, such rural mobility declined from 1550 and 1812.[3] Even local movements of people disrupted village life. Between 1650 and 1820, migrants into one large rural parish in West Yorkshire faced hostility from local residents, who did not easily accept outsiders into their small communities. Migration also rose and fell in tune with minor economic changes. Two isolated nineteenth-century rural towns in the Yorkshire hills, Wensleydale and Swaledale, contained three economic sub-areas of lead mining, diverse mining and agriculture, and pastoral farming. Patterns of labor migration in the Yorkshire dales, especially over short distances to other localities, vibrated with the separate fortunes of each of these sublocal economies.[4]

By the early nineteenth century, Yorkshire contained three major areas of productive activity: worsted and woolen manufacture in the western half of West Yorkshire or the West Riding, coal mining in the south, and commercial agriculture and fishing in the East and North Ridings. Each had differing expressions of the local dialect and distinctive cultures. Early industrialization appeared to strengthen regional identities and interests at the expense of national popular and political movements.[5] Regional sources of capital for West Riding industrialization between 1750 and 1850 came from mortgages on land and in capital raised from farming, the rural putting-out system, and wool selling rather than from urban merchants.[6] Important advances in wool-spinning technology run by water power, in addition to easy access to coal to run more dependable steam engines, helped shift the center of worsted production by 1850 from the flatlands of Norwich to hilly Yorkshire. In 1910 economic historian J. H. Clapham categorized this change as "probably the classic case of industrial migration in English history."[7]

The worsted town of Bradford, with only one sizable beck or stream for waterpower, depended on local sources of coal for its steam engines, while the nearby textile towns of Halifax, Keighley, Leeds, and Huddersfield relied on abundant waterpower, delaying the technical transfer to steam and the necessity of buying coal from south Yorkshire mines (see map 1). These coalmines, stretching from Leeds southward to Nottingham, became the largest developed in England. Migrants from the Midlands, Nottinghamshire, and Derbyshire worked in the deep pits. Although many were internal migrants, they joined streams of other migrants from across the Irish Sea, and from Germany. Together they represented part of the "proletarian mass migration" within the nineteenth-century Atlantic economies. The fleeces necessary for the tightly twisted worsted yarn had to be obtained from long-haired Lincoln sheep raised in the Cotswolds, Kent, and Leicestershire in southern England or imported from Australia.[8]

The demands created by industrial change in West Yorkshire altered both distant and local agrarian economies. Rural East Yorkshire farmers provided beef, milk, and other foodstuffs for the developing textile cities and towns of the West Riding. Yorkshire novelist Phyllis Bentley described the scene.

> The West Riding links of this [Pennine hill] chain were part white limestone, part hard dark millstone grit, coated with peat, fringed with coal, pocketed to the south with iron ore. . . . Millstone grit . . . cannot grow rich grass or deep abundant grain. But coal and grit country are rich in springs and streams. . . . These . . . are the cause of the textile trade. Wool and soft water; coal and iron . . . no good living to be had by farming alone.[9]

Map 1. Nineteenth-century Yorkshire and principal cities. Courtesy of Paul Coppens.

With the construction of local canals, which created a system of commercial waterways, and the introduction of railroads, Bradford grew from 13,000 in 1800 to 100,000 inhabitants in 1850 and became the driving force in the economic activity of the West Riding.

"Worstedopolis" Creates Change and Conflict

Spinning firms organized in the 1790s and 1800s turned rural handicraft areas into weaving villages such as Wilsden, where Hedley Smith placed the Denby family in his novel, "The Mill Folk," before they migrated to Rhode Island. Such firms used local waterpower for spinning frames in centralized shops. Early nineteenth-century Yorkshire mills sold their yarn in the West Riding, in Norwich, to the hosiery industry in the English Midlands, and on the Continent. Trade in yarn and later in cloth developed commercial contacts within the Atlantic economies. Power looms run by steam engines were adopted during the late 1820s. Within Yorkshire, Bradford became industrially dominant in the "plain goods" worsted trade, while Leeds, Keighley, and Halifax continued to make "fancy stuffs" or fine worsted cloth.[10]

During the mid-1830s, Bradford manufacturers led by the firm of Titus Salt and Sons decided to produce mass quantities of worsted dress cloth called "mixed" goods using strong, cheap cotton warp. The combination of cotton warp obtained from local and Lancashire spinning mills with heavy, warm hard-twist alpaca or mohair yarns yielded an inexpensive fabric of a high "lustre" finish and stiff drape suitable for use over crinolines and hoopskirts. The mill owners intended to sell their mass production of women's dress goods in a transatlantic market to the English, European, and American middle classes and the respectable working classes. They would compete with all-cotton dress goods in price but surpass them in warmth and style.[11] Bradford capitalists ceded the production of all-wool worsted manufacture for the upper-class luxury market to French technical and aesthetic superiority. These decisions to concentrate on mixed goods as the staple product and the resulting heavy investment in cap and throstle spinning machinery would become a financial liability when ladies' fashion inevitably changed. Between 1830 and 1860, however, great success in the mass selling of mixed goods banished caution.

Changes in handicraft production of worsted cloth in Yorkshire beginning in the 1780s slowly altered class relations until an explosion of resistance occurred in 1825. Sharp bursts of industrial innovation applied to one worsted occupation at a time marked a long-term pattern of succeeding waves of work reorganization and worker displacement. Before mechanization and centralization in the early nineteenth century, domestic production had centered in the family and the artisan shop, often located in weaving villages where wives and children provided hand-spun yarn to the weavers. When weavers owned their own wool in the eighteenth century, they slung rolls of cloth over their shoulders and walked to market towns, where the bridge parapets were built especially low to accommodate their passage.[12] Wool staplers "put out" or provided wool fleeces to the woolcombers who worked together in small artisan shops. They cleaned and straightened the fibers by hand, then passed the combed wool on to handloom weavers. The staplers, who often became early nineteenth-century manufacturers, owned the wool but had little control over the pace or quality of the work. They had to wait to collect and sell the woven cloth in special markets called piece halls.[13] Women assisted by their children spun the combed wool into yarn on single-thread wheels for the handloom weavers in their families.

In the mill village of Horton in Bradford Parish, Daniel Dracup, born in 1786 and a forebear of Hedley Smith, organized his household to support his handloom weaving. Smith often used the names of his ancestors in his Briardale fiction. Dracup had no idea that his snug little cottage and hard-working family was part of a "proto-industrial" system, doomed to oblivion. The subsequent decline of this system of rural industry in Yorkshire reflected similar developments in other European textile cities, such as woolen centers in France. Rural deindustrialization in Europe, which withdrew capital from countryside manufacture and prompted migration, became fully as important a component of the nineteenth-century society as the urban factory system.[14]

The first application of mechanization in Yorkshire came in spinning, inspired by innovations in cotton textile technology. Between 1787 and 1810 a dozen spinning mills appeared in the Bradford area. By 1830 steam engines, repaired in Bradford iron foundries and fired with local coal, powered thirty large spinning mills. Domestic spinning became extinct, but former spinners, young women and children, entered the new mills to tend steam-powered throstle spinning frames. The handloom weavers became dependent on these spinning mills for yarn. Many West Riding spinning mills sold their yarn throughout England and on the Continent, and thus local supplies became stretched. To insure their access to yarn, by the 1820s the weavers began to work in centralized shops attached to spinning mills. Centralization preceded mechanization but introduced new forms of work discipline. Their employers owned the handlooms, while overlookers both repaired the looms and regulated a new pace of work. The old weaving villages, in which workers also hand-sheared or cropped the finished cloth, began to disappear.

Expanded spinning and weaving operations demanded additional combed wool. In a reversal of craft custom, which carried with it bitter resentment, the woolcombers shifted out of their small shops, which had once nurtured the rituals and privileges of artisans, into their individual households. Until woolcombing became mechanized in the 1840s, woolcombers slogged away, separated in their cottages and forced to use the tools provided by employers. Furthermore, each man had to pick up and return the wool to the spinning mills, as well as carry back his supply of charcoal for heating the combs. Former artisans now did the degrading, exhausting job of porter. After carrying heavy weights of coal, which were often wet by the time they reached home, the combers faced both new deadlines for delivery of combed wool and deteriorating family health from charcoal fumes.[15] In 1824 steam-powered looms were set up in one Bradford mill in spite of the smashing-up of the first loom by Luddites two years earlier.

Phyllis Bentley, the Yorkshire novelist so admired by Hedley Smith, captured the rage and scorn with which each class viewed the other in her 1932 novel *Inheritance*. "Mester" Oldroyd, owner of the Syke mill in "Ire Valley," refuses angrily to call for military troops to deliver his woolcropping machinery safely into his mill.

> "The Luddites! Curse the Luddites! . . . A few stupid ignorant men that don't know what's good for them, that's what your Luddites are. . . . I'll work those frames in this mill if I have to ride in Luddites' blood up to my saddle-girths."

To recruit Joe Bamforth as a Luddite, hand-cropper George Mellor shows him his wrist.

> "Feel this!" . . . Joe winced as he felt the "hoof" which, formed by constant pressure of the "nog" of the shears, always marked the hand-cropper. "Aye, shrink from it!" cried Mellor. "It's the cropper's mark, tha knows; it shows he's worked t'shears for mony a year. It's a man's job, is a cropper's; it needs strength and skill. And then they want to bring in them cursed frames to take bread out o' wer mouths and spoil t'cloth. . . . How can wood and iron and water work better nor a man?"[16]

In the novel, Luddites kill Oldroyd, but the machines are set up at the mill now run by his son.

Building anger over displacement, disrupting changes in family life, and the loss of control over work shaped the 1825 strike led by handicraftsmen. Combined action by woolcombers and weavers' unions quickly organized in

1824–25 drove the six months' strike that spread throughout the woolen and worsted districts of Yorkshire. In Bradford several thousand woolcombers, 3,000 factory workers, and 13,000 handloom weavers were on strike within a six-mile radius. The extent of this strike, "one of the most massive and protracted industrial conflicts" in nineteenth-century England, reflected profound discontent among 20,000 textile workers. Their goal was equalization of wages among hand workers and factory workers, nothing less than a denial of the labor cost advantages of centralized and mechanized production. The mill owners responded with lockouts and blacklists. When the strike began in the spring the cloth market was high, but by the fall of 1825 prices had declined, while unemployment grew after the strike ended in November. The operatives won brief recognition of their unions but no wage increases. Still, the many who resisted in 1825 "provided the backbone" for new forms of union activity and for political reforms championed by the Chartist movement in Bradford in the 1830s and 1840s.[17]

After the 1825 strike, Yorkshire mill owners decided to abandon most hand work and began to buy and install steam-powered looms, including some jacquard looms for fancy patterns, concentrating mechanized production in factories. They meant to keep wages low by hiring females as factory weavers. Among the workers were many of Hedley Smith's female relatives including his mother and grandmother. By 1837 the factory system prevailed in worsted production. Bradford's textile workers became, according to Theodore Koditschek, divided between a minority of skilled adult men and a "largely silent, unorganized, and increasingly feminized mass of industrial operatives isolated within the confines of the factory's walls."[18]

The Industrial Workforce

Industrial change in Yorkshire represented a sharper break with the preindustrial sexual division of labor than in the Lancashire cotton textile industry. Except for supervisory and mechanical work, adult men found few jobs in steam-powered factories. Women and children dominated spinning and weaving. Displaced weavers and men from rural areas and from Ireland, plus woolcombers from declining Norwich, had flocked into West Riding woolcombing until its complete mechanization. Artisan woolcombing was then reduced to casual labor with male combers bidding against each other for work. While the mechanization of spinning, weaving, and woolcombing forced rural producers into factories, after 1845 as many as 20,000 displaced hand woolcombers migrated out of the region in a desperate search for any kind of work. In the late nineteenth century, adult females during the day tended washing, carding, and combing machines in combing sheds, composing as much as 60 percent of the total combing/carding workforce.[19]

Children of both sexes under the age of seventeen represented the vast majority of industrial workers in Bradford in 1833–50. Factory owners and overlookers believed that children and young females could be easily subordinated to the rules of mechanized factory life. The great reservoir of cheap labor would be replenished with migrants, a rising birth rate, and early marriage. Working-class family income depended on the pooled wages of low-paid children, adolescents, and married women with children who often returned to the mills.[20]

Between 1851 and 1881 percentages shifted in the makeup of the Bradford textile factory workforce, yet confirmed into the twentieth century the pattern established in the early nineteenth century of the majority as young and female. Seventy-eight-year-old weaver Amy Collins Bainbridge, Hedley Smith's aunt, remembered entering the Bradford mills at twelve in 1914. "When I was a girl there was no saying nay. It was work and earn your keep and do as you are told."[21]

The employment of boys, eighteen and younger, slipped from 26 percent in 1851 to 15 percent in 1881. Likewise, the employment of girls declined from 37 percent in 1851 to 23 percent in 1881. The employment of both girls and boys under the age of fourteen had become regulated by the 1874 Factory Acts. Mandatory education meant that "short-timers" under fourteen split the day between the factory and school.[22] Hedley Smith's paternal grandmother, Mary Holmes (Smith), was seventeen in 1874, born too early to benefit from factory regulation, as was Smith's maternal grandmother, Jane Holdsworth (Collins), born in 1850. When Jane Holdsworth Collins died in 1889, Mary Parkinson (Collins), born in 1853, became Hedley Smith's step-grandmother.[23] These Yorkshire lasses probably started in the mills as early as ten years old. Yorkshire dialect poet John Hartley captured the general lament over the child laborer in "Th' Short Timer."

> At hauf-past five tha leaves thi bed,
> An off tha goes to wark;
> An gropes thi way to mill or shed,
> Six months o' th' year i' th' dark.
> Tha gets but little for thi pains,
> But that's noa fault o' thine;
> Thi maister reckons up *his* gains,
> An ligs i bed till nine.[24]

The employment of adult women, largely between the ages of eighteen and thirty, held almost steady, but declined between 1851 and 1881. The total number of females of *all* ages represented 70 percent of the workforce in 1851 and, after factory laws, 56 percent in 1881. Males represented about 42 percent in 1881, down more sharply from 73 percent (including many woolcombers) in 1851. When boys reached the age of eighteen, they either left the mills or were lucky enough to find employment that led to supervisory or skilled work. Female spinners and weavers unable to advance or earn a living wage searched around for better places in other mills or dropped out, creating a high turnover rate. In 1911 the Bradford factories still hired a workforce predominantly young and female, 70 percent of the spinners and 81 percent of the weavers, the majority of the jobs. During the first decade of the twentieth century, married women represented 10 to 15 percent of the total workforce in worsted production.[25] Among them was skilled alpaca weaver Alice Collins Smith, Hedley's mother.

Hedley Smith's kinfolk in Yorkshire experienced all of these changes, shifting their occupations as the local economy moved toward centralized and mechanized factory work. John Dracupp of Horton village, born in 1688, was both a cloth dealer and an artisan joiner or furniture maker.[26] Two succeeding generations of Dracups drew on this man's carpentry skills to make wooden shuttles for hand looms used in household production as the West Riding slowly intensified cloth-making. Shuttle-maker Nathaniel Dracup, born in 1728, became swept up as a young man in waves of evangelical religion and preached John Wesley's Methodism in Horton. Hand-loom weaver Daniel Dracup relied on the spinners in his family, including his wife, Mary Briggs, to supply his production. Succeeding nineteenth-century generations of men, however, left the rapidly industrializing textile work to become stone quarriers, laborers, delvers or manual excavators, and artisan-trained workers, while the female generations shifted to factory work as spinners and weavers. Hedley Smith's father, Ernest, was an artisan brushmaker, born in 1883, while his mother, Alice Collins, also born in 1883, entered the mills as a weaver. Her mother-in-law, Mary Holmes, born in 1857 and married to Sam Smith, an interior painter, also had become a skilled weaver. But when widowed in 1903, she left the mill to take care of her grandchildren, Sam and Hedley, while their mother worked.[27] Some of Hedley Smith's relatives made short migrations of about ten miles from rural areas in West Yorkshire to Bradford Parish. Others remained where they had been born, such as the Dracups of Horton, and the industry grew up around them.

Migration Streams to and from Bradford

By 1835 Bradford's twenty-five mills employed 4,200 workers, while Halifax had only fourteen worsted mills employing fewer than 800.[28] Bradford's expansion over the next two decades attracted rural people from Devon and Cornwall in the West Country and Irish migrants in large numbers, some to work as woolcombers. F. W. Jowett, Socialist and Labour MP for West Bradford first elected in 1906, remembered migrants from Southwest England "coming as children to work in the mills," some with their parents and others sent by the Poor Law authorities. His own mother, born in Devonshire, arrived as a child of seven with her two older brothers. "Like many other children in those days, she had been deposited for exploitation, fatherless and motherless, alone among strangers and regardless of consequences."[29]

By 1820 migration into the West Riding, especially from Ireland, had replaced natural population increase. Bradford more than doubled in size between 1831 and 1851, boasting 206 mills in 1861, while the number of mills in Leeds rapidly declined. In 1850 West Yorkshire contained 90 percent of all worsted operatives in England of which 50 percent or 25,872 resided in Bradford Parish.[30] This migration represented part of an international labor force, such as the Irish who entered the cotton factories of Lancashire and Belgian migrants who worked in the woolen mills of Roubaix, France. In 1851 Irish migrants in Bradford represented 21 percent of all Irish-born persons in the West Riding. One-third of these people, especially in the peak years of migration, 1841–51, came from Queen's County, where the established woolen and linen textile industry had employed many. Irish textile workers and manual laborers in construction who ended up in Bradford came in stages by way of Lancashire or other towns in Yorkshire. They resided in the Irish quarters of Bradford characterized by density of population and poverty. Many Irish men became manual woolcombers, thus crowding one of Bradford's most rapidly mechanizing occupations. Yorkshire-born woolcombers, already facing tremendous pressure on their wages, resented deeply the Irish migrants and their Catholicism. The resentment of these men, who were rapidly being replaced by machinery, did not, however, result in open assaults on the Irish community.[31]

One of those displaced woolcombers was Hedley Smith's great-grandfather, John Holmes, born in 1819 and married in 1842. Holmes lived in the weaving village of Horton near Bradford, until industrial change turned woolcombing into machine work and forced him to move about Yorkshire searching for work. After his daughter Mary was born in 1857, Holmes moved his family to Leeds, where he worked for several years as a "foundry laborer." His son

George was born in 1864. By 1871 the family returned to the Bradford area to reside in the neighborhood of Allerton, a small village absorbed into expanding Bradford. That same year daughter Mary entered the spinning room of a local mill at the age of thirteen. For over a decade, John Holmes competed for work as a "laborer" until he and his wife died in 1883. Mary Holmes, who married Sam Smith, was Hedley Smith's grandmother. Other male relatives tried tenant farming for local landlords; the lucky ones entered trade apprenticeships. Dracup Collins, Hedley Smith's maternal grandfather, worked beginning as a ten-year-old lad driving a donkey in the coalmines of Durham, far north of Bradford. When the family returned to the Bradford area, young Dracup was apprenticed as a stone mason. Deprived of sunshine and milk as a child, Dracup Collins was a tiny man with famously bowed legs, who, it was said, could not "stop a pig in an alley."[32] His female children became weavers in the mills.

During the early nineteenth century mill village life had given way to the rise of West Riding industrial towns devoted to worsted manufacture. Bradford-born J. B Priestley recalled them as

> built of a dark stone that makes them look like strange out-croppings of the native rock, as if the Pennines had suddenly pushed out mills and streets and tripe shops. . . . [The industrial workers living there, who] ought to have been sluts and brutes, . . . were not—they were decent and kind, humorous and hopeful.[33]

Sam Smith, Hedley Smith's grandfather, apprenticed as an interior painter. After receiving a savage beating from his strict Methodist father for whistling forbidden music-hall tunes, Sam left home for good, immigrating to the United States. He arrived in the 1870s at the age of nineteen to work on the American railroads, trying hard to earn enough to settle. Sam Smith expected his sweetheart, Mary Holmes, to join him for a new life, but she refused. Many other skilled British interior painters and decorators and miners made seasonal transatlantic passages as "birds of passage" but, unlike Sam Smith, never intended to settle. When his savings were stolen in 1875, Sam Smith found work as an interior decorator in Utica, New York, earning enough for a homeward passage. In 1882 he married Mary Holmes in Bradford where his only child, Ernest, was born. Jobs in his trade led Sam Smith, his workmates, and sometimes his family to various locations throughout the West Riding. He itched to relocate overseas until his dying day in 1903.[34]

The borough of Bradford led the other major textile centers in percentage of residents born outside of Yorkshire. Young single females from English towns and from Ireland made up about a quarter of the local migrants.

They often lived in lodging houses run by widows or pooled their wages to rent rooms together, returning periodically to their families. These women formed part of a temporary labor-migration system, which unless they married probably ended with a return migration.[35] They do not appear to have become domestic servants in Bradford. Internal migrants from Lancashire and Lincolnshire traveled on the developing railroad lines in the 1840s connecting Bradford to Manchester.

As industrialization continued, Yorkshire worsted merchants congregated in Bradford, abandoning the grand Piece Halls of Halifax and Leeds. Among these merchant traders were several hundred Jews from Germany and Central Europe, including the provinces that would compose modern Czechoslovakia, forming a "foreign colony" in Bradford. Financed by German banks, they made on-the-spot decisions about the quality and quantities of worsted goods for the Continental markets and therefore must have returned periodically to Europe. These commercial migrants, many of whom came to settle, represented a traditional merchant diaspora, networks of whom were incorporated into expanding systems of European capital. Their warehouses formed a district called "Little Germany." Some of them, caught up in German nationalism, sent their sons to fight in the Franco-Prussian war in 1870. In 1873 they established one of the first Reform Jewish synagogues in England and became active in civic, charitable, and cultural life of Bradford. Their cultural interests blended with long-established traditions in this music-loving community, including working-class brass bands and choral groups, which revered the high canon of English music, especially Handel's oratorios. As Yorkshire author J. B. Priestley noted, "[a] dash of the Rhine and the Oder found its way into our grim runnel—'t' mucky beck.'"[36]

In the late nineteenth century, English-born members of the Jewish community intermarried and integrated into Yorkshire life. The congregation of the synagogue declined, while some members became Zionists. As naturalized citizens, foreign-born Jews in Bradford participated in municipal government and served as aldermen and mayors. In 1910 ardent Zionist Jacob Moser from Schlesweg-Holstein became Lord Mayor of Bradford. Yorkshire workers rated these merchant traders highly, and there was no trouble with their union warehouse men. As highly respected merchants, they expected only the best quality worsted cloth and formed bonds with small manufacturers who came to depend on them to meet their weekly wage bills. One well-known member of the community was Jacob Behrens, who came to Bradford from Hamburg in 1832. Behrens became influential among the great free trade English Liberals and advised the government on the 1861 commercial treaty with France. He helped found the Bradford Chamber of Commerce and in 1882 was knighted by Queen Victoria. The House of Behrens grew to handle much more than Yorkshire goods and did business in Manchester, Glasgow, Calcutta, and Shanghai.[37]

Other German Jews worked as wool staplers or wool sellers. Julius Delius migrated to Yorkshire in 1855 from the Westphalian town of Bielefeld, married a woman from his hometown, and became an English citizen. He bought and sold bales of Australian wool, expecting his three sons to join the trade. As a young man the composer Frederick Delius, born in 1862, tried to comply with his father's wishes but became far more fascinated with the Yorkshire dialect, which he picked up from the warehouse men, and the music he heard in London and on the Continent during his selling trips. Although Delius the musician rarely returned to England, he regarded Yorkshire as his home and considered setting Emily Brontë's *Wuthering Heights* to music.[38] This German-Jewish community in Bradford and the cultural "leaven" and diversity they provided disintegrated in the 1930s.[39] Nazi-era German banks no longer advanced credits to Jewish merchants. Where they went is unknown, but the circumstances suggest individual and family dispersal. Although Hedley Smith makes no mention of these merchants, his fiction includes German working-class residents of Bradford who worked as dyers and chemists, mostly from Halle, Germany, a group overlooked by Bradford's historians. They organized their own brass bands, provoking local friction during the political tensions leading up to World War I.[40]

Industrial Change and Bradford Class Society

Some Yorkshire-born manufacturers in the worsted industry specialized only in spinning operations. Born in 1830 as the last of ten children, Joseph Benn of Queensbury, near Bradford, assisted his father, a handloom weaver, until he got a chance to learn the worsted trade as a young man in Germany. Relative technical superiority within the Atlantic economies often prompted temporary British migration to Western Europe.[41] In 1860 Joseph Benn set up the Oak Mills spinning operation at the town of Clayton, west of Bradford, as Joseph Benn and Company. Benn sent his son Harrison, born in 1851 and one of his five sons, to Germany for his education. Harrison worked at the spinning mills for his father and his partners until the partnership was dissolved in 1882. With the financial backing of their father, Harrison and his brothers, Joseph Jr., William Henry, Arthur, and Alfred, purchased the worsted properties of the old Turner family at the Beckside mills in Great

Horton, Bradford. In 1881 Joseph Benn and Sons, Ltd., employed about 900 workers to manufacture alpaca and mohair fabric.[42]

Harrison and Alfred prospered, building suitable mansions on family land in Clayton at Oakleigh and at Upper Syke Farm.[43] Joe Benn Jr. left the family firm to set up an independent mill in 1893 to manufacture dress good, coatings, and linings. Alfred died in 1896 and Joseph Sr. in 1897. Harrison Benn, with his brother William Henry, was the energetic textile capitalist who in 1903 built the mill at Greystone village, North Providence, Rhode Island, the site of Hedley Smith's "Briardale" tales.

Within a twenty-five-mile radius of the worsted capital of Bradford, the other important sites of the Yorkshire textile industry—Leeds, Keighley, Halifax, Huddersfield and Dewsbury—manufactured diverse woolen products (see map 1). The district of Bradford, which at mid-century manufactured 80 percent of English worsted goods, included mill sites at Great Horton, the site of the Benn operation, and at Manningham. Surrounding the district dubbed an "industrial Milky Way" were the worsted operations of Shipley, Saltaire, Wilsden, Clayton, and Queensbury (see map 2).[44]

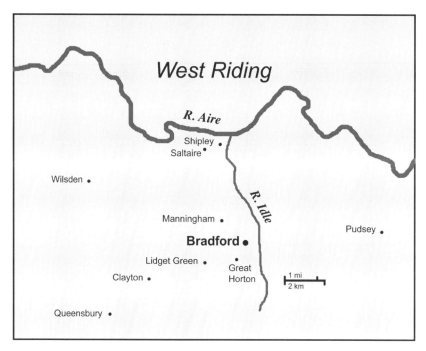

Map 2. Bradford area and principal centers of worsted and silk production, c. 1890. Courtesy of Paul Coppens.

Bradford's mixed goods continued to sell well until events in international trade and politics intruded, upsetting nearly thirty years of prosperity. Cheap cotton warp depended on bales of raw cotton shipped from the American South, which were cut off by the U.S. naval blockade of southern seaports during the Civil War, 1861–65. Wartime ravages to the Cotton South's agricultural system reduced the postwar cotton supply. In England this cotton "famine" in the 1860s depressed Lancashire industry, while cotton warp nearly disappeared. Bradford firms returned to all-wool worsted cloth, now cheaper than scarce cotton fabrics. They successfully competed in markets even with the French but only during the market upheavals of the Franco-Prussian War. By positioning themselves within the transatlantic cotton trade and the Atlantic economy of the worsted trade, Bradford area firms faced serious challenges at mid-century.

Economic change reshaped Bradford society but the old culture hung on. By 1870 some manufacturers from humble origins had bought villas in the countryside. John Foster of the Black Dyke Mills even renovated a nearby castle, although, as William Byles, editor of the *Bradford Observer* and Liberal politician observed, he and others still spoke in the dialect and disdained to wear gloves.[45] These men sent their sons to university to learn the classics, however impractical for the future of the worsted trade. Their sons preferred life in the Army or as gentlemen to running textile mills. By the 1880s the luxurious consumption habits of the second generation of mill owners had undercut paternalist practices and managerial concern for class harmony in the West Riding.[46]

The nineteenth-century expansion of Bradford attracted elements of a small middle class, although more heavily weighted with those engaged in textile manufacturing, retailing, and the building trades than professionals, such as lawyers, physicians, and accountants.[47] Skilled workers, providing services as cabinet-makers and printers, increased rapidly by 1851, but Bradford was becoming an overwhelmingly working-class industrial community. The *Bradford Observer* represented middle-class interests, while the *Yorkshire Post* sided with wealthy mill owners and the gentry. As Liberals the new middle class vied for local political leadership with the Conservative landed and corporate elite, a conflict that revolved around how best to deal with factory workers in the new industrial order.[48] Still, some of the heads of the biggest textile firms, such as Titus Salt, were Liberals who supported industrial paternalism, leading to the Factory Acts in 1874 that established the half-time system for child workers under fourteen.

Phyllis Bentley was one of Hedley Smith's favorite Yorkshire writers, along with the Brontë sisters. Three of Bentley's Yorkshire novels follow the fortunes of early nineteenth-century worsted manufacturers who head dynastic families, such as the Oldroyd family of the "Ire Valley." Bentley, born in Halifax, Yorkshire, in 1894, grew up in a "middle of the middle class" family who worked for small textile manufacturers. She spent most of her life in various Yorkshire towns. Well regarded as a regional novelist, Bentley plotted struggles over dominance that involved homicidal revenge and embittered class relations.[49]

In *Inheritance* local Luddites murder the Oldroyd patriarch for installing in his mill wool cropping machines that mechanically sheared the surface of woven fabric. His son Will takes over the Syke Mill and gleefully watches his father's murderers hang, well aware that according to law their bodies would be used for anatomy classes. Will avenges his father's murder but loses his pregnant lover, Mary, whose brother dies with the others. Will Oldroyd builds his great fortune expanding the Syke operations. The "days before McKinley" mean riches and ostentatious acquisitions leading to heavy personal debts after the new American protective tariffs on worsted beginning in 1890.

Contests of will and power between masters and workmen, insurmountable class and cultural distinctions, passionate if often mismatched sexual attachments, and declining industrial fortunes echo through Bentley's Ire Valley novels *Inheritance* (1932), *The Rise of Henry Morcar* (1946), and *A Man of His Time* (1966).[50] Her treatment of the twentieth century charts the decline of the old firms and the rise of small mill owners who struggled with demands for design innovation, world wars, domestic competitors, and family members unsuited or unwilling to run worsted mills. Her works probably inspired Hedley Smith's Briardale trilogy, "The Millmaster," "The Lion and the Eagle," and "The Tongue-Tied Town," all three set in Rhode Island. Bentley's focus on upper- and middle-class characters meant a minimal use of dialect in her novels, but they powerfully convey what she understood best: the various ways class shaped Yorkshire society.

In her 1962 autobiography, *O Dreams, O Destinations,* Bentley wrote that two events ruined her family: the McKinley tariff and trade unionism. In spite of her drift toward atheism and idealistic Socialism at age nineteen, she insisted, "The General Strike [in 1926] killed my father." During the devastation of the worsted trade at the turn of the twentieth century, the Bentley family lost its money and servants, forcing her mother to do housework, cook, and make clothing. This was an embittering time for the class-conscious Bentleys who regarded themselves as Tory and Church of England. Still her father, revered as the central figure in *The Rise of Henry Morcar,* started up his own small company in 1910. Phyllis was sent to all-female private schools, which trained their students to be "admirably fitted for the tasks [of wife and mother] the British Empire then imposed on them." A social and psychological casualty of these family upheavals, Bentley remained emotionally dependent on her mother until she freed herself by becoming a published writer and later volunteering in 1939 as an ambulance driver.[51] Her novels and collections of short stories are rich in perceptive observations of Yorkshire life and character. Hedley Smith so admired her work that he dedicated his second collection of stories, *More Yankee Yorkshiremen* (1974), in "Homage to Phyllis Bentley."

Gender Antagonism and Working-Class Life

In nineteenth-century Yorkshire, young females systematically denied access to skills in the worsted industry faced a sexual division of labor that relegated them to poorly paid, unskilled work. Even female-dominated burling and mending, the skilled removal and repair of surface flaws with needles and other trade tools, which determined the price of the goods, was not recognized as skilled or well paid.[52] Adult males in the weave sheds served as overlookers or loom mechanics on whom the female weavers depended to speed their work. Both paternalist employers and skilled unionists deliberately perpetuated this situation by denying craft training and union membership to women and attempting to drive the more experienced and skilled married weavers out of the workforce. Many young Yorkshire wives left their jobs and thus gave up chances to gain experience and skill. Women weavers who managed to stay at or return to work developed reputations as skilled, efficient teachers able to "tune" (repair) their own looms and earn higher wages.[53] Still others, like Hedley Smith's mother Alice and like his fictional characters Sally Greaves and Cissie Croft in *Yankee Yorkshirewomen* (1978), advanced to complicated jacquard weaving in Yorkshire mills. The majority of low-paid, young female labor in the spinning and weaving departments remained unorganized, while skilled male workers, such as dyers and wool sorters, enjoyed strong craft unions. The lure of privileges in the harsh new industrial order drowned out the idealism of early nineteenth-century craft cooperation and Chartist reform. Hierarchical rankings among the male operatives also blended well with employer paternalism.

The paternalist ideology of mid-nineteenth-century Yorkshire, which meant controlling the relations between the "master" and his skilled male workers, regarded the working-class home and its harmonious domestic arrangements as central to industrial order. Titus Salt, owner of the 1853 model industrial village of 5,000 at Saltaire in Bradford, viewed the small preindustrial village with its beer, lust, and freedom of moors and fields as the source of riotous Chartist and antifactory agitation in the 1840s.[54] Indeed, courting couples had free access to secluded woods and village lanes in the early nineteenth century. Providing cricket teams and brass bands for male workers as well as strict regulation for behaviors in factory, parks, and dwellings, employers like Salt intended to divert and control working-class passions. Mid-nineteenth-century paternalists in the West Riding provided domestic training to mill lasses who, once married, were expected to drop out of the workforce. Typically "when young people had fallen into sin," their employers expected them to marry or quit. But even wives dependent on their husbands' earnings at Saltaire stoutly refused to use the mills' bathing and washing facilities, calling them inconvenient and an "invasion of their privacy." Resistance to these conveniences by females in working-class families contradicts acceptance of paternalism. Deference and paternalism among male textile workers in Lancashire and the West Riding appeared to channel the discontents of the early nineteenth century into a quiet period of mid-century accommodation and harmony.[55] But this deference and accommodation by skilled male workers had consequences for relations between working-class men and women.

The early nineteenth-century mass displacement of skilled handicraftsmen had been traumatic on the deepest level. The sexual division of labor in work and in unions produced gender antagonisms that shaped Yorkshire factory and village life. Violent sexual conflicts between the growing female factory workforce in Bradford, Yorkshire, and "attacks by men on women operatives" were commonplace during early Yorkshire industrialization. Young factory lads "shouted naughty and pert obscenities," when "lassies" in textile mills removed their stockings before work; the lads then pulled up the clothes of female sleepers during rest periods. In most accounts, sexual tensions during industrial change seemed to victimize females into the early twentieth century. Hedley Smith's Aunt Amy remembered going into the mill when she was twelve. She "hated every minute of it. When I look back at the horrors, the bullying and the dirt—the ignorance and filthy talk that was our daily lot, not to mention the tears I shed."[56]

In his fiction Hedley Smith used sexual antagonisms to explore the emotional conflicts among working-class men and women. Patriarch Grandfather Denby, one of Smith's strongest characters in his novel "The Mill Folk," often clashes with female family members. He regards all women, including his faithful wife, his daughters, and his daughters-in-law, as objects of his more or less controlled lusts. Insisting on his rights as master of the house in the late nineteenth-century mill village of Wilsden, Yorkshire, he spanks his impudent daughter Martha like a child on her bare backside in front of the family. In retaliation and partly for his refusal to let her continue her schooling, Martha threatens the family economy by withholding her wages as a weaver. She then boards with another family and becomes sexually active to great village scandal. Even worse, she lands herself an older wealthy husband and leaves Yorkshire for Rhode Island. Smith's Briardale fiction also offers dramatic evidence on Yorkshire working-class sexual customs transferred to Rhode Island.[57]

Despite family efforts to direct their sexuality in the interest of family economic welfare, Yorkshire lasses became sexually active in their teens with various partners. Female subculture made abortion an accepted part of working-class life. Joanna Bornat's concept of the marginalized lives of Yorkshire women offers an explanation of the sexual behaviors of mill lasses far more convincing than merely their status as wage earners.[58] Girls as young as ten or eleven entered the worsted mills as doffers. Between fifteen and eighteen as they reached puberty, young women became throstle spinners or weavers. For as long as they remained mill workers, these lasses could expect no advances in skills or in wages or any role in changing their situation through union activity. Most female workers in the worsted factories would marry and drop out of the workforce. Yorkshire society widely condemned working wives.[59]

For most mill lasses with little future for advancement in the workforce, sexual experimentation would seem the next logical step on the road to marriage and female adulthood, while she turned over her Saturday wage packet to her family. Young women workers, like Hedley Smith's rebellious Martha Denby, thus defined for themselves the onset of courtship and adulthood knowing that, unlike many Lancashire working wives, marriage often meant an end to paid work. Indeed pregnancies among brides in mill villages in both Yorkshire and Lancashire were commonplace. Illegitimacy rates in Bradford remained "fairly constant" between 1851 and 1881, averaging between 6 and 8 percent, while female-controlled networks of sex information and abortion became the major means of family limitation in late nineteenth-century Yorkshire.[60] "Courters" often hurried up their wedding day because "a child was on the way." Alpaca weaver Alice Collins, Hedley Smith's mother, wed twenty-one-year-old artisan Ernest Smith on July 2, 1904, when she was twenty. Four months later, on October 20, 1904, her first son, Sam, was born. The marriage lasted forty-eight years.[61]

Despite the condemnation of working wives by the middle class and trade unionists, older married women weavers in Yorkshire forged a direct connection between family limitation and their return to the workforce. In response to declining wages and depression in the worsted industry beginning in the 1870s, a generation of working-class wives who had found the means to control fertility generally through abortion returned to weaving. Participating in this trend, Hedley Smith's relatives had small families, and wives, such as his mother, returned to the mills. In 1851 29 percent of married women over the age of thirty-five worked in textiles, while thirty years later, in 1881, 63 percent of women working in textiles (presumably largely as weavers) were over thirty-five. Indeed, as Karl Ittmann argued, "the pace of fertility decline continued to increase in Bradford up to the First World War." By then the curtailing of fertility probably reflected a mutual choice by husband and wife.[62]

During the first decade of the twentieth century married women represented between 10 and 15 percent of the total worsted labor force.[63] These mature women workers possessed the experience and judgment that made them leaders in incidents of late nineteenth-century Yorkshire labor protest. Whether Alice Collins Smith participated in strike activities or labor protest is unknown, but Smith's Briardale fiction refers indirectly to such activity and includes many strong, mature female characters central to Yorkshire and Rhode Island mill village life from weavers and storeowners to midwives.

Market Protectionism and Yorkshire Industrial Decline

In the 1870s Western European fashion abandoned the crinoline for softly draped costumes arranged to fall backward over the bustle, a padded, wired cushion tied around the female waist. French production of all-wool worsted cloth, using yarns spun in varying light "counts" (a measure of fineness) on mule spinning machines and inspired by Gallic coloration and design made Bradford manufacturers increasingly "sick with envy." Woolcombing by machine in Yorkshire required oiling the wool, making the even dyeing of worsted fabric difficult, while mule spinning frames were far too costly in price and wages. Some mills employed patternmakers, such as Hedley Smith's ancestor, Samuel Dracup of Horton, and used jacquard looms as early as the 1830s for fancy patterns, but their designs often copied those from the Continent. Expensive French all-wool worsted cloth made at Roubaix penetrated the English home market.[64] Thus began the long period of Yorkshire's depressed trade in the late 1870s and early 1880s.

Years of poor markets forced Bradford manufacturers to diversify their product. Led by the sons of Titus Salt, owners of the industrial complex at Saltaire, John Foster's Black Dyke Mills at Queensbury, and G. and J. Turner of Great Horton (later Joseph Benn and Sons, Ltd.) made worsted coatings, coat linings, and suitings for men's wear, which proved successful.[65] Titus Salt and Sons and Samuel C. Lister's operations at Manningham in Bradford also shifted to silk plush production.

By the 1890s foreign tariffs to protect emerging industry in the United States and Germany, both key export markets for Yorkshire, cut into the worsted and silk trade. Support for "free trade" ideology waned as Yorkshire manufacturers demanded retaliation and sought new markets at home and within the British Empire. Just before Titus Salt and Sons was taken over by new owners, management had attempted to open operations in Bridgeport, Connecticut, to evade American tariffs. Still under the punitive McKinley schedules, the Salts' American trade both in men's coatings and silk plush disappeared. The "infamous" McKinley tariff in 1890, passed by a Republican-controlled U.S. Congress, cut in half worsted and silk imports into the United States, followed by three years of more relaxed tariffs under Democrats during the economic depression of the 1890s. With the election of Republican William McKinley as president and a Republican Congress in 1896, the Dingley tariffs even further slashed Bradford worsteds for American markets.[66] Only some yarns and raw wool survived. McKinley's name became anathema throughout the West Riding.

State protectionist policies that reflected partisan domestic political contests in the 1890s deeply undercut Yorkshire manufacturing and created widespread unemployment. Carl Strikwerda argued that state policy trumped national economic interests in the nineteenth century by easing laws on international trade, finance, and commerce, and promoting freedom of trade, navigation, and communication, thus opening the way for global migrations.[67] Nineteenth-century tariff protection of worsted, woolen, and silk plush manufacture by the United States was, however, the result of intense political lobbying of the emergent post–Civil War majority Republican Party by textile manufacturers, bankers, and investors in the Northeast. In this case, state policy, responsive to and shaped by industrial and finance capitalism, resulted in new state bureaucracies and regulations. The economic power of emerging national industrial interests motivated these changes.

Facing the threat of higher American tariffs, silk plush operations in the Bradford area ran flat out, demanding compulsory daily overtime in 1889 and 1890 to allow the firms to stockpile goods in New York warehouses. Wages rose with threatened strikes. With the enforcement of the McKinley tariffs on plush and worsted goods imminent, the Lister firm at Manningham expected its workforce, not its restless shareholders, to assume the burden of cutting costs in an unreliable market. The Yorkshire textile world remained complacent. Until textile manufacturing in the United States reached higher technical and aesthetic standards, Yorkshire goods could not be equaled, but no one knew yet what the effects of the American tariff would have on Yorkshire.[68] On December 9, 1890, Samuel Listers's Manningham mills cut wages for all "workpeople" in the velvet department between 20 and 35 percent.[69] To the plush workers, the wage cut was enormous and totally unjustified. Meanwhile, the firm briskly sold its New York stockpiles, and shareholders could anticipate short-term higher profits.

The immediate effect of the wages cuts would equalize the wages of silk workers with the less-skilled worsted workers of Yorkshire. Anticipated losses and long-term competitive advantage in plush production in the transatlantic trade drove these deep wage cuts. The silk plush weavers vowed to prevent this. The editors of the *Textile Manufacturer* called Bradford's Manningham mills strike in 1891 the most "prolonged struggle . . . in Bradford for a quarter of a century," in which women workers played a key role. The participation of women workers in the activities during the Manningham strike defied their marginalization and subordination in trade unions. Despite its defeat, the Manningham mills strike reflected the potential of gender and skill cooperation in the silk plush trade, especially among weavers, not realized in Yorkshire until World War I but central to weavers' unions in Lancashire. It was a memory some weavers would take with them when Yorkshire textile workers migrated to Rhode Island and confronted unfair treatment (see chap. 2). Meanwhile, they faced a long-term regional crisis of industrial depression in the Yorkshire worsted and silk trades that created the conditions for transatlantic labor migration. Large numbers of Lancashire cotton textile workers and Yorkshire worsted workers had already left their districts for the United States beginning in the late 1860s.[70]

During the Manningham strike, at least three hundred skilled workers left Bradford, headed for the developing silk industry in the American Northeast. The head of a Philadelphia silk firm who himself had worked as a dyer for a year at Manningham hired fourteen of the firm's best dyers and paid their passage. Some husbands and fathers left their families behind in Yorkshire, while migrating sons and daughters likewise promised to send for their families once settled. As early as the sixth week of the long strike, strike funds were tapped to send skilled workers to Lancashire, Scotland, and the

United States.[71] A Manningham mills velvet weaver, J. Gath, and his wife left Yorkshire for New York City just weeks before the collapse of the strike. They traveled by steerage class surrounded by smelly, seasick Irish "foreigners," "feeding the fishes." Repelled by dirt and bad food, Gath deftly avoided the "jabbering" Irish, Dutch, German, and Yorkshire people desperate to get off the ship and telegraphed his brother, who met him at the dock. Yorkshire plush workers, he learned, were coming "too quick." Jobs at silk looms were scarce in Bridgeport, Connecticut, but the workforce at the Philadelphia silk mills was on strike and resented the flood of experienced English workpeople. Choosing Bridgeport as his destination, Gath wondered about his fellow strikers and coworkers and their fates and requested that the *Yorkshire Factory Times* be sent to him.[72] When Ernest Smith emigrated with his family in 1923, he also expected to find work in an American mill, following the customary path of many Bradford textile migrants.

After the Manningham mills strike, Lister's operations entered a period of sharp decline. Titus Salt, Bart., Sons & Co., Ltd., had reorganized into a family-controlled joint stock firm in 1881 but was taken over by new managers until the death of Sir Titus Salt in 1887. These men had decided to build the unsuccessful operation in Bridgeport, Connecticut. This failure and the McKinley tariffs forced the family to sell out the whole operation to a syndicate of Bradford manufacturers in 1892 when the eldest Salt heir died.[73] The new owners of the Salt firm, like Lister, faced a bleak market. In late 1892 the market for silks and plush exports was declared "practically dead" and trade with the Continent "extremely dull."[74]

The fate of Manningham mills and Saltaire together reflected the general decline of Yorkshire textiles. The Bradford trade in silk and worsted had collapsed. Thousands of worsted looms fell silent, more than during the last bad "period of depression" in the late 1870s. In 1892 firms shipped 20 million fewer yards of worsted fabric to New York City. By the end of 1893, however, the American economy descended into the worst industrial depression in its history. Depression proved more damaging to Yorkshire textiles than high tariffs. After surveying the situation, the new owners at Titus Salt advised their fellow manufacturers to operate as if no American market existed "or ever would exist." "[A] chronic state of dullness" continued to plague Bradford firms and their workers.[75] Not until the British cornered the world market in raw wool just before the outbreak of the Great War in 1914 did fortunes truly revive. By then British migration to the United States had slowed almost to a halt.

During the Tariff Commission hearings in 1905, Joseph Benn Jr. of the J. Benn and Co. at Clayton complained about the fifteen years of banishment from the American market and the difficulties of relentless competitors, "as thick as flies in summer," for the home trade. Coat linings, finely woven of cotton warp and Peruvian alpaca or Turkish mohair, became one successful line of domestic goods, as did tightly woven mackintoshes for men and women's wear in the English rain. Waterproofed worsted flannels became the emblems of English sporting clothes. Coatings required wider looms and new processes of waterproofing but not a shift to expensive mule spinning machinery for wool. Developing sources of mohair wool from British South Africa freed Yorkshire of their dependence on Greek and Turkish traders, while crossbred merino sheep from Australia, New Zealand, and South Africa fed the English appetites for mutton and long staple wool. These shifts in the wool supply changed the wool stapling trade in Bradford. Instead of just sorting and selling certain kinds of wool fleeces, "topmakers" washed, combed, and wound "tops" of mixed wool for sale to spinning firms. American tariff schedules may have blocked worsted cloth but admitted Yorkshire tops. Some went to worsted firms in Rhode Island.[76] When the Benn operations opened in Greystone, Rhode Island, Yorkshire tops like the ones they used at the Great Horton mills were already available.

British Migration to the United States in the Late Nineteenth and Early Twentieth Centuries

Accounts of English settlers in the United States in many general surveys of immigration usually end with the early nineteenth century, shifting to consideration of the Irish and German immigrants.[77] Although quantitative measurements indicate that English, Scots, and Welsh people arrived in the United States in significant numbers prior to 1850, the peak periods of English migration occurred between 1851 and 1913. Marcus Lee Hansen left the impression that only limited numbers of English immigrants arrived in late nineteenth-century New England textile centers, far outnumbered by French-Canadians and Irish.[78] Maldwyn Jones argued, however, that beginning in 1869 English "immigrants" (many of whom were labor migrants) to the United States began to outnumber those from Ireland: in 1880 by two to one. So many English returned home, however, that net emigration from England scarcely changed in the 1870s and 1880s.[79] J. Gath, the migrant velvet weaver from Manningham, Yorkshire bound for Bridgeport, Connecticut in 1891, might well have returned home during the severe industrial depression in the 1890s. Many Lancashire migrants certainly returned during those hard times.[80]

Maldwyn Jones pointed out that late nineteenth-century English migration included high proportions of single men and women migrants, "largely temporary and transient." This "impermanence" among English migrants was little different from the "new immigration" from southern and eastern Europe, an argument supported by the research of Dudley Baines. Walter Nugent suggested that by the 1880s English migration represented the beginning of the wage-seeking "birds of passage." But as early as 1850, numbers of skilled British (English) workers, especially in the building trades of masons, plumbers, carpenters, interior painters and wallpaperers, and stone quarry workers, were employed seasonally mostly in and around New York City. English birds-of-passage migrants came in larger numbers between 1879 and 1893. Dirk Hoerder argued that British and German emigrations during the transatlantic proletarian mass migrations of the late nineteenth and early twentieth centuries were comparable in terms of absolute numbers. Both streams of migrants, especially the English, represented numbers of skilled and unskilled urban workers who shared among themselves a sense of superiority to the receiving culture.[81]

Between 1906 and 1911 British immigration shifted away from the United States to British North America, some to settle the wheat-growing areas of western Canada with rising numbers to Australia and New Zealand. By 1911 69 percent of British emigrants headed for destinations other than the United States.[82] Although Baines criticized the serious discrepancies in comparing data on English migration supplied by American and British government statistics, he concluded that large-scale migration of the English in the 1880s and early 1900s matched similar mass proletarian migrations from other parts of Europe, especially southern and eastern areas. Baines also argued that if these English migrants came largely from a few important regions, then the comparison with other European nations is even more apt. He surmised, however, that between 1854 and 1900 "relatively few emigrants came from the rapidly changing industries, like textiles."[83] According to Baines, many of these migrants, especially in the late nineteenth century, were male construction workers and miners, traveling alone as temporary or seasonal migrants. Most left Liverpool bound for New York City.

Peak periods of English migration fluctuated with the ups and downs of the American economy. Charlotte Erickson used the data on occupations from the manifests of American ships, especially in 1885–88, indicating that among English adult males the percentage of textile workers fell from 17 percent in 1846–54 to 8 percent in 1885–88, while percentages of white-collar and construction workers increased. Baines concluded that after the 1860s, the long-term rate of returns by British migrants from the United States "was always high," regardless of American economic conditions but never represented a majority. Still, he argued, it was possible that some migrants returned because a "*particular*" overseas industry, such as cotton or woolen textiles, disappointed. In the 1880s emigration from urban areas in England, including Yorkshire and Lancashire, greatly increased over rural areas and proved exceptional in comparison with other urban counties. Aggregate figures provide general patterns but do not reveal the impact of migration on specific industrial locales, occupation by industry, or information on most women migrants.[84]

Qualitative evidence on late nineteenth-century English migration is scarce. Baines argued that during the late nineteenth century English newspapers supplanted the personal letter as a source of information. Charlotte Erickson's research on nineteenth-century British immigration used carefully selected primary sources of private letters and diaries, passenger lists, English and American population censuses, and county histories in both countries. In her many books and articles, especially *Invisible Immigrants: The Adaptation of English and Scottish Immigrants in Nineteenth-Century America* (1972) and *Leaving England: Essays on British Emigration in the Nineteenth Century* (1994), Erickson recovered the detailed experiences of British immigrants settling on farms and in small businesses, largely in rural American society. Explicitly choosing to avoid issues of class consciousness or labor conflict in either nation and in spite of her repeated warnings that her chosen few were not representative, her work on these immigrants has assumed great weight among historians, such as Baines, Nugent, and Hoerder. Rowland T. Berthoff's *British Immigrants in Industrial America, 1790–1950* (1953) followed working-class immigrants into American industrial cities but dealt with no particular industry, city, or region in depth. Based on the work of Berthoff and Erickson, British immigrants have become defined as a culturally invisible and predominately conservative people who adjusted easily to American society. The fiction of Hedley Smith, the activities of the textile workers of North Providence, and the research of Richard Stott on the ethics of work contradict this generalization.[85]

Brinley Thomas analyzed nineteenth- and early twentieth-century British migration cycles in the context of economic changes in the Atlantic economy, primarily the United States, Britain, and Germany. He indicated that lags occurred in the direct correlation between economic growth and transatlantic migration. His measures of American development, while quite general, are indirectly related to textile production: railroad construction and the production of bituminous coal. The availability of British investment capital for this U.S. growth is measured by data on building construction in England and on London share prices.[86] Increased numbers of European migrants who became cotton textile workers in the United States, Thomas argued, reflected the automation of machinery and consequent decline in skills required for the industrial production of cloth. He also noted the changes in migration patterns between the two world wars. In 1928, five years after the migration of Hedley Smith's family, the tendency for English migrants to shift from the United States to the Dominions strengthened until the Depression of the 1930s proved a turning point. British people then ceased emigration, while British society received return migrants from the United States, Canada, and Australia.[87]

Migration Patterns of the Smiths and Collinses

Hedley Smith's family, relatives, and in-laws participated in these historic and shifting migration patterns. His grandfather, Sam Smith, had initiated the idea of immigration to the United States but failed to gain the support of his sweetheart. He returned to marry her and settled down in Yorkshire. Still, just before he died suddenly of pneumonia in 1903, he seriously considered relocating his wife and nineteen-year-old son Ernest to South Africa. Ernest completed his apprenticeship as an artisan brushmaker in 1903 and married Alice Collins in 1904.

Alice Collins was raised in a family of loss and upset. Her mother died of heart failure when Alice was five; one of her three brothers died as a baby and another drowned at twelve. Her stepmother had two daughters. The house was crowded and affection was scattered among several small faces. Alice went off to the mills young and excelled as a weaver. After she married Ernest Smith, her mother-in-law watched her two sons as Alice continued to weave. She appeared to be a valuable worker, a doting mother, and a tender, loving wife.[88] Her brother, Arthur Collins, immigrated at a young age to Philadelphia in 1906, married a Yorkshire-born woman from North Providence, and worked as a machinist in Providence. Arthur Collins provided crucial support for the Smith family when they arrived in 1923. He became an American citizen in 1918 and witnessed the naturalization of his sister's family in 1929. Other Smith and Collins relations had migrated to homestead on the frontier of Saskatchewan, Canada, and still others to Australia and New Zealand. Like many other British migrants at the turn of the century, movement was on their minds. As such, they joined hundreds of thousands in the mass proletarian migrations across the Atlantic beginning in the nineteenth century and stretching into the early twentieth.

For Hedley Smith at thirteen in 1922, talk of migration was a subject for adults. A photograph taken by brother Sam that year, probably after a good Yorkshire Sunday dinner, shows a drowsy, well-fed father Ernest in a worsted suit with tie and watch chain, Alice benignly maternal in soft blouse and long skirt, and sturdy Hedley between them, alert and wearing the jacket and short pants of a school boy (see fig. 1).[89] In January 1921 Hedley had confided to his best friend Tom Cromwell about his attempts at poetry, his delight at winning a huge dictionary in a spelling contest, and "my favorite retreat," the library. His other close friend, Horace Sharp, shared their intense literary interests and close attention to local cricket teams. Quotes from his first diary, 1920–21, revealed Hedley's healthy love of holiday food and of impromptu football [soccer] games with "my mates."[90] Born, raised, and first schooled in Lidget Green, a Bradford neighborhood close to Joseph Benn and Company's Beckside Mill at Great Horton where his mother worked as a weaver, Hedley was happy in this comfortable world that he understood very well.

In 1922 young Hedley enjoyed a week's August holiday with his brother, parents, and their friends on the Isle of Man. He kept a diary of his journey, his first on "a foreign soil," even if located just off the coast in the Irish Sea.[91] His diary is highly organized and precise day by day, reflecting a lad's interest in trolleys, trains, ships, forts, caves, and castles. But dominated by the adults, the holiday was filled with walks, drives in horse-drawn vehicles, visits to pubs, and the anticipated scenic views, which Smith attempted to capture with literary flourishes. More to his liking were the memorably thick slices of cream cake and rich custards at dinner and the outbursts of fun and laughter during an improvised cricket game on the beach. The crossing by ship from Liverpool had been rough, sickening most of the passengers but not Hedley. At the island's special wishing spot, he gleefully hoped for a similarly rough return. Back in Bradford he anticipated other exciting holidays, as he resumed studying German, French, history, science, and mathematics at the Grange Road Secondary School for boys. With its grammar school curriculum, his education at the Grange School assured him and his friends social distinction and a path to university, worlds apart from many envious, resentful working-class youngsters.[92]

But that fall his mother, who had worked for years as a skilled weaver, had a physical collapse diagnosed as anemia. This required an expensive three-week stay in a nursing home at seaside Blackpool. Her loss of strength raised questions about her ability to work in the future. Hedley Smith recalled his

Figure 1. (*Below*) Ernest Smith, Hedley Smith at thirteen, Alice Smith, Aberdeen Place, Lidget Green, Bradford, c. 1922, courtesy of Sam Smith and Portia Thompson. (*Above*) Hedley Smith at fourteen, Johnston, R.I., December 1923, courtesy of Sam Smith and Portia Thompson. Thanks to Bruce Lepore.

awareness during his last summer in Yorkshire of the impending emigration as a "double shadow" cast across both his future and his schooling. Still he enjoyed "a very happy time" during the unusually fine summer weather.[93] By August 1923 Alice and Ernest were selling their household goods to leave for the United States and had spent the holiday funds to visit all their Yorkshire relatives to say goodbye. In Rhode Island, Hedley would forgo holidays until he could personally afford them.

Both emotional and economic factors shaped Ernest and Alice Smith's decision to leave Yorkshire and when to do so. They were both forty years old and their son Sam was eighteen. The family was part of a post–World War I wave of workers from a depressed Yorkshire textile industry. The Smiths came to settle. Alice Smith had worked as a skilled weaver but listed her occupation on the ship's manifest as a housekeeper.[94] She considered emigrating as early as 1913, but the family decided to wait. Ernest's widowed mother lived with them, and he was her only child. When she died in 1921, the family began seriously to consider a move. Donna Gabaccia and Hasia Diner both argue that a mother's death as in this case can precipitate a family decision to migrate.[95] Alice's father, Dracup Collins, a retired stone quarry worker, died in March 1922. Links with the older generations of Smiths and Collinses were dissolving. With Alice's physical collapse in the fall of 1922, pressure mounted for a move.

In 1923 Ernest Smith lost his job as a brushmaker for a worsted mill. By the 1920s 65 percent of British emigrants were traveling to the Dominions, but the worsted mills that had taken the trade from the West Riding were in the United States.[96] Alice and Ernest's concerns and dilemmas included the interests of their sons. Sam Smith had completed two years at Bradford Technical College with an accompanying apprenticeship with a Bradford firm. He knew that the worsted industry in Yorkshire was in decline and thought that the United States offered brighter opportunities. For Hedley Smith, however, the North Country was full of historically rich and dramatic literary associations. The landscape of the West Riding was exciting and well explored. His family and kin seemed to be embedded in Bradford society and comfortably well off. He had passed the crucial exams, won a scholarship, and was bound for university. His future appeared bright. Yorkshire was his land of promise.

Immigration Restriction and the Smith Family

By 1922 American policy toward immigration had shifted sharply toward restriction. The adoption of a literacy test in 1917 meant little to most Yorkshire migrants, although Hedley's grandmother Mary could not write her name. Still, advocates of this step toward restriction predicted a 25 percent decline in immigration.[97] More important, the legislation that passed in 1917 set up a large bureaucracy to regulate the immigration of aliens, including the expansion of inspection points at ports of entry and, working closely with the newly organized Department of Labor, the use of fines to discourage contract labor.[98] When postwar restrictionist policies emerged, the administrative infrastructure was already in place.[99] The United States' involvement in World War I, which produced domestic discord despite the government push for national unity, sparked a revival of antiradical nativism and programs for Americanization. Postwar labor upheavals intensified both impulses.

Fears of a huge flood of migrants from postwar Europe shaped the new policy of racial restriction based on nationality adopted in the Immigration Act of 1921.[100] This provisional legislation was extended in 1922 to last until 1924. Annual quotas for entry to a maximum of 355,000 annually beginning in 1921 restricted each nation of origin to 3 percent of the number of persons born in that country and listed in the U.S. Population Census of 1910.[101] The Quota Act of 1924 reduced the annual number to 2 percent among a total of 150,000 for Europe, but the designated census enumeration shifted back to 1890. English immigrants were still favored, but the *numbers* admitted by percentages alone had dropped by a third between 1921 and 1924. The window of opportunity was closing fast. Brinley Thomas described the summer of 1923 as a "panic-driven rush" to enter the United States before the new quotas of 1924 were imposed.[102] Family sources do not reveal any concern by the Smiths about immigration restriction, but Yorkshire people, who had migrated before World War I and continued to do so during the postwar period, were likely to know all about it.

As a lad of fourteen, Hedley Smith arrived at Boston from Liverpool with his family in October 1923 after a rough, gloomy ten-day crossing. A fourteen-year-old involuntary migrant character in one of his novels voiced his remembered heartache. "It was all so English, so like the place I had come from; but there was a difference, and it was this likeness in unlikeness that hurt the most of all . . . that was harder to bear than utter strangeness would have been."[103]

Smith's father, Ernest, a master brushmaker, had become unemployed during the postwar depression. A Yorkshire-born friend and former workmate, Bill Shann encouraged him to seek similar skilled work in a woolcombing operation that he managed in North Chelmsford, Massachusetts. Ernest's emigration might have been that of a nineteenth-century venturesome conservative, hoping to escape the destruction of his craft.[104] The ship's manifest listed all of this information and Shann's address, which was handed over to the Boston immigration inspectors. In his decision to emigrate, Ernest Smith acted as an agent for his family's interests. With a job in his trade secured, Alice could give up weaving, Sam might continue his technical studies at the nearby Lowell Textile School, and Hedley could resume classes at the local high school. But in 1923 state intervention disrupted this commonplace chain migration. When Ernest and his family arrived in Boston, the immigration service officials told him that in arranging to guarantee a job, both he and his friend were involved in an illegal "conspiracy to deprive a native-born American citizen of an employment opportunity."[105] They threatened Bill Shann with a heavy fine of $200 for violating contract labor laws and Ernest and his family with deportation.[106] Why Ernest did not know this or why no one in Yorkshire tipped him off to conceal this arrangement is not clear. As Adam McKeown has pointed out: "All migration moves through [unpredictable] social and political landscapes."[107] During the following two weeks, zealous immigration officials of Irish background continued to harass both Englishmen in North Chelmsford.[108] Ernest's son recreated this incident by "the blasted" immigration officials ("and them Irish to the last man jack of 'em)" in part 1 of his Briardale trilogy, "The Millmaster." As a result of these threats, Ernest quickly moved his family to an unknown address among the English settlements in Rhode Island near his brother-in-law, where he, his wife, and oldest son sought work in the Providence area worsted mills.[109] Ernest Smith never forgot what he saw as an injustice. According to his son's recollections, subsequent Fourth of July celebrations of America as the land of freedom, justice, and opportunity made his father grimace.[110] Although Ernest Smith along with his family became citizens as early as possible in 1929, his was a cynical convenience, not a commitment. His wife and sons apparently never spoke about their own feelings, but it is hard to believe that the boys did not blame their father for failing to avoid the infamous contract labor law.

Facing a material and emotional crisis in their immigration plan, they rearranged the family economy. Ernest's skills were technically obsolete; immigration, as it turned out, had cost him his trade. He searched for other kinds of jobs in the various Providence mills, including a mechanized brush factory. He had skilled hands but was not used to being bossed. Alice Smith never found any skilled jacquard weaving jobs, but once very briefly demonstrated her skills in the window of a department store. Sam had completed two years at the Bradford Technical Institute in Yorkshire while serving an apprenticeship at a local engineering firm. Arriving in Providence on October 20, two weeks after the family docked at Boston, Sam worked very briefly in textile mills located in the villages of Esmond and Centredale in North Providence, Rhode Island. This was not the work life he or his parents had hoped for. Within a year, probably helped by Uncle Arthur Collins, a machinist, Sam applied for the position of apprentice draftsman at Brown and Sharpe in Providence. In the meantime he worked as a lathe operator while the family rented furnished housing in Johnston where Uncle Arthur and his family lived.[111] With mixed hope and trepidation on leaving Yorkshire, Sam got a job with this well-known Providence machine design company. Furthermore, with the decline of Bradford textiles, many of his shop mates were Yorkshire-born.[112]

Hedley's hopes for continued education ended abruptly. In Bradford at fourteen he had passed the eleven plus exams and obtained a scholarship to attend a school with a curriculum that prepared its students for university.[113] When he arrived in North Providence as a "school boy" in short pants during the fall of 1923 and applied for admission to classes, the local high school refused to provide additional formal education to this son of working-class parents. Hedley was prepared for an advanced curriculum of Greek, Latin, and mathematics, but his family had no money for a classical high school. In the eyes of the Johnston school officials, however, fourteen was the typical age that children in millworker families entered the mills.[114] Hedley and his family were profoundly disappointed.

For months in his earliest letters to his friends in Lidget Green, Hedley could not bring himself to mention it. Emigration for him represented an incalculable loss of educational opportunity that destroyed his life. The fact that at fourteen he became the first steady wage-earner for the family crushed his aspirations.[115] Parting his slicked-backed hair straight down the middle and donning his first long trousers and a cheap, ill-fitting suit jacket, he went to work in late December 1923 as a file clerk in Providence (see fig. 1 above). Indeed his recommendation from Headmaster Denby in Bradford included both teachers and employers.[116] His whole demeanor as a well-educated, properly brought up English lad made him an attractive choice to prospective employers for a job he desperately did not want.

As a result Hedley Smith did not experience the acculturation process of American schooling. He never obtained a high school diploma but subsequently attended classes at a small local business school. Unlike other English immigrants, neither language nor skills nor educational attainments nor aspirations helped the Smith family adjust to a new culture. They faced unanticipated harassment by the state carried out by Irish American immigration officials, doubtless motivated by revenge over English policy toward Ireland. Their immediate hopes for an easy settlement and family economic security and advancement vanished. Expecting skilled work for Ernest in North Chelmsford, the Smith family brought few possessions with them. While they moved about the Providence area, they lived "poor" and sought work and friends.[117]

Carl Strikwerda has pointed to the state and the economy as the major determinates of international migration in the nineteenth and twentieth centuries.[118] From the perspective of Hedley Smith and his family, those factors provide the context of migration, but the intent and motives of the migrants themselves remain primary. Planning strategies and family agendas, saving travel funds and disposing of household goods, saying farewells to friends and relatives, and then carrying out these decisions, the migrants themselves became the agents of timing and movement and the recipients of whatever were the consequences. Furthermore, the Smith family's decision to leave Yorkshire in 1923 occurred during the "huge break" of nineteenth-century global migrations after World War I. Their decision was first delayed by dependent family members, then triggered by a friend's promise of a good job with excellent prospects. These human considerations overrode ongoing economic trends. Rowland Berthoff's sturdy Yorkshire immigrant artisans, such as machinists, as well as worsted workers and carpet weavers, were welcomed to American shores for their skills and the aspiration of their children.[119] In the case of artisan Ernest Smith, officials of the U.S. Immigration Service in Boston with Irish backgrounds and memories of homeland persecution seized the opportunity to punish two Englishmen. Personal political reprisal colored state action. The consequences of migration included the unexpected. Dashed hopes did not result in return migration but profoundly shaped the migration experience. The life and imaginative work of Hedley Smith emerged from these circumstances.

2

Migrations of Capital, Industry, and People, 1891–1922

In April 1891 William Smith of Leeds, Yorkshire, set out from Liverpool on the *Majestic* bound for the United States to write a book about his travels. Sharing the luxurious accommodations of saloon class was the director of the Titus Salt firm at Saltaire, determined to assess the American market after the passage of the 1890 McKinley tariffs as well as the firm's operations in Bridgeport, Connecticut. He would later conclude that the U.S. market for Yorkshire goods was dead, currently and for the foreseeable future.

William Smith did not visit Bridgeport but proceeded dutifully to both Lawrence, Massachusetts, and Philadelphia, Pennsylvania, for a brief look at the American worsted industry. He inspected the huge Pacific mills in Lawrence and talked to Yorkshire immigrant workers among the firm's 5,000 operatives. Most of them had been in the United States for one or two decades and told him of their "perfect satisfaction" with the work and the city. In Philadelphia his dialect was immediately recognized while he searched for acquaintances: "Eh! Ye're through [from] Leeds or Huthersfield [Huddersfield] way?" Smith reported to them on the "Old Country" but left Philadelphia unimpressed with the managers, the quality of the fabrics, or the competitive threat from the United States. In 1891 at least, there were American jobs for English worsted workers. Facing the reality of the McKinley tariffs, some Yorkshire worsted and plush firms sent agents in 1891 and 1892 to survey the prospects for branch factories in the Northeast in Utica, New York, South Portland, Maine, and Providence, Rhode Island. The industrial depression beginning in late 1893 ended the export of international capital to the United States but only temporarily.[1]

Early twentieth-century European capital investment in textile manufacturing in the United States built major centers of production in the Northeast and attracted migrants with experience and skills as well as many others new to the industry. American capitalists, counting on years of high protective tariffs under the new majority Republican Party, also hastened to invest money in textile expansion. Capital movements prompted a complicated labor migration to these growing textile centers that defies classification as either "old" or "new." Better described as a mixture or medley of people from diverse nations of origin, these textile workers came from widely varying cultural and industrial backgrounds. They formed a workforce for worsted production in Massachusetts, Rhode Island, New Jersey, and Pennsylvania far more culturally complicated than in English, French, German, or Italian textile cities. For example, the workforce of the worsted industry in Roubaix, France, was regional and largely from nearby Belgium.[2] The implications of the mélange of migrants with transatlantic connections and multiple political perspectives shaped community building, mill floor organization, ethnic conflict, acculturation, and multicultural radical labor politics in early twentieth-century New England worsted communities. Not even the transfer of small numbers of Yorkshire worsted workers with a homogeneous background to a tiny Bradford-style mill in Greystone village, North Providence, could isolate them from these complexities.

Empirical data on these developments in Rhode Island mill villages when compared with Hedley Smith's fiction on early Briardale provides a diverse picture, often as contradictory as enriching. These contradictions allow insight into the author's intent for his imagined Briardale. Together the lived and the imagined complicate an understanding of early twentieth-century Yorkshire migration. Furthermore, placing this fiction in the context of early twentieth-century Rhode Island industrial development and labor conflicts provides new evidence on the lived experiences of working-class migrants who came to adopt a multiethnic or transcultural labor politics even as they cherished and defended their homeland culture. Probing the connections between ethnic enclaves and multicultural class coalitions can deepen an understanding of the relationship between translocal experience and transcultural ties.

Transatlantic Investment and Migration

As the American industrial depression eased by 1896, the passage of the 1897 Dingley tariffs ended all hope of the resumption of Yorkshire exports to the United States. E. M. Sigsworth estimated that total Yorkshire worsted exports fell by 50 percent between the 1880s and 1913.[3] Some English and West European firms frozen out of the American worsted market in 1890 began to move to New England, specifically to establish branch factories in Rhode Island. Belgian and French capitalists developed the French-style worsted industry in Woonsocket, Rhode Island, in the early twentieth century. Earlier in the 1880s English investors and experienced workers from Macclesfield had built a thriving silk textile industry in Paterson, New Jersey, while German companies in the early twentieth century invested even more heavily in worsted mills in Passaic, New Jersey, drawing their skilled workers across the Atlantic to join a workforce of unskilled migrants from southern and eastern Europe.[4] At the turn of the twentieth century, skilled textile workers, including experienced French and Belgian worsted workers and northern Italian silk workers from Lombardy and Piedmont, migrated simultaneously with rural migrants from southern and eastern Europe seeking jobs in American worsted and silk mills. These industries provide additional evidence to dissolve the traditional distinctions between "old" and "new."

Although the numbers of French and Belgian migrants in Woonsocket, Rhode Island, never rose above 2,000, the presence of both Franco-Belgian capitalists and skilled workers provided the city with heavy investment for new mills and with a small experienced workforce inclined to strike action and radical politics. The French investors from Roubaix and Tourcoing remained absentee mill owners who visited once a year, but Belgian capitalist Joseph Guerin became an American citizen, community leader, and paternalist manager. The majority of Woonsocket's textile workers came from Quebec, Canada, creating a vast social and economic distance from the French managers and "aristocratic" Franco-Belgian industrial workers, especially the mule spinners. Other industrial communities that attracted transatlantic workers such as Belgian glass makers developed, then readjusted—in their own interests—specific cultural and political frameworks in which those migrants lived and worked.[5] Yorkshire migrants to North Providence mill villages followed this pattern.

In 1903 Harrison Benn, head of Joseph Benn Ltd. of Great Horton, Bradford, began to rebuild the decayed Rhode Island mill village of Greystone in the town of North Providence. Initial capital investment in the new Greystone mill far exceeded any worsted operation established by French and Belgian investors in Woonsocket between 1899 and 1904. Benn intended to manufacture English-style worsteds: goods "equal, if not superior to the same goods made in our mills at Bradford, England."[6] Greystone and the surrounding mill villages of Esmond, Graniteville, Centredale, and Georgiaville, clustered along the Woonasquatucket River that flowed eastward toward Providence harbor, became the immediate basis for Hedley Smith's fictional Briardale (see map 3).

But Smith also intended through the Briardale stories to represent Yorkshire immigrants and their cultural and economic settings that stretched from the worsted mill villages in Harrisville near the Massachusetts border, to the worsted towns in central Rhode Island, and south to the Peace Dale

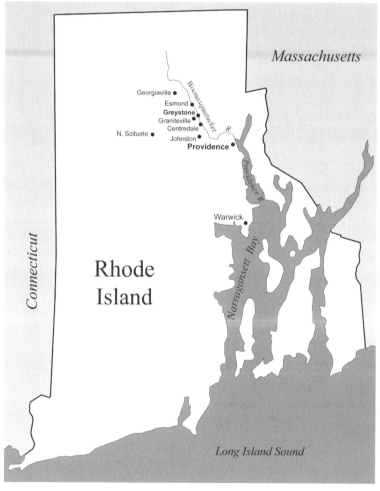

Map 3. State of Rhode Island, important features, and the mill villages of North Providence, c. 1922. Courtesy of Paul Coppens.

mills in Washington County.[7] Smith also provided transatlantic vignettes of working-class and middle-class society in fictional "Silsbury" and in the Yorkshire mill village of Wilsden and the city of Bradford.

The industrial economy of Rhode Island had prospered during the American Civil War and expanded during the postwar years. The workforce in textiles grew from 16,000 in 1865 to 23,000 in 1880. Machine tool producers and the Corliss steam-engine company in the capital city of Providence helped advance the technology of making cloth. Lancashire immigrants worked in numerous cotton-mill sites located in the Blackstone River Valley in northern Rhode Island. By 1900 the thirty-mile radius around Providence, including the Blackstone Valley and the town of Woonsocket, contained the largest concentration of textile manufacturing firms in the United States. By 1905, profiting from tariff protection that had begun in 1890, the twelve worsted mills in Providence boasted the largest capitalization in the city (63 percent of the total capital invested) and the highest value of product in the city's total textile production.[8] Trade journals insisted that worsted cloth made from hard-twisted yarns would dominate the future of men's wear at the expense of New England's woolen mills.[9]

Between 1905 and 1911, the huge American Woolen Company in Lawrence, a firm that specialized in Bradford-style worsted cloth, established its dominance in New England worsted production. Employing 14,000 workers in 1912, American Woolen, in combination with the Arlington and Pacific worsted mills in Lawrence, set regional wage rates for the New England worsted industry. During those years, American Woolen owned a total of twenty-nine worsted mills in New England, nine of them in Rhode Island.[10] German investors in five large worsted mills in Passaic, New Jersey, had the future potential to challenge the position of the firms in Lawrence in the worsted production market. To avoid this withering competition, the Benn operation in Greystone sought a niche in black mohair and alpaca coat linings, using its established commission house in New York City to sell its products. This marketing strategy allowed them to avoid hiring the mixture of ethnic groups in the huge workforces of most large textile operations, as in Lawrence and Passaic.[11]

Developing American Worsted Centers

In 1905 Rhode Island woolen and worsted production ranked third in the nation. Massachusetts was first in value of product at $110 million, Pennsylvania second at $83 million, and Rhode Island third with $53 million.

Six other Northeastern states together produced $113 million. New Jersey ranked seventh; the Passaic mills had just begun to enter the contest.[12] Massachusetts employed 50,000 operatives in the industry, Pennsylvania had 40,000, and Rhode Island 22,000. Those numbers included many English immigrant workers as well as many naturalized citizens of English and Scots background. Compared with other immigrant groups, they were a minority but possessed, as did Germans, Franco-Belgians, and Scots, industrial experience and skills.

According to the 1911 Immigration Commission's study of one-quarter of the national total of employees in the woolen and worsted industry, English-born males represented 17 percent of the total number in the study, while English-born females represented 13 percent.[13] By 1900 the mills of Lawrence employed nearly 70 percent foreign-born workers in which operatives from Ireland, England, Scotland, Germany, and French Canada predominated. Native-born workers of Irish and English parents dominated the Philadelphia workforce. The mills of Providence, Rhode Island, employed 4,701 operatives in 1900, of whom 55 percent were foreign-born, much larger than Philadelphia and second to the Lawrence percentage. In Providence, as in Lawrence and Philadelphia, the largest proportion of workers had northern and western European background, but the number of southern Italian-born workers in Providence and Lawrence was much higher than in Philadelphia.[14]

The same 1911 study of employees reported a total of 58 percent male workers, of whom 87 percent were foreign-born or were second-generation immigrant. Similarly, of the 42 percent females workers, 86 percent were of foreign birth or background. Of those male operatives previously employed in "textile manufacturing," workers from France topped the list with nearly 90 percent, followed by the Germans, English, Scots, and Russian Jews. Among the females previously employed in textiles, the French and English represented nearly 90 percent with very high percentages for Scots and German workers. Only 10 percent of the southern Italian females and less than 1 percent of the southern Italian males had previous textile experience, but by 1911 they were entering American worsted production in large numbers. The commission study included only the foreign-born workers who represented at least 5 percent of the male employees in the 1905 industry: French Canadian, English, Irish, South Italian, and Polish. But forty additional groups were listed by "race," actually by national birthplace.[15] The majority of workers in the best jobs were well trained and experienced.

The established "races" in the worsted industry, according to the Immigration Commission study, were however being displaced by new migrants.

The study of Community A—quite obviously Lawrence, Massachusetts—demonstrated this shift. The pre- and post–Civil War expansion of the (Lawrence) textile mills had attracted a "heavy immigration" of English workers from Lancashire and Yorkshire to join others from Scotland. Irish immigrant construction workers who in the 1840s had built the dam on the Merrimack River, the mills, and the tenements constituted a separate community. Waves of French Canadians and Germans joined the postwar workforce. By 1890 new groups of workers from Poland, Portugal, "Hebrew" Russia, South Italy, Syria, Armenia, Lithuania, Belgium, and France complicated the structure of an already culturally mixed workforce. Numerically French Canadians ranked first in the city's total population with the English residents second to the Germans, but all British migrants (English, Scots, and Irish) had slipped in number since 1890. Still, this commission study on the eve of the Lawrence Bread and Roses Strike of 1912 listed "the English and South Italian races" as the most important among the total of 73.2 percent foreign-born workers in the city. Data from the Lawrence Worsted Mills in 1909 also indicated that English and southern Italian immigrant workers dominated this company's workforce.[16]

The Bradford-style processes in Lawrence worsted production remained familiar to the English migrant, but their workmates in the city were nothing like the West Riding. While the small village of Greystone with its Yorkshire workforce in 1910 did not represent the multicultural American worsted industry in Woonsocket, Lawrence, or Passaic, neither was it isolated from regional wage rates or strikes. When Yorkshire immigrants in Greystone went out on strike in the early 1910s, their key allies were Italian immigrant worsted workers in nearby mill villages.

In his study of the ethnic communities in Lawrence, Donald Cole endorsed the social invisibility of English immigrants in the late nineteenth-century city. "The English did not quickly establish societies because they encountered no linguistic or religious conflicts with the natives." Given class and cultural divisions, close social connections between Yankees merchants or lawyers in Lawrence and Yorkshire-born textile workers seem unlikely. But in contrast with German, Irish, and French Canadians, Cole insisted that the English migrants "had an easier time."[17] Still, evidence on the nineteenth-century activities of the English-born residents belies Cole's invisibility argument.

The Yorkshire community in Lawrence had its own newspaper, the *Lawrence Journal* (1871–77), edited and published by Yorkshire immigrant Robert Bowers.[18] Bowers became notably active in the ten-hour working day reform movement through state and local politics, mobilizing the Yorkshire-born.

Richard Hinchcliffe, Yorkshire-born labor reformer who migrated in 1849 to Lawrence from Bradford with his working-class parents, wrote poetry critical of chattel slavery and wage slavery. Also a dedicated supporter of radical politics, Hinchcliffe lobbied vigorously between 1869 and 1874 for the passage of the Massachusetts ten-hour legislation. His friend Robert Bowers published Hinchcliffe's volume of radical poems, *Rhymes Among the Spindles,* in 1872. The early organization of cricket clubs and chorale groups in the 1860s and 1870s suggest an expression of interests peculiar to English workers. They lived together in an ethnic enclave near the Arlington mills, voted Republican, and dominated city politics in Ward 5. The quick establishment of a cooperative store on the English Rochdale plan in 1866 gave shareholders access to household goods at cost. For years, Cole noted, the cooperative at the Arlington mills was the largest in the United States.[19] Migrants to Greystone also quickly organized village activities specific to Yorkshire culture.

Once built, the Greystone Mill produced fine alpaca and mohair linings for custom-made men's coats, which the managers sold both directly and through New York and later through Chicago commission houses. Shareholders and banks in Bradford and Providence provided the investment capital, while the town of North Providence assured tax-exemption status for ten years. In comparison, the neighboring American-owned worsted spinning mill in Centredale, even with its own tax exemption, had capital assets of a mere $100,000 in 1905. By 1905 capital assets in the Benn mills of Greystone increased from $1 million to $1.5 million, rising after the profits of World War I to $2 million and to $3 million in 1924, after which they declined until the mill was sold in 1939.[20] Harrison Benn became the president/treasurer and his brother William Henry Benn vice president, thereby maintaining tight control over the operations in Great Horton and in Greystone.

Harrison Benn hired Frank P. Sheldon of Providence to survey various sites. On his advice, Benn chose the abandoned Greystone cotton mill and its water rights and dam on the Woonasquatucket River. In 1904 Sheldon's engineering firm began to build the Benn operation at Greystone, which included a large four-story brick mill flanked by two towers and an imposing chimney of 160 feet. The mill owners introduced steel (not cast iron) beams into local brick mill construction and concrete (not the traditional granite) foundations between seven and ten feet thick. Using state-of-the-art electrification technology, the managers organized production to duplicate, and even better, the technical standards in Yorkshire. In addition, a distinctive saw-tooth roof with huge glass windows to cast light on the looms topped the spacious ground-floor weave shed. Benn made sure that there would be no trouble with illumination or vibration for his weavers. The dye house emptied its black waste into the river.[21]

The onsite mill superintendent, George Keralake, and his wife arrived in 1904 with an English maid. They subsequently resided in a large green and white painted Colonial house with a big porch, surrounded by wide lawns and old rhododendrons. Two other English-born managers followed as the mill expanded its operations. The management of the mill consisted of a designer, two bookkeepers, a timekeeper, a paymaster, a cashier, and a shipping clerk, all English-born. The overseers of the various major divisions of work were likewise experienced men of English birth, most arriving in 1904 and 1905 and one via the worsted mills of Pennsylvania. The Benns also enlisted the aid of North Providence lawyers, bankers, and insurance agents.[22]

The initial complex for the village featured fifty semidetached rental cottages for 100 operative families, but the company expected to hire more than a thousand workers and quickly built wooden, Bradford-style back-to-back tenements. The old, dilapidated cotton mill was refurbished to house a Westinghouse steam turbine to generate electric light both for the mill and the cottages. A branch track of the New York, New Haven and Hartford Railroad ran a spur line through the boiler room to deliver coal (see fig. 2).

The Rhode Island Company extended its trolley line from nearby Centredale to provide freight cars to deliver merchandise to Providence for shipment across Long Island Sound to New York City. Those trolley cars carried back imported mohair and alpaca and later would provide a commuting service for workers from Providence.[23] Benn inspected his property in the late summer of 1904. These decisions, made by telegraphed correspondence between Bradford and Providence on bank loans, mill construction, and transportation links, turned Harrison Benn into one of Rhode Island's most energetic and well-connected industrial capitalists.

Work continued into 1905. In February 1906 Harrison Benn personally supervised the starting up of mill operations, delayed for months by his insistence on importing English machinery. Benn purchased new textile machinery but insisted that it all be run in the Bradford mills to qualify as lower-taxed used machinery for importation into the United States. Coincidently, pieces of worsted cloth on these looms intended for the huge Greystone weave shed had been woven by Alice Collins Smith, Hedley's mother, in 1903 and 1904. Benn built forty more cottages and a village store. An initial contingent of twenty-nine Yorkshire men and women had arrived in the summer of 1904 to help set up operations.[24] Three experienced wool sorters trained local men in English methods for judging color and texture in imported alpaca and

Figure 2. Greystone Village, North Providence, Rhode Island, n.d., courtesy the Rhode Island Historical Society. *Inset:* The Greystone Mill, 1925, courtesy of Sam Smith and Portia Thompson. Thanks to Bruce Lepore.

mohair. They favored Yorkshire immigrants. No American supplies would be used in production, even to the soap for scouring dirt from the fleeces. Where William Benn got his ideas for this mill village is unclear, but mill engineer Frank Sheldon contributed his experience from constructing mill villages around New England. It is doubtful that Yorkshire workers who came to Greystone from Bradford had ever worked in such a setting. Benn had constructed for his own purposes an idealized version of a Yorkshire mill village. Hedley Smith's fiction would expand that idealization.

English-born men performed the skilled work in the mills, including engineers, steamfitters, and firemen for the steam engines, dyers (except for one experienced forty-eight-year-old French Canadian dyer, possibly from Lawrence), cloth inspectors and finishers, loom fixers, machinists, electricians, carpenters, masons, and warehousemen. Benn carefully avoided American anticontract labor laws by personally recruiting a workforce, family by family, in Bradford.[25] Walter Rotherey and his family of four arrived in 1906. All members worked at the new Benn mill, most of them as weavers. In 1907 Simon Priestley brought his wife, two daughters, and his son to Greystone. He and all of his children worked in the Benn mill, while his wife, Mary, obligingly boarded English-born weaver Ethel Greenwood.[26]

Brinley Thomas observed that between 1905 and 1913 the numbers of British migrants to the United States both declined and shifted toward skilled workers and middle-class professionals. The New England cotton textile industry required fewer skilled workers from Lancashire as automated machinery, such as the Draper loom, took over production processes, but William Benn had no trouble hiring experienced worsted workers. Union wool sorters particularly considered themselves as a skilled elite. By July 1905 Benn and Sons advertised to manufacturers and buyers alike the availability of Bradford-quality black and white linings and yarns of mohair and alpaca as well as facilities for custom dyeing and finishing.[27]

After worsted production began, the village grew quickly as the company laid out a pattern of streets, one named Beckside Road after the Benn mill in Great Horton, Bradford. Hundreds of dwellings were built, provided with both running water and electric light by the mill. Most were multiple-family attached rowhouses with a few single and semi-detached or double residences. A large, very utilitarian boardinghouse provided housing for single male and female workers. Several privately owned stores opened. Rhode Island Yankee Alfred Sweet opened a general store with a young English-born butcher who knew how to cut a proper Sunday joint. Massachusetts Yankee George Charette barbered the men, while his wife (born in New York) helped keep the mill's books. By 1910 a family of Italian American merchant tailors, Angelo Rossi and his sons Alexander and Frank Rossi, with their extended families, relocated via New York City and Providence to Greystone, where they made suits and coats. Angelo and Alexander Rossi had emigrated in 1878 and 1879 and were naturalized citizens. Southern Italian immigrants including weavers in Providence, hostile to priests from northern Italy, had engaged in struggles in 1902 to protect their religious culture and forge their community.[28] By 1910 a few Italian weavers resided in Greystone village and more probably worked in the Benn mill and lived in Providence.

Despite efforts by the Benn management to build a mill and a village like the Bradford district, residing in Smith's "Briardale" was not the same socially or physically. For many young Yorkshire men, the other textile workers in

Rhode Island mills seemed a "tame lot," while village social life proved so dull that those wishing excitement had to walk miles through a seemingly empty New England landscape to Providence.[29] And many characters in the Briardale fiction felt they had had no choice but to emigrate.

> "Aye, it were a black day for the West Riding, were that," Grandfather Denby would say. . . . "It were a case of sit at home and starve to death, or else pack your traps and get a move on. We didn't come here 'cause we wanted, but 'cause we had to. I'll never forget the day. I comed home to mother there, and I said, lass, we're bound to go."[30]

The wooden houses also prompted many complaints. The earliest residents of the village of "Briardale" according to Hedley Smith's "The Mill Folk" found:

> a little bit of a place when they arrived, a two-three houses at the most, and a little old shoddy mill with whitewashed stone walls and a red slate roof. The second hand machinery was being set up in it and soon the looms were rattling away. Streets were staked out in long rows one behind the other up the slope of the hill, trees were felled, and the company houses began to rise in rows in their place, much the same as you see them today. Flimsy things they looked, with their wooden boards and green shutters, to folks who'd known nothing but solid stone and slate, and many were the scornful remarks that were made about them.
>
> "Tumbledown affairs they were," Grandfather Denby said. "It seemed the first puff of wind would blow them all away." And he never tired of telling the story of [weaving overseer] Sam Knowles, even at times and places when he should have known it would be good manners to keep his mouth shut. "I mind when they were having a hassle over the weavers' rates, when George Curtis was overlooker. It was supposed to be a great secret till Binns-Cockcroft wanted it known. But somehow it were all round the village, and George was in a mad hig to think anybody dared set his wishes at nought. So he called Sam into his office and he said to him, "Now, Sam, it's all over the place about the new piece rates, and that were a secret between thee and me. So one of us two must have talked and I'm damned sure it wasn't me." And Sam, he stood right up to him and said, "Well, there's nobbut one way that I can think on. The only soul I've breathed a word to is my own wife, and I told her while we were ligging in bed t'other night, and it must be that somebody in the next house heard us through these blasted paper-thin partition walls. That's all I can say." And George sort of smiled, and all he said was, "Well, Sam lad, it just goes to show, a man can't ever be too careful, even when he's i' bed with his own wife."[31]

In Smith's fiction, Briardale village in the pre–World War I days represented a successful if temporary transplantation of Yorkshire culture and custom. These days

> had been the good ones. All the fowk had been more like one big, happy family, wi' the bairns running in and out of each other's houses . . . ; the fathers and mothers setting on the doorsteps . . . ; the men reading under the long summer twilight the newspapers from England and calling across to one another the cricket scores, til the voice of Pea Wally swelled up like a Chapel hymn of benediction as he trudged the streets in his long white apron, his great tin kettle of hot peas swimming in spicy pork gravy balanced on his shoulder.

Wally Sugden was a Briardale institution; he was

> another link with the old Bradford life where a man could addle a comfortable living peddling hot victuals up and down the districts where whole families worked in the mills in rotating shifts that left no time for cooking hot dishes at home.[32]

Hilly woodlands owned by the Benns surrounded the whole village. Those Yorkshire workpeople, who had arrived on the isolated construction site during the summer of 1904, almost immediately organized a social club and built a Primitive Methodist Chapel by 1905. The building of social networks prompted the expected chain migrations. As other workers arrived with their families, the club grew and sought a place to meet. The club's board of directors raised funds, but Harrison Benn offered to both build and equip a large structure for the Greystone Social Club. The Whitehall Building with its own janitor opened its doors in June 1907. The four-story white clapboard building, including a street-level basement, sported a wide, sweeping porch with one balcony overlooking the river and the cricket field beyond for sipping beer and reading newspapers.[33] The first floor for men only housed separate rooms for billiards, reading, dartboards, and smoking in addition to a secretary's office. A bar sold bitter beer made on the premises and Scotch whiskey. A large assembly hall on the second floor with restrooms for men and women shared the second floor with a men's gymnasium. After a meeting or a dance, members came downstairs for Yorkshire teas and collected their belongings from the cloak room.[34] The design suggested the arrangements without the fancy decorations for saloon-class passengers aboard the ocean-going steamships familiar to Harrison Benn.

The grand new building provided a community center with shops on the street floor but did not wholly contain the sociability of Greystone residents.

By 1911 the mill employed 1,400 hands who acquired in 1912 their own much smaller clubhouse, "The Working Men's Club." Men and women of the village used this place for other more exclusive activities, such as complaining about wages and conditions and organizing labor protests, which peaked in 1912 and 1913. A small elementary school opened in 1910 with one teacher and an enrollment of about twenty-five pupils.[35]

Housed in one of the shops in the Whitehall building, the Greystone cooperative store served English families living in the surrounding mill villages: Graniteville, Centredale, Esmond, and as far north as the cotton textile town of Olneyville in the Blackstone Valley. Workers from the Centredale Worsted Mills, a spinning operation with English machinery, shopped at the co-op. The Esmond mills, expanded in 1906, made fine blankets of cotton and wool and employed many English-born workers. Following Yorkshire practice as at the Arlington mills in Lawrence, members of the Greystone Cooperative bought shares to finance the purchase of household goods at cost and received annual dividends based on the financial success of the transactions.[36] The co-op provided a network of community contacts within the river valley and beyond that served well in strike activities and in spreading news of jobs openings and social activities.

As in Lawrence, migrants to Greystone quickly organized other village activities specific to Yorkshire culture. The Social Club sponsored annual contests held by the Greystone Fanciers' Association for the best breeds of poultry and for the best dogs as well as special holidays including the American Thanksgiving and the Yorkshire-style Whitsuntide in the spring. Dialect songs and recitations and other entertainments accompanied the Social Club's monthly "feeds" of roast beef. A Christmas tree and gifts for the village children were followed on Christmas Day by a celebration at the clubhouse with traditional richly spiced Christmas cake frosted with marzipan and white icing, and plum puddings with brandy sauce provided by the members' wives and daughters. During the year the Providence Young Women's Christian Association held classes each week at the smaller social club, offering the girls gymnastics. The Whitehall gym was reserved for men and boys, but the YWCA provided young females with lessons in the domestic arts of sewing and millinery at the Whitehall Building. The Loyal Greystone Lodge of the Odd Fellows, Manchester, England United, and their auxiliary Odd Ladies could choose whichever meeting place suited. Both the English and American sports of cricket, English football, baseball, and a troop of Boy Scouts diverted the men and boys. Each year in July, the village held a Greystone

river carnival, attracting contestants locally and from other states and sometimes from Canada by offering competitive rowing and swimming contests.[37]
Outwardly, sociability included the bicultural, but many Yorkshire migrants
clung tightly to their own institutions, culture, and social networks.

Hedley Smith's fiction describes the three religious organizations available to Briardale residents. They included two Methodist churches: the small
Primitive Methodist chapel, and the larger, more moderate Methodists who
offered a range of religious and social activities, such as the Whitsuntide
festivities. According to the census of 1910 John Singleton, the thirty-two-
year-old minister of the Greystone Methodist Church, with his wife Sarah
and their Massachusetts-born three-year-old son had emigrated in the 1890s
from England, probably from Yorkshire. The Primitive Methodists took care
of preschool children for their working mothers. Both of these religious services featured "lots of plain speaking and rough eloquence, plenty of Bible
language and references to things of simple, everyday living that would bring
the message home . . ., and a spice of hellfire and brimstone seasoning to
make it savory to their palates."[38]

An Episcopal church in nearby "Middleton" (actually Centredale) offered
Anglican-style services primarily for the mill's owners, their managers, and
other professionals. By 1912, however, a rising and dissenting Yorkshire middle class in Middleton had organized a Methodist church. In another story,
Smith also invented a nineteenth-century Episcopal Chapel in Briardale with
so few members that a curate was sent over on Sundays from a town ten miles
away.[39] If there was a church in Greystone before the Benn operations, it was
more likely to have been Congregational or Baptist.

Based on his study of Spanish immigrants to Buenos Aires, Jose Moya
proposed using his model for English immigrants to the United States. Both
groups faced the dual collective identity of belonging to the founding culture but of entering a society where they were perceived both as cousins
and strangers, relatives and outsiders.[40] Moya's work impressively assembled
both qualitative and quantitative data on macro (meso when necessary) and
micro levels. Greystone in comparison is miniscule in scale, but its community institutions, organized both by the residents and the corporation, had
a similar impact on the villagers of maintaining and promoting Old World
customs and ways of thinking and a sense of separateness for the newcomers. The Benn corporation intended to isolate its workforce, and the social
and cultural isolation worked at least for a while.

Greystone in 1910

While running an eye over the 1910 population census columns on microfilm to find the street names in North Providence that define the mill village of Greystone, it becomes clear that the village was surrounded by neighborhoods in adjacent villages, such as Centredale with a mixture of English, English Canadian, French Canadian, Belgian, and Italian families.[41] But Greystone itself was overwhelmingly populated with "English-born" people who worked in the local worsted mill. Here is the basis for fictional Briardale.

Of the total population of Greystone village in 1910, which was 842 people living in 166 households, the English-born represented well over three-fourths or 84 percent of the residents (see table). In addition, there were fifty-four Rhode Island-born children and infants, forty-eight of whom were the children and grandchildren of English-born residents. The village was indeed an enclave of English immigrants (no doubt from Yorkshire) and their immediate families.

Nineteen Rhode Island Yankees constituted the next largest group, one of whom was seventy-year-old Sarah Hopkins who lived on her own income, probably in her ancestral home, with her Irish-born servant Catherine Welch. The three French Canadian resident families were naturalized citizens, far longer settled in Rhode Island than their English-born neighbors. Joseph Cote, for example, had emigrated in 1870 and worked as a skilled dyer for the Benn operation. Likewise, the three Italian-headed families, although not all naturalized citizens, had migrated before many of the Yorkshire people who worked in Greystone. These residents found themselves scarcely visible, except by the census taker, in a Yankee Yorkshire village. Male-headed nuclear families with or without children dominated household structures in 1910, while the dates of immigration within families suggest an abundance of chain migration. More than one-quarter of the families had boarders.

The total number employed in the Greystone mill in 1911 was 1,400, indicating that the firm hired part of their labor force, probably weavers, spinners, and less-skilled workers, from adjacent communities. These networks of textile workers who lived outside of Greystone would supply vital support during labor protest activities and would include geographically mobile boarders. Eight-four other boarders, or 10 percent of the residents, lived with Greystone families or in the large boardinghouse that held thirty-two plus staff. The census also lists twenty-two male-headed nuclear families without children, boarders, or in-laws, possibly young newlywed mill workers who had met at the boardinghouse or at the mill. Presumably Yorkshire-born persons were

Nationality of Residents of Greystone Village, North Providence,
Rhode Island, 1910

Nation	Number of residents	Percentage
England	707	84.0
Italy	11	1.3
Canada: French/English	10	1.2
N. Ireland/S. Africa	8	1.0
Scotland	2	0.2
Ireland	1	0.1
United States:		
Rhode Island	73[a]	8.7
Massachusetts	11	1.3
Other states	17	2.0

[a]Forty-eight were children of English-born parents.

Note: Male-headed nuclear families with or without children dominated household structure in the total population of 842 residents in Greystone village in 1910. This result is not surprising. The dates of immigration among the members of many extended families suggest an abundance of chain migration. Of the total families, 28 percent contained boarders. By 1920 three-fourths of the 1910 Greystone residents had left the village.

Sources: U.S. manuscript census of population microfilm records for 1910, Greystone Village, District 112; town directories for North Providence, R.I., for 1913, 1916, and 1924; U.S. manuscript census of population microfilm records for 1920, Greystone Village, districts 125, 126. All 842 residents of the village in the 1910 census were recorded by hand in 166 households, including one large boardinghouse. This admittedly primitive technique allowed me to reassemble the managerial structure of the Benn Company in 1910. For 1920, each name over ten years of age except for servants was traced in the 1920 census and the town directories of North Providence. The town directories offered some occasional information on the deaths or relocations of former residents (see chap. 2). My thanks to Janet Pohl for data entry on Greystone village residents.

preferred as employees, but a small number of other nationalities, probably from Rhode Island worsted mills or from Lawrence and Pennsylvania mills, lived and worked in Greystone. The census did not name the mills at which textile workers were employed although I have assumed that those listed as worsted and woolen workers who lived in Greystone worked at the Benn mill and walked to work. With no surviving mill records, the census gives the barest snapshot of the village residents in 1910. Patterns discernable in the census are most valuable, but details provide interest.[42]

By 1910 English-born immigrants living in Greystone could have become naturalized citizens, if they had filed their first papers as a declaration of intent, waited five years, and then filed a petition for naturalization. After mid-

1906, the Naturalization and Immigration Service had to obtain verification of the date of immigration from the ship's manifest, delaying the process. The filing of first papers was indicated in the census by the mark "PA." The boss of the combing room, Squire Kershaw, who immigrated in 1903, was an American citizen by 1910. The very busy mill manager George Keralake was listed as entering the United States in 1904. He was not yet naturalized in 1910 but had submitted his first papers. Some waited. Sam Wood, his wife, and daughter arrived in the United States in 1902. They all worked in the Benn mill: Sam as a warp twister, his wife as a weaver, and their sixteen-year-old daughter as a spinner. When Wood had taken out his first papers was unclear. At any rate, he had not yet decided to proceed to naturalization, and the decision would affect his wife and daughter.[43]

The 1910 census took no notice of the citizenship of women and inconsistently reported the status of dependent adult males. Information on naturalization in the 1910 census on the 151 male heads of resident families indicates that nearly a quarter, or 23 percent, were naturalized citizens; nearly half, or 44 percent, had applied for first papers; and only 29 percent remained aliens. Apparently many had intended to make their immigration to the United States permanent. Among the less settled sixty-five male immigrant boarders, 14 percent were citizens, 18 percent had filed first papers, 58 percent remained aliens, and 9 percent were unreported or unknown. Even if British-born men became U.S. citizens, they did not cease to be British subjects. They would have to formally renounce their allegiance in a declaration of alienage before British authorities.[44] The rights of dual citizenship were valuable to English men if they chose to return to Yorkshire with their families.

Unrest in Greystone

Community institutions that maintained Yorkshire customs and contacts with the homeland contributed to labor unrest and class identity in Greystone, unlike similar institutions in Moya's Buenos Aries.[45] The concept of "fairness" embedded in work traditions were among the Yorkshire customs maintained by union wool sorters and worsted weavers in Greystone. Furthermore, their sense of cultural separateness did not prevent Yorkshire worsted workers in their class interests from joining with textile operatives of other nationalities to resist their employers when they refused to honor homeland work rules.

In 1906 managers at the Benn operations altered Yorkshire-style wages and working conditions in an apparent attempt to undercut their New England

competitors. Yorkshire textile workers in Greystone reaffirmed homeland connections by defending work traditions that contradicted the policies of New
England textile capitalism. In April 1906 the entire workforce of Greystone's
worsted weavers, men and women, went on strike to oppose unfair cuts in
their piece rates and changes in their work customs.[46] The Greystone weavers opposed a management order changing their allowance of two broken
threads per fifty yards of alpaca and mohair cloth, an order backed up by new
fines. Broken threads in worsted cloth required the services of skilled burlers
(menders) to maintain quality. But the Benn operation had not set up the customary mending room and continued to pass the work back to the weavers,
a practice that reduced their earnings and penalized male weavers without
the traditional needle skills or experience to mend. The weavers declared the
new order impossible but bided their time. By 1910 the Benn operation hired
three women burlers, two of them the wives of cloth inspectors, to address
this grievance.[47] Other Greystone worsted workers were also disaffected.

Union wool sorters, who had relocated from the Benn mills in Bradford,
sent word back to the West Riding in December 1906 by private letter and by
cablegram that they were at "loggerheads" with their employers. The cablegram sent to the secretary of the National Woolsorters Union in Bradford
appeared to be an effort to build "an international scheme of organisation"
to oppose national wage differentials for skilled workers.[48] The dispute was
resolved when the company agreed with the Greystone union to drop its
plans to import English wool sorters to settle labor disputes. But the wool
sorters had other grievances that demanded recognition of transnational
union standards.

Greystone wool sorters struck twice in February 1907 over the wage rates
for handling "rubbishy" imported wool.[49] English law regulated the industrial use of organic materials likely to carry anthrax, one of the great hazards
of wool sorting. When management refused to respond, most of those dissenting wool sorters left the village and easily found work elsewhere. In the
census of 1910, the Benn mill in Greystone employed seventeen wool sorters,
eleven of whom had helped set up operations in 1904 and 1905. After the 1907
disputes, four more English-born wool sorters joined them, notably in their
early thirties or younger. Two American citizens of English birth, immigrants
in 1867 and 1885, had been hired away from other U.S. worsted operations.
Apparently the Benn mill handled their wool sorters more carefully thereafter.
Most wool sorters had become American citizens or had filed first papers.

Back in Bradford, the Benn managers tried to protect their sources of
skilled workers by using a clumsy hoax in the form of a dialect letter sent to

the labor newspaper *Yorkshire Factory Times,* signed by a "lad" who claimed: "Awve bin i' these States nah fer aboon a duzzen year, an' know a bit." Indeed few were fooled by the awkward rendering of dialect or by the round-about message that conditions in Rhode Island were fine and the pay good.[50] Additional strike activity among discontented worsted workers in northern Rhode Island mill villages, many of whom were English immigrants, occurred in 1907 and again in 1910.[51] In addition to labor unrest, Yorkshire workers in Greystone had been joined by other immigrant groups. In addition to the skilled dyer of French Canadian birth, the 1910 census indicates that a few Italian workers resident in Greystone had entered the Benn mill. Mike Carnacum at fifty-seven, an immigrant in 1901 with his family who spoke only Italian, worked as a coal-heaver in the mill, but his twenty-one-year-old son, Mike Jr., was a weaver. Roke Lyrosa, an immigrant in 1904 who was married with two children born in Rhode Island, worked as a wool packer.[52] All no doubt had contacts with other Italian immigrants in Providence. Whatever William Benn had intended for Greystone village, changes beyond his control were beginning to occur.

British Workers in the American Textile Labor Movement

Once the expensive Greystone mill complex went into full operation, the Benn managers moved quickly to adopt the political and economic policies of other New England textile operations. Harrison Benn, now established on the opposite side of the Atlantic, became an outspoken protectionist. He warned in 1911 that he would close the Greystone mill if the tariff reductions on worsted cloth in the pending Underwood bill became law. He argued in classic protectionist language that the tariff-protected wages he paid to his 1,500 operatives in Greystone were double those paid in Yorkshire.[53] As Harrison Benn joined other textile capitalists in Providence to lobby Congress for the preservation of high protective tariffs on American-made worsteds, the Greystone managers altered work practices customary in Bradford. Their Yorkshire mill workers immediately rejected these changes by demanding homeland work rules or threatening to leave Greystone. In effect, they were asking Harrison Benn: was this community really a transplanted Yorkshire village or a Lawrence-style industrial city? In doing so they joined a long tradition of labor activism among British immigrant workers in the United States.

Herbert G. Gutman's work on waves of nineteenth-century immigrants from preindustrial peasant cultures to industrializing America laid a foundation in social and labor history for the study of this first generation of immigrant opponents to American industry. However, he rejected the passive peasantry of Oscar Handlin's *The Uprooted* for the vibrant peasant culture and distinctive adjustment of Rudolph Vecoli's *contadini*. Just before his death in 1985, Gutman began to study the contribution of the second generation of those immigrant workers with experience in industry and urban life.[54] Textile workers from the urban areas in Lancashire and Yorkshire working in the Northeast had already brought their own experiences, skills, ideologies, and practices of labor protest when they migrated across the Atlantic as early as the 1840s. Recent studies of nineteenth-century Lancashire and Yorkshire spinners and weavers, Scottish and Welsh colliers, and Irish industrial workers reveal a complex mix of radical politics within cultural enclaves. Based on John T. Cumbler's work on Fall River, Horst Rössler argued that British migrants disseminated textile trade unionism and "radical consciousness and ideals" in the Atlantic economy and played a decisive role in the development of the American labor movement.[55]

Indeed skilled English and Scottish immigrants proved essential to the development of the American textile industry as fancy weavers, makers of machines, mule spinners, dyers, and cloth printers.[56] Immigrant calico printers from Manchester, Lancashire, filled Fall River printing works and "English Row" in Lowell, Massachusetts.[57] Handloom weavers of cotton and woolen cloth from England and Scotland, both men and women, found skilled work producing fancy checked, plaid, or twill cloth. Nearly every New England cotton mill had some skilled British "help," and many of them aspired to become small manufacturers or at least overseers. Lancashire workers had also immigrated to the textile industry of Philadelphia in the 1820s and 1830s where they contributed their skills and experiences of radical politics to local labor protest. American manufacturers of carpets and hosiery tried to use machinery to avoid paying the costs of expensive English workers, but in Philadelphia skilled hand work by English immigrants remained important through the 1880s. By the 1850s immigrant labor from England, Scotland, and Ireland had settled in and dominated the workforce in New England factories. Lancashire cotton operatives in Fall River and New Bedford "abounded as nowhere else," and later rose to managerial positions. Rhode Island mills filled up with them. When the Lawrence mills began to manufacture worsted rather than woolen goods in the 1860s, Yorkshire immigrants from the West Riding arrived in large numbers.[58]

Although many English immigrants guarded the secrets of their skills, native-born workers, in spite of tensions with the newcomers, learned from them different work techniques and new protest tactics in strikes. English workers also brought with them, depending on the timing of their emigration, varied experiences of political activism and labor protest that included strikes, mass demonstrations, and in the early 1840s working-class demands for the ten-hour day and manhood suffrage, the keystone of the Chartist movement. When the Chartist movement was repressed in the mid-1840s, its leaders were jailed or hounded from politics. Many immigrated to the United States. Lancashire Chartists headed for Fall River and Lowell, and Yorkshire Chartists for the mixed woolen and cotton city of Lawrence, built in 1848. Meanwhile Lancashire mule spinners in Fall River maintained transatlantic contacts by contributing funds to the 1853–1854 Preston strike in Lancashire that disrupted a mid-Victorian period of conciliation and compromise.[59]

Although English workers had been commonplace in American textile operations, the post–Civil War surges of Lancashire and Yorkshire spinners and weavers, many blacklisted for labor agitation and encouraged by their own unions to emigrate, thus reducing the labor surplus, seemed overwhelming. English immigrants in masses were now entering the New England mills as spinners, weavers, carders, and in other jobs among the general workforce of Yankees, Irish, and Scottish immigrants and immigrants from English and French Canada. These men and women migrated in successive waves before and after the American Civil War to the textile cities of Massachusetts, Rhode Island, Connecticut, Maine, New York, and New Jersey. Their growing numbers and the depth of their experience appeared ominously threatening. In 1869 a woman weaver in Lowell stated her fears in the *American Workman*. "Great numbers of skilled English operatives are on their way to compete with us for bread . . . to still further lengthen our hours, or reduce our pay."[60]

English immigrants joined Yankee labor reformers agitating for the ten-hour day in Massachusetts and other northeastern states. In response to an 1869 wage cut by the mill owners in Preston, Lancashire, the weavers and spinners of Preston, Blackburn, and other Lancashire mill centers organized to promote the emigration of 1,000 weavers and additional numbers of spinners to the United States. England had adopted a ten-hour law in 1847; reinforcements for ten-hour reform activity were on their way. Ten-hour men developed a statewide coalition in Massachusetts to organize the votes of native-born and naturalized industrial workers to achieve a partial victory in 1874.[61] Crucial to this coalition were powerful organizations of textile workers from the woolen and cotton districts of Yorkshire and Lancashire. Most active in Lawrence and Fall River, they had set up their own labor press, the *Lawrence Journal* and *The Labor Journal* in Fall River. Once ten hours became Massachusetts law in 1874, the Yorkshire-born labor reformers in Lawrence planned to introduce the English half-time system of education for factory children and other reforms while they built cooperative stores for industrial workers.[62] They also agitated for a ten-hour day in Rhode Island.

In the late nineteenth century English immigrant workers seized control of labor politics in northeastern textile mills. Each fresh wave of immigrants, especially weavers and carders, brought with them English standards and practices to compare with American conditions and labor policies. They judged the New England mills as badly managed, much too large, and extravagant in dividends. Weavers entering the Fall River mills faced working conditions, long hours, and opposition to labor protest unheard of in Lancashire since the 1840s. During a strike in 1875 a Lancashire-style demonstration marked the return migration of ten mule spinners and their families, their fares paid by the local spinners' union. Before they boarded the train to Boston to catch the ship to Liverpool, a procession of strikers escorted them with music and flags flying from the union headquarters, through the streets, conspicuously circling the besieged textile mill while carrying a banner, "I'm Going Home." This thumb-in-your-eye gesture characterized Lancashire-style protest. Fall River became the American epicenter not only of late nineteenth-century cotton textile production but also of agitation for cotton textile unionism. By 1890, after a long series of lost strikes, a conservative trade union approach led by the mule spinners and affiliated with the American Federation of Labor (AFL) prevailed.[63]

While other less-experienced migrant groups began to replace the English and Irish in the American cotton industry, the numbers of Yorkshire workers in woolen and worsted persisted. In Lawrence, the "Bradford of America," in Rhode Island, and in Philadelphia, Yorkshire men and women ran machines, oversaw operations, and built new equipment. Some mills established with British capital routinely contracted with groups of English workers until forbidden by Congress in 1885. Yorkshire worsted workers preferred agreements with established mills to risk, and consequently their numbers began to decline.[64] More important, the 1893 industrial depression in the United States discouraged migration until the early twentieth century.

By 1906 worsted worker discontent had spread throughout Rhode Island. The American Woolen Company in Lawrence, Massachusetts, had raised wages by 10 percent in 1905. Between 1905 and 1911, the manufacturing dominance of the American Woolen Company in the New England worsted industry set regional wage rates, and American Woolen owned nine worsted mills in Rhode Island.[65] Unrest fed on the refusal of smaller mills in both Massachusetts and Rhode Island to comply with regional wage standards.

Workers at two worsted mills in Harrisville in northern Rhode Island, at the Namquit Worsted in Bristol in central Rhode Island, and at the Peace Dale worsted company in southern Rhode Island struck for higher wages and against changes in their work rules.[66] Many had been trained in Yorkshire.

In late 1912 and 1913 the restive Greystone weavers, men and women, joined by others in the adjacent mill villages of Esmond, Centredale, Georgiaville, and Graniteville, played a key role in organizing worsted workers in North Providence to increase wages. Historical Greystone proved far more culturally elastic than Hedley Smith's exclusive enclave of Briardale (see map 3). First, worsted workers in the Benn mill extended their support to English-born labor activists in the other four mill villages along the Woonasquatucket River, class and culture linking them together like a string of beads. These activities led them to join attempts by the multicultural Industrial Workers of the World (IWW) to organize the textile workers in the Northeast in 1912 and 1913. These skilled worsted workers thus anticipated a similar alliance between skilled and unskilled worsted workers emerging in Passaic during 1919.[67]

English Immigrants and the IWW

In the numerous studies of the IWW textile strikes in the Northeast, the long-term engagement of English immigrants remains unappreciated. Although English workers participated in both worsted and silk production in Lawrence and Paterson, their possession of skills appeared to rule them out of direct involvement in IWW activity. However, English-born worsted workers helped to organize the first IWW local in Lawrence, Massachusetts, in 1905. Melvin Dubofsky argued that although English immigrant workers generally backed the Lawrence United Textile Workers (UTW) in the AFL, he also reported that William Yates and Thomas Holliday from Lancashire became "key leaders" for the IWW during the 1912 strike. In addition, Yorkshire-born Jeannie Bateman helped organize supporters for the IWW among the English-dominated workforce at the Arlington Mills. David Goldberg pointed out that some experienced labor activists among the skilled English worsted and silk workers from both Bradford and Macclesfield remained involved in the IWW through 1919. For example, Thomas Holliday reemerged as a leader in Lawrence labor activity in 1919 and 1920, joined by the influential chair of the 1919 strike committee, Lancashire-born socialist Samuel Bramhall.[68]

English and German workers in Paterson who dominated silk-ribbon weaving and other skilled work cooperated for the first time with the multicultural broad-silk weavers in the January 1913 strike. Although David Margrave insisted that by 1913 English silk weavers from Macclesfield no longer played a significant role in the Paterson industry, David Goldberg found that their descendents remained skilled warpers, loom fixers, and ribbon weavers.[69] The multicultural labor coalitions of these Paterson operatives continued until 1919. Similar cooperation occurred in mill towns of the Woonasquatucket Valley.

Following the multiethnic victory of early January 1912 in the Lawrence Bread and Roses Strike by textile workers guided by the IWW, demands for a similar 10 percent wage increase surged among Rhode Island's worsted workers. Insisting that their weaving skills were "wholly different" and irreplaceable "in this country," following Yorkshire strike traditions, and relying on support from English-born sympathizers in neighboring mill villages, the 250 weavers and 150 throstle spinners at Greystone struck on November 12, 1912, for the 10 percent wage advance won in Lawrence. As in Yorkshire, the "great body" of workers marched behind their strike committee, crowding the mill gates while their representatives negotiated with management. Strikers in Greystone used the fire stations and public halls in neighboring Graniteville and Centredale for meetings to appeal for strike funds. They insisted that it had been "understood" that they were to receive "an advance in wages at the time other New England mills gave a wage increase to their weavers." Rhode Island worsted mills, such as the Benn operation in Greystone, gained a competitive advantage by denying or at least delaying wage increases after the early 1912 Lawrence victory.[70]

This labor activity among weavers and spinners in North Providence contrasted with the sluggish pace of Yorkshire union organization. Historians ascribe the "retardation" of unionization in the Yorkshire worsted and woolen industry in the late nineteenth and early twentieth centuries to both employers and male trade unionists who denied skilled work and union membership to the vast numbers of low-paid, young female workers who dominated weaving and spinning while driving the more experienced and skilled married women weavers out of the mill workforce.[71]

These traditional patterns of Yorkshire labor politics provided a point of departure for new forms of activity in New England. The immigration of Yorkshire worsted workers to Rhode Island mill villages seemed to loosen the strict sexual division of labor in worsted production, to increase the age of female workers, and to open new opportunities for their involvement in labor protest. Data on Rhode Island strikes between 1906 and 1913 and from the 1910 census of Greystone suggest that the numbers of male weavers and older females in weaving sheds increased. The sex composition of strike-prone weavers, men and women, and the throstle spinners, usually described as "boys and girls," suggest that North Providence worsted workers represented a mix of males and females somewhat different from Yorkshire, the proportions of which however are difficult to reconstruct.[72] Male weavers composed 25 percent of the 1910 Greystone residents, while female weavers dominated with 75 percent. Some families, such as the Lancasters, were all weavers, including James, the husband and father, his wife Sarah, and his sixteen-year-old daughter Mary. Other weaving couples, such as John and Mattie Muloannsh had two boarders, Elizabeth Naylor and Louisa First, who were weavers.[73] Weavers resident in Greystone in 1910, however, made up only 60 percent of the Benn mill weaving workforce in 1912. More weavers came from the adjacent mill villages, and these networks proved strong. Still, male workers alone spoke to the press on behalf of the strikers, thus continuing the Yorkshire tradition of female subordination in public affairs.

Initially resisting the advice of both IWW organizers and the representatives of the UTW-AFL in Providence, the Greystone strikers settled on December 19, 1912, for a 7.5 percent wage compromise. They continued to ignore the conservative leaders of the UTW-AFL who, like John Golden, were English immigrants from the Lancashire cotton district.[74] On December 14, the strikers had formed the "Greystone Textile Local," representing all jobs in worsted production rather than divided by craft as in the federated UTW. This move suggested attempts to overcome skill and wage divisions among the weavers, spinners, and the more skilled worsted workers, such as wool sorters. After the settlement the Greystone strikers organized Local 838 of the IWW's "United Textile Workers of the World," thereby linking the customs and practices of Yorkshire labor activity with the most radical, inclusive, and multicultural movement in American textile unionism. IWW locals also appeared in Esmond, Centredale, and Georgiaville, mill villages that flanked Greystone on the north and south, while the mill workers of neighboring Graniteville lent material support to strikers in Greystone and Esmond. According to the Socialist press in Providence, Harrison Benn's hopes to isolate his Greystone mill workers from the American labor movement had been "rudely shattered."[75]

At first Benn "personally" took the November 1912 work stoppage in Greystone "so lightly" that he left for England the following day as planned. After the strike settlement and in retaliation for the 7.5 percent wage increase in his absence, he telegraphed orders in early 1913 from Yorkshire to raise house rents in Greystone by 13 percent. On May 1 he had a notice posted on the Greystone mill properties to halt production as a result of the newly proposed higher U.S. tariffs on worsted in the Underwood Act. Benn did not, however, follow through on his threat. At the same time, he devised a transatlantic strategy to pit his mill workers in Bradford, out on strike in May 1913, against those in Greystone by threatening to send production to Rhode Island. But with outbreak of war in Europe in August 1914, the economic effects of the lower Underwood tariffs were never tested. Orders for woolen and worsted cloth from the Allied military services provided two years of "heavy business at profitable prices." American involvement in the European war would stimulate demand much further.[76]

At first, betrayed by their angry Yorkshire managers, Greystone mill workers turned to each other and later reached across cultural boundaries to protect their class interests. By joining the IWW in late 1912 and supporting local strikes, English immigrants in North Providence forged transcultural ties with other ethnic groups, notably southern Italian workers. Paul Buhle regarded 1913 as the period of "high excitement" among Rhode Island's Italian migrants, which brought together "supporters of labor and radicalism across ethnic lines."[77] The activity of English worsted workers in North Providence demonstrates the crossing of ethnic boundaries to serve class purposes. The activities of skilled English silk workers in Paterson also crossed cultural lines during the 1913 strike. Despite the English heritage of British imperialism and racism, the lived experience of Yorkshire worsted workers involved in labor activity in 1912 and 1913 contradicts the cultural chasms fundamental to Smith's imagined Briardale and his own sense of English superiority. Indeed, having themselves been racialized as ignorant "jickeys," English worsted workers could disregard for the moment their own British racial heritage for the sake of their class interests.

Yorkshire immigrants in North Providence mill villages behaved no differently during these strikes than "new immigrants," much as the Italians who became the most prominent supporters of the IWW with its transnational allies and strategies in organizing New England textile workers. English immigrants, however, had the advantages of language, skills in textile work, and experience with labor activity in the industry. In comparison with English people, southern Italians as "inbetween people" ranked lowest among European groups in racial terms. Working-class Yorkshire immigrants in Hedley Smith's Briardale fiction and the strikers in North Providence mill villages regarded themselves, as did Smith himself, as both culturally distinct from and superior to American values and New England mill practices. As labor activists, they seemed indifferent to American racial values and racialized ethnic distinctions, especially the extreme racialization of Italian workers in

New England. They demonstrated their willingness in 1912 and 1913 to join with these and other immigrant groups to achieve mutual class aims.[78] James Barrett and David Roediger acknowledged that some "new" immigrants, such as Italian socialists in the IWW, a "multi-national, multi-racial" union, could be "indifferent" to American racial distinctions and "abstain *from whiteness*." In a debate on the historical meanings of whiteness, Eric Arnesen called for more nuanced understandings of local events to provide context and specificity for the use of the concept "whiteness" associated with race, class, and ethnicity.[79] The events in North Providence in 1913 support the additional inclusion of these Yorkshire labor activists as abstainers from "whiteness."

In January 1913 members of the newly organized IWW local in Greystone supported striking weavers in Esmond, a mill village just north of Greystone with a workforce reportedly one-half Italian immigrants, one-fourth English immigrants, and the rest German, Portuguese, and French Canadian workers. An Italian-speaking IWW organizer from Lawrence arrived in Esmond, and about half of the men and women workers in Esmond quickly formed the third IWW local in the town of North Providence.[80] The IWW's National Industrial Union of Textile Workers, meeting in nearby New Bedford, Massachusetts, offered support through its local in Olneyville, Rhode Island. Two IWW organizers from Lynn, Massachusetts, Giullo Mazziallo and P. Giaconnelli, were "in charge of the Italian section" during the Esmond strike. Franco-Belgians had been active during the Lawrence strike of 1912, and one interested Franco-Belgian worker from Woonsocket appeared in Graniteville in support of the Esmond strikers. While deputy sheriffs from Providence armed with pistols and clubs protected the Esmond mill, the neighboring mill villages of Graniteville and Centredale, home of many Yorkshire immigrants, provided food and safe meeting sites for the Esmond strikers who demanded a 20 percent wage increase and recognition of the IWW.[81]

Unequal pay for weavers who did not speak English became one of the key issues in the multiethnic Esmond strike. With no posted price lists for piecework, payroll accountants at the Esmond mill issued meager wage packets that convinced the sixty-five Italian men and women weavers of their calculated deceit. Under pressure from the strike committee headed by Herbert Whitehouse, the Esmond mill superintendent quickly offered to post all prices and address all grievances. As in the 1912 Lawrence strike, transcultural labor politics featured the activism of women weavers, English and Italian, who became members of the IWW local in Esmond, attended public meetings, and picketed and participated in the work of the strike committee. Fearing the imminent spread of IWW influence in northern Rhode

Island, the Esmond managers offered a 5 percent wage increase to all—if the strikers rejected the IWW and joined the UTW-AFL. The strikers settled for the 5 percent wage increase but kept the IWW local.[82]

The Esmond strike settlement in mid-February 1913, with concessions for all workers, reflected a primarily English agenda. "A local unionist," probably Herbert Whitehouse, announced,

> The tea kettle has arrived, also the [warming] oven. We are going in for 9 o'clock breakfasts [English-style second breakfast], a good hot dinner, also afternoon tea. What do you think of that, you guys at Centredale and Georgiaville? We'll show you how to make a mill a pleasure to work in.[83]

The settlement also included a grievance committee, special pay for overtime, for waiting for work, and for teaching new weavers, plus a twenty-minute smoking break. The agreement guaranteed that no rents would be increased to offset wage raises as in Greystone and contained plans for a consumer cooperative and a social club.

The settlement also featured a special provision for Italian and other immigrant textile workers who lived in the ethnic neighborhoods of Providence. The Esmond managers agreed to refund trolley carfare to commuting workers when the mill could not provide them with work on that day. Although Italian immigrants represented one-half the workforce in Esmond, the skills, experience, and work culture of English weavers dominated the 1913 Esmond settlement. Still, both groups supported the IWW, all strikers returned to work, and English and Italian men and women workers joined together to gain concessions that helped all weavers, such as limiting the assignment of difficult weaving using black yarn. Furthermore, during the Esmond strike, the English overseer and assistant overseer of weaving was fired (later rehired) for being too sympathetic to the strikers, while "English-speaking employees" opposed certain concessions on account of the objections of "Italian weavers."[84] As in the 1912 Lawrence strike, transcultural cooperation of men and women textile workers led to success in Esmond.

One month later, in March 1913, strikers in the Centredale Worsted Company's spinning mill, just south of Greystone, formed their own IWW local with the help of Esmond striker John Greenwood.[85] These young male and female throstle spinners were attempting to build an alliance with workers in the company's Olneyville mill in Providence. Using Graniteville as a sanctuary for strikers, they demanded a 10 percent wage increase and, clearly aware what had prompted the Lawrence strike more than a year earlier, a guarantee that wages would not be cut when Rhode Island's new fifty-four-hour workweek law came into effect on July 1. Providence police easily dispersed the small group of men and women strikers from Centredale who had gathered near the Olneyville mill. Esmond and Greystone weavers struck again in April 1913: in Esmond to protest the firing of Italian mill workers branded as IWW "troublemakers" and in Greystone to protest additional changes in work rules. In Esmond the Italian workers associated with the IWW were fired, and on April 15 the remaining workers signed cards reportedly abandoning membership in the IWW. Most of the Providence press quickly announced the end of the IWW in North Providence, but in gleeful secrecy, according to the Socialist *Labor Advocate,* the weavers kept the IWW alive and useful in Esmond into 1914.[86]

Extending the IWW's transcultural labor politics into southern Rhode Island in March 1913, English and Italian migrants also worked together during a strike at the Peace Dale worsted complex in South Kingston. An alarmed state government, fearful of IWW organization statewide, especially in the garment factories and jewelry industry of Providence, banned the display of the IWW flag, while both the city's AFL labor council and the town officials in South Kingston condemned the organization. Efforts to get the IWW weavers reinstated failed in South Kingston, while the IWW organizing drive in Providence collapsed.

During the early summer of 1913, local police successfully prevented Socialist Party organizers from addressing audiences in the streets of Centredale until in late July when "the largest assembly ever held in the town" loudly shouted encouragement to the speakers, forcing the police to desist. This incident included organized class resistance to the misbehavior of town police and Providence deputy sheriffs during local strikes. As in Esmond, other IWW members and sympathizers in Rhode Island went underground. During the conflict-ridden spring of 1913, the massive strike among the silk workers of Paterson, New Jersey halted the IWW organizing drive in the textile industry.[87]

At first, Yorkshire immigrants to Rhode Island worsted mills, faced with wage grievances and unfair changes in work customs, attempted to defend Old Country values in the increasingly adversarial industrial context of Rhode Island. When this appeal to transnational work customs failed to protect rights and sustain privileges, transcultural labor politics offered the militant solidarity necessary to win strikes, even if—as in Esmond—largely on English terms. Victories in North Providence mill villages in 1912 and 1913 propelled labor activity by migrants far beyond the retarded union traditions of Yorkshire. Transcultural ties reinforced translocal community values to reshape the pre-World War I labor movement among New England's immigrant populations. The key leaders of this labor protest represented a blend of seasoned textile workers from Yorkshire industrial centers and southern Italians, not unlike Donna Gabaccia's militant Sambucesi migrants.[88] Two heady years of this growing success in New England based on IWW strategies to overcome ethnic, skill, and sexual divisions frightened textile capitalists in all divisions of the industry into stern political opposition throughout the region by 1914. When in the 1970s Paul Buhle interviewed Italian immigrant Al Sisti, who had worked as a boy in a Providence worsted mill, Sisti recalled the impressive "leadership qualities" of "oldtimers speaking with an English accent or Irish brogue. . . . We used to listen and be inspired by them."[89]

Hedley Smith's fiction offers few clues to explain either the labor unrest or these transcultural connections. As a financially precarious member of the middle class, emerging from the Great Depression and periodically unemployed during the postwar years, Smith clung to his superior Englishness and "whiteness" (see chap. 3). Privately, he often referred to Italians as "Blacks." Smith's short story "Minnie Kettlewell's Husband" explores a controversial Yorkshire-Italian marriage in Briardale. The tale reflects the increasing presence of Italian migrants in the worsted mills of North Providence. The Italian men in the story, however, were stone masons. The Kettlewells of Briardale felt vastly superior to impoverished "Eyetalian" immigrants. As extreme Protestant sectarians, they shuddered at Roman Catholicism. Not only did Briardale folk "hold themselves" far above Italian migrants, they felt suspicious of English mill "fowk" from unfamiliar mill villages in Yorkshire. After a good deal of difficulty, the arrival of Kettlewell grandchildren soon melts their Yorkshire hearts if not their prejudices.[90] Emotional links forged through marriage and considerable patience provide the solvent for some cultural boundaries.

On the issue of labor protest, Smith seems more ambivalent. Simon Hardacre, in "'The Millmaster," the first of the Briardale trilogy novels, takes a secret pride in his own daughter's strength and courage as she helps well-known labor activist Ann Burlak organize the New England cotton textile industry during the early 1930s. Jailed for assault on strikebreakers, his daughter joins, according to her father, "[h]er Yorkshire grandmother, and generations even earlier than that, [who] had probably done the same thing—and more." On the other hand, my own correspondence with historian Paul Buhle indicated that while at Brown University, Hedley Smith's son Duncan offered him a typescript of an earlier novel, which does not appear in Smith's canon, by his father that included a character based on Ann Burlak. Buhle considered the characterization of Burlak nearly a libel. It appears that I was not offered a chance to read this novel, but the textile strike in 1934 was repressed with particular violence in Rhode Island.[91] I am not surprised that Hedley Smith might view Communist Ann Burlak, the incendiary speaker called the "Red Flame" of Ukrainian background, with alarm. An inability to reconcile the attitudes of Simon Hardacre and the unread novel leaves conclusions about Smith's views impossible.

Mass migrations of working-class men and women at the turn of the twentieth century led to various strategies of resistance, as Dirk Hoerder has argued. Day-to-day acts of rebellion and strikes ranged globally from immigrants to North America, Hawai'i, Malaysia, and elsewhere. Resistance involving multiethnic and multiracial militancy occurred in particular work-places and locations, suggesting the primacy of class, as in North Providence mill villages. But the outbreak of World War I in August 1914 disrupted these moments of transcultural connection as Yorkshire immigrants shifted their energies to homeland mobilization, fierce patriotism, and the assertion of a more exclusive "English" identity. During the Great War, the political allegiances of Yorkshire people who stayed in Rhode Island strengthened their trans*national* connections; certainly this was the case in the Briardale fiction. Many young men of Greystone and in the Briardale stories returned to England to serve in World War I, while those who stayed behind added outbursts of English patriotism to their energetic organization of material support.[92]

Many other ethnic groups in New England textile mills, such as Poles, Italians, Jews, and Syrians, believed that Allied victory would aid their homeland regions and create new nations from old empires. Michael Topp concluded that the events surrounding the 1912 Lawrence strike intensified the political conflicts among Italians over loyalty to nation or region. Indeed, labor politics among textile workers after World War I became a contest between "revolutionary socialism and ethnic nationalism."[93]

Imagining Briardale

Hedley Smith arrived in Rhode Island with his family in late 1923, almost twenty years after the establishment of the Benn operation in Greystone. Most of the early settlers of Greystone and the surrounding mill villages had gone. World War I and the fluctuations of prosperity and postwar depression had reshaped the communities, although the physical settings of the mill villages remained intact. Harrison Benn died in 1921. Hedley Smith set most of his Briardale fiction prior to the emigration of his family, embracing Benn's constructed Yorkshire-style mill village and renaming it. Harrison Benn's planned Yorkshire village and grand mill complex in Greystone did not suit the residents in many ways. It took only a few years for Benn's dream to become an illusion. Hedley Smith turned his dream into fiction.

This fiction captures both the Yorkshire migrants' homeland experience, their forced transference, and their endurance during the settling-in phase into Rhode Island society. Smith's stories and novels preserve customs and dialect, portray community power hierarchies and family strategies, mourn the loss of friends and opportunities, and explore the intense emotional climate of memories, sexuality, and family. In the preface to an unpublished third volume of short stories, he called his writings a blend of memory, hearsay, and imagination "about family relationships, the comedies and tragedies, that were interminably in progress in this secluded place outside the gates of the world." Smith wrote: "What applies to Hardy's countryfolk is just as true of Briardale's Yorkshire textile workers . . . it leads me on to think of Thomas Hardy and his novel, *Far from the Madding Crowd*."[94] He was thus explicitly both modeling himself on Thomas Hardy and reaffirming his Yorkshire identity.

On weekends during the late 1920s when Hedley and his brother, Sam, lived with their parents in Centredale village in North Providence and earlier in Johnston, they listened to "front porch stories" in the surrounding mill villages about the bitter regrets and experiences of friends and neighbors forced to relocate to New England from an economically declining Yorkshire. As Smith put it in "The Mill Folk":

> [W]e'd sit around the stove and listen to the old folks talking. Children hear more, and understand better at a very early age than grownups give them credit for doing, and I think they'd have been surprised if they'd ever realized how much of both of good and bad we young ones picked up.[95]

Based on what he heard, Smith describes a Yorkshire people who experienced the forced dispersal to New England as a labor diaspora, accompanied by potential cultural rupture. The tariff business was always "sleazy" American politics, and the Briardale mill itself "a crouched Juggernaut" in the midst of them as "an inescapable brooding presence" with a breath of greasy wool, soap, and chemicals.[96] Smith created the patriarch Grandfather Denby, a major character in "The Mill Folk," as a prime example of forced labor migration and cultural resentment as he and his family moved from their village of "Silsbury" to Briardale and the new "Binns-Cockcroft" mill.

> We didn't think they meant it seriously, about moving the plant, till all the new machinery started coming in. Aye, that very machinery you can hear at

this minute rumbling and thumping in the darkness. Every piece of it, they brought it into the mill at Silsbury and set it up and ran it for two-three days, then knocked it down and boxed it up and shipped it across here. That made it used machinery, you know, and they didn't have to pay duty on it that way. The bloody Yanks were smart enow to stop us earning our livings by taxing the cloth we made, but they weren't smart enow to catch us out in that trick! There weren't no flies on Binns-Cockcroft.[97]

Grandfather Denby combined homesickness with pride of English history and Yorkshire shrewdness. His granddaughter Rhoda interjects to the reader:

Binns-Cockcroft was the name of the big plant in Yorkshire. It had been running for more than a hundred years, I reckon: for I remember Grandfather [Denby] telling me how his grandfather had woven cloth for the soldiers that fought Boneparte [sic] with Wellington, in the little black stone mill beside the river up among the hills.

"Aye, it was a bonny spot, Silsbury," he would say, for he carried a secret homesickness with him to the end of his life. "We worked hard and long. But then, we laiked [played] hard, and all: what with our cricketing and footballing, our knurr and spell [ball and bat], and our cockfighting up on the moors on a Sunday afternoon. And there was always enough brass for a Bank Holiday weekend at Morecambe, choose how we had to pinch for it. . . . Eh! There's folks living along this very street here hadn't been as far from home as Bradford till they were put on the train and shipped off to Liverpool and America. In fact, folk were so clannish that every village had its own language, or its own way of talking, and when in course of time other factories were set up around Briardale and brought more workers from England, people meeting one another on the streets for the first time would say, Eh, thou'll be from Wilsden, or, I reckon thou comes from Horton way."[98]

One key purpose of Smith's fiction was to capture and preserve the variant of Yorkshire dialect used by the migrants in North Providence mill villages. Phrases such as "choose how" (regardless of what one prefers), "we mun thoil it" (we must endure it), "summat for nowt" (something for nothing), "I'll be glad and fain," or "shift for myse'n," and expressions such as I'm "throng" (busy) and "sitha!" (look here!) mark identity and remind the listener of the beloved homeland culture.[99] Emotional excitement or intense personal affection provoked or accompanied Yorkshire words, such as "Champion!" (just great!) and "Aye!" and "Nay!" and continued the use of thee, thy, and tha (for thou) in intimate address. Smith depicted these sturdy, practical, taciturn mill villagers as cherishing and preserving the language, music, religion, and social customs of the Bradford worsted districts. Yorkshire novelist Phyllis Bentley praised Smith's rendering of both Yorkshire dialect and female character as "perfection." She appreciated his depiction of Yorkshire character as a "special blend of strength and warmth coupled with an outward dislike of too much expression."[100]

Smith's Briardale "fowk" had little contact with Rhode Island Yankees, who fled the developing, increasingly immigrant-dominated mill villages of North Providence. But Yorkshire people did confront, especially in response to their dialect or public shows of English patriotism, condescending Yankee voices deriding them as "jicks" or "jickeys." This slur, peculiar to southeastern New England, identified an English immigrant mill worker as a poorly educated, dialect-speaking lout. In return, Yorkshire men denigrated the "bloody" Yankee way of "brag and shout." Working-class immigrants expressed their scorn for Yankee beer and baseball and remained loyal to English bitter at the Social Club and cricket playing on Greystone's field. Some Bradford migrants, however, eagerly sought advantages in American society. In "Miriam Ainsworth," set in 1912, Smith distinguished between two responses to "Briardale Valley." The first group "heartily disliked their native Yankee hosts and wanted nowt to do with them," keeping "clannishly" to themselves. The second disliked the natives "just as much" but admired their "bustle and go" and "their way of getting on and up in the world." These middle-class strivers, such as bank clerk Miriam Ainsworth, found "the Land of Promise a land of promise indeed, and not just a land of empty promises."[101]

Smith used both middle-class and working-class characters, such as Grandfather Denby, to capture the Briardale dialect as well as to portray the social and cultural distances in Rhode Island. In "The Lion and the Eagle," part 2 of the Briardale trilogy, Walter Barraclough, wool buyer for Binns-Cockcroft, confronted the stodgy Yankee relatives of his beloved young wife and, lapsing into Yorkshire dialect, criticized their narrow-mindedness.[102]

> And isn't it time we thought on that we're not a bunch of silly, sulking, peevish bairns, but grown up fowk wi' brains in our heads and manners and decency in our ways. I know Aunt Marian, you and your lot hasn't that much love for us English, and thinks you're a cut above us and all that; and happen there's more reason on your side, 'cause we're not an easy lot to get to know and there's a touch of roughness in our words and our ways that doesn't go down with your smooth manners. Same way, there's things about your class that seems a bit too loud and self-conceited for t' likes of us. But what of it?

> Personally, I dunnot give a rap what you thin o' me and my sort, and you shouldn't what I think o' you. And ower and above that, there's one thing to be said: it's silly to judge owt by t' lump—it's matter of individuality. In all things! All fowk is different just like all pieces o' cloth is different. They're all t' same stuff, but some—cloth of fowk—is woven on a balky loom and comes out a bit rough, while others is almost without a flaw.

But what the Yankees thought *did* matter. Earlier Barraclough confided to his visiting friend Yorkshire lawyer Eric Sutcliffe how his relatives from the Rhode Island "Codfish aristocracy" felt about his marriage.

> You know, of course, deep down at the bottom these oldtime Yankee families have no use for us English, and they make no bones about showing it whenever they can—or happen it comes so natural they don't even know they're doing it. In fact, I've had it shoved into me so often that I think I knew more about George Washington an' Bunker Hill than I do about Waterloo and Trafalgar. . . . It was a bitter pill, I can assure you, when Laura flung her cap over t' house-tops and wedded me; though I've never heard 'em complain abut my brass, or object to my waring [spending] it on things and causes that they fancied themselves. Allus in a tolerant, condescending way, of course.[103]

For Smith, cultural more than class antagonisms created the briars in Briardale. Despite his grandmother and mother's experiences as worsted weavers in Yorkshire and Rhode Island, his stories do not explore working-class life inside the textile mills where he himself was never employed. According to Smith, paternalist Yorkshire-born managers ran Briardale's "Binns-Cockcroft," owned by the parent company in Bradford, and textile workers had few grievances.[104] His fiction reflects the intense cultural isolation of an immigrant enclave and conveys a sense of time and place, which the author, as an outsider in the dominant Yankee culture, connects with the larger Atlantic world. Smith captures the sights, sounds, and smells of Briardale. The stories accurately reflect the female networks in English working-class neighborhoods often bounded by only a few streets that provide Elizabeth Roberts's definition of a woman's sense of place.[105]

> No matter which way you went, you had to run the gauntlet of Briardale village in one direction or the other, coming or going; and whatever the state of the climate, and choose how many folk were penned up in the mill, Briardale back yards and streets were always lively with humanity. Women looked out over the rampart of rugs or bedclothes hanging out to air at upstairs chamber windows; in kitchens and parlors frilled and looped curtains twitched to

the touch of crooked fingers; sharp eyes looked out through these peepholes or through the groves of glossy aspidistra blades; women emptying their rubbish into dustbins, or harvesting the milkman's or the postman's bounty, would halt in their occupations, their knowing eyes would follow . . . [any] "outsiders," marching together down the sidewalk. Eyes would roll upward under eloquent eyebrow-twitchings, looks of frank or grotesque curiosity or suggestiveness would clash like weapons crossing from one side of the narrow street to the other. . . . In the heart of the village the pressure was even more overwhelming. There was always neighborly fraternization of housewives on the threshold of the Co-op; while the big queues waiting on Fridays in the hot, rancid smell of grease and frying food for an order of fish-and-chips-to-go, were practically a town meeting in themselves.[106]

Smith, describing the stories in his first collection, *The Yankee Yorkshireman* (1970) as "largely autobiographical," characterized Yorkshire immigrants as people "with . . . ingrained habit[s] of understatement . . . dour and taciturn way[s] of accepting and grappling with their personal adversities in private, . . . shrinking from the torture of ever betraying emotional tenderness." But, his handling of the characters of Lemuel Briggs and his wife, Emma, in his short story "Uprooted" suggests a far more complex view of human relationships. Briggs (like Smith's father, Ernest), is depressed by his inability to get work as an artisan brushmaker and dependent on his wife's earnings as a weaver (like Alice Collins Smith). He takes a walk on a glorious fall afternoon through the countryside near Briardale. When a kindly old Yankee farmer hires him as an odd job man and offers a cottage to rent, Lemuel regains his standing as a man, a wage earner, and head of family. This change of fortune leads to a passionate sexual encounter with his willing but embarrassed wife as they recline on a country hilltop to watch a sunset made more brilliant by the "great flaming masses of trees, scarlet, saffron and orange."[107]

> Then suddenly he couldn't help himself. He pulled her against him hard and his arms went round her in pure hunger, and he began kissing her. . . . "Don't!" she said again, as his hands found her bare flesh. "Shame on thee! My best skirt, and all! And here in broad daylight!" But it was only her tongue that fought. . . . [S]he was a passionate lass when the depths of her were stirred. . . . "Shame nothing! It was not a bit shameful, Emma, it were natural. It were beautiful. Everything! The day, the little cottage. . . . Thee. Everything's beautiful in the world, and I've nobbut just realised it."[108]

Smith's tender story of reconciliation to change represents an unusual sexual frankness in a son's tribute to his parents' resilience.

Smith's "Uprooted" portrays the consequences of being forced to leave the homeland and the disappointments and difficulties of settling-in. The husband, an artisan worker, has been ripped out of his work culture and never finds his place again. As a man, as a husband, and as an immigrant, he is uprooted. His wife easily finds work as a weaver and moves among her Briardale coworkers and neighbors without trouble. She is transplanted. Within this marriage and depending on the fortunes of migration, the basic concepts of two major immigration historians are found side by side in one bed. Although Handlin's *The Uprooted* dealt largely with the movement of rural people to nineteenth- and early twentieth-century America, he observed that during the process defined marital roles became "altogether confounded" both in the family and in the sexual relationship to each other.[109] In Hedley Smith's story, the reconciliation was far swifter and joyous than the slow, painful, and uncertain reaffirmation described by Handlin. Smith's own cultural and marital problems were more complex.

Donna Gabaccia and Dirk Hoerder call for new perspectives on the sexuality of female migrants and the inclusion of friction and conflict within families and among kin.[110] In addition to Smith's perceptions of sexuality, his fiction also explores the powerful tensions among these immigrant working-class men and women over sexual expression and choices. Grandfather Denby, the lusty, patriarchal father in "The Mill Folk," regards all women as fair game.

> His mind was quick and his nature fun loving: happen both were a bit coarse by today's standards, but nobody thought any the worse of him for that. And there were two sides to him. He was equally ready to take a lass behind the bushes on a dark night or sing in one of the Sacred Cantatas at the chapel in holiday times, and he used to say it was just the same kind of feeling he got out of both.[111]

In his old age, the close living quarters of the family afforded Grandfather Denby many glimpses of female flesh, according to his granddaughter Rhoda.

> Naked to her middle with her upper clothes pushed down below her navel and her heavy breasts swinging, she [Nance, his daughter-in-law] bent over the tub and thrust her arms in the soapy water. Over in the corner by the stove I heard a sudden, throaty chuckle, and looking that way I saw Grandfather Denby, whom I hadn't yet noticed, sitting in his rocking chair. I hadn't seen him for a good while, and felt a shock at the sudden sight of his aging. . . . It seemed all the life that was left in him was in his eyes, and they were as young and lively as ever, greedily twinkling as they watched Nance, taking

in her bare arms and shoulders and the swing of her big, smooth paps as she bent over the tub, minding him no more than if he were a bairn or a puppy watching her. But even in his old age Grandfather Denby was Grandfather Denby still!

Daughter-in-law Nance's careless dismissal of the old man's leers as utterly harmless undermined his cherished virility, an old tactic used by women to disarm aggressive males.

Yorkshire immigrant men of Briardale openly disdained Yankee female bodies as too thin and sharply bony, their skin sallow, and their grim faces shaped by hard jaws and long noses. Sam Knowles, a weaving overlooker from Yorkshire who plays the sage in many of Smith's stories, likened the experience of bedding them as cuddling so many "razor blades." The female Yorkshire eye likewise rejected Yankee men. In Smith's short story "Miriam Ainsworth," Epenetus and Ambrose Hanley, descendents of eighteenth-century Providence merchants, were lanky, ungainly, dried-up sticks with withered hearts and untidy hair, an insult to the fine worsted cloth they could afford to wear. In contrast with the Hanleys, Isaac Bond, an immigrant stonemason, typified the Yorkshire male with his fresh complexion, lively eyes, bodily energy, open-heartedness, manly vigor, and nimble skills.[112]

The male ideal of Yorkshire female beauty meant women with heavy breasts, big hips, and ample "bums," long, luxuriant blonde or auburn hair, and fair, rosy complexions. Yankee women, often portrayed as moral hypo-crites, were either sexually calculating or prudish, while Yorkshire lassies and women embraced sexual encounters spontaneously, eagerly, and unasham-edly, as a part of their essential female natures.[113] Female refusals however to respond, pay attention to, or behave according to male expectations about their "nature" proved effective weapons in the sexual politics among the in-habitants of Briardale. In 1937 Smith himself married a Yankee woman who had lived with her parents for years in Greystone. Their daughter Portia once slipped into the house, declaring that she had located evidence of her mother's English roots in Yorkshire, to which her father replied dryly, "I always knew that I had married a Yorkshire lass."[114] His wife was not amused.

Yorkshire lasses were both sexually knowledgeable and active. In "The Mill Folk," before Rhoda Denby's family immigrates to Rhode Island, her Aunt Martha violates Yorkshire custom by moving out of her family to great village scandal. In the Briardale tales, mill villagers in Yorkshire expect working-class lads and lasses to have "their fun" until a mutually desired pregnancy leads to a chapel wedding. For a lass like Martha Denby to use sexuality to climb out of her class or for her to be educated beyond village norms provokes public denunciations of the upstart as a whore or of her family as "uppity."[115] Mill lasses learned from each other ways of countering conception, for example with herbal abortificients such as pennyroyal.[116] Martha Denby's experiences as a weaver shape both her sexual experimentation and her rebellion. She claims that she wasn't "built" to conceive but brags to her niece that she also controls access to her body.

> Of course I had my fun with the lads in my time. But I were smart enough to know when to keep the gate shut. . . . And it's been a lot happier and more sensible life than tewing your guts out at a loom all day, and then coming home to breed babbies all night to follow on in your footsteps at the mill.[117]

One sympathetic reviewer compared Smith's Briardale chronicles with D. H. Lawrence's novels about sexual relations in working-class England. The reviewer suggested that Smith understood the "uncanny ways in which . . . emotional and sexual attachments" can become "the glue that holds the culture together."[118] The frank exploration of sexual tensions between men and women and sexual customs, expectations, and behavior in community life distinguishes Hedley Smith's work from the indirection or reticence about sexuality in much ethnic fiction set in the early twentieth century.

World War I and Its Aftermath in Greystone and Briardale

Together Hedley Smith's fiction about Briardale and the empirical data create a composite picture of Greystone village during the war period, enriching but often contradictory. The contradictions offer clues to the author's intent. Smith's desire to convey Yorkshire migrant society in North Providence as an ethnic enclave resistant to acculturation obscured the village's more complicated ethnic texture, increasingly altered by labor conflict and the impact of wartime production.

Orders from the military for cloth brought prosperity to American worsted factories in Rhode Island, Massachusetts, Pennsylvania, and New Jersey. By mid-1918, government purchases consumed nearly 70 percent of domestic production. Wartime inflation, however, quickly undercut the value of periodic wage increases granted as a result of threatened strikes beginning in 1916. Still, labor shortages increased the bargaining position of skilled worsted workers, such as the Greystone workforce. Indeed the original capitalization of the Benn mills in 1903 of $1 million doubled by 1919 and rose to $3 million in 1924. When the textile workers of Lawrence went out on strike in 1919, the strike committee tried to organize support in the Providence area, but the disappointing response indicated that, unlike 1912, these strikes lacked reliable regional connections.[119] There is no evidence of strikes or unrest in the Greystone area in 1919 and 1920. High profits and wage increases may have tamed or transformed the workforce.

By 1920 75 percent of Greystone's residents (excluding boarders and children under ten) in 1910 had left the village. One hundred and forty-eight residents were traced in the 1920 census and three North Providence city directories, thereby locating another eighty-two persons at their new residences (see p. 67). Of this small number who had moved, nearly half (41%) resided in neighboring towns or mill villages, such as Johnston, next door to Greystone and may have continued working at the Benn mill. Another half (49%) stayed in Rhode Island, moving to mill operations in places such as Pawtucket, Smithfield, Woonsocket, and Providence. Nine former residents moved to Pennsylvania, and the rest scattered to Maine, Massachusetts, Oregon, Michigan, and Connecticut. Methodist minister John Singleton and his family ended up in Lowell, Massachusetts. The movement of three-quarters of Greystone residents between 1910 and 1920 marks the failure of the Benn project. One by one, families appeared to abandon the village for better jobs and working conditions in larger communities or left the industry entirely. If they could not change their working lives in Greystone, they chose geographical mobility or return migration.[120] Still, in the late twentieth century, traces of Yorkshire dialect still informed the Rhode Island voice.[121]

Where had those former Greystone residents gone? A few had died, some perhaps of the deadly 1918 influenza. Others relocated to other Rhode Island mill towns. Earlier, young men had volunteered to serve in the British military during World War I and never returned to the United States. Others might have seen better wartime or postwar opportunities in Canada, Australia, or New Zealand or returned to Yorkshire with their savings. The women might simply have married and followed their husbands elsewhere. Three Greystone residents went to Oregon; two weavers married each other. A worsted comber from Greystone became a paving (stone) cutter on the West Coast. Wool sorters tended to remain wool sorters, but spinners became weavers; weavers became dyers and loom fixers; learning new skills paid off for many. Historical Greystone proved far more geographically and socially mobile than Hedley Smith's enclave of Briardale.

During the war years, Harrison Benn and his brother William Henry Benn suspended their transatlantic visits to Rhode Island, resuming them during the winter of 1920. In the summer of 1921, however, Harrison Benn died at seventy of heart trouble at his residence in Devonshire, far from the soot and smoke of the West Riding. Determined to keep the Rhode Island operation going as his brother had wished, William Henry Benn managed both the mills in Bradford and Greystone until his death in 1939 when the Rhode Island mill and its property were sold to American interests.[122] But the 1920s brought hard times to New England textiles in general, especially in cotton production, which had shifted to the American south. Silk mills faced the threat of cheap, cellulose-based, artificial silk called rayon. High-quality worsted cloth of mohair and alpaca seemed less affected.

After the war, the village of Greystone honored the eighty men and one woman, Bertha Holt, who had served in American military units between 1917 and 1919. The Benn Company had donated the land and paid for the granite marker and bronze tablet, which stands on Route 104 in North Providence. Smith's fiction conveys the belief of Briardale residents that Binns-Cockcroft had amassed huge profits from the war and, unwilling to let their "brass" go in taxes, built a "Victory Building" as well as the war memorial. Whatever the actual motives of the Benn managers, almost all of the names on the actual memorial tablet were English, except four: three of Italian background, Umberto Di Christoforo, Ralph De Lucia, Michael Leoncallvo, and one of French lineage, Homer Porier.[123] Although the village had a reputation as a Yorkshire stronghold, by 1917 at the latest, other family groups of different nationalities had established a foothold, strong enough for their sons to volunteer to serve in the American military. None of these families, however, were found in the 1920 Census of Greystone. On the tablet, the names of the five dead, all of English background, were marked with stars.

Hedley Smith used but altered the content and the context of the Greystone war memorial. Set in 1922, "The Tongue-Tied Town," part 3 of the Briardale trilogy, explores the cultural tensions arising in the village within the first generation of Yorkshire migrants over political and cultural loyalties during World War I. The Briardale War Memorial, built in the village square to honor military sacrifice, names the servicemen and the dead regardless of which nation they had fought for or with which military they had served. The square is to be dedicated to Yorkshire-born Silas Bradford, "the first from Briardale to win the Military Medal with the West Yorkshires on the Somme in 1916," later missing and presumed dead in 1918.[124]

Silas Bradford's character is an imagined blend of Hedley Smith's uncles Horace and Fred Holmes, members of the Kings' Royal Rifles Regiment during the war. Horace had made the English army his career but before the war had in anger struck the officer he served as a batsman. This was a very serious offense, and Horace served six months hard labor in a Gibraltar prison, after which he had retired with thirteen years service. Horace was well known around Bradford for his capacities to drink and fight.[125] He reenlisted at the beginning of World War I. In 1916, as Smith recalled:

> Uncle Horace [on leave] was entertained by my family and took quite a fancy to me, then a very small shaver [of six years who was] barely recovered from a fearful hospital stay with a broken thigh. And his parting gesture was to leave with me his cap badge: the Maltese Cross which he had carried in Italy, Malta, Gibraltar, Egypt, Africa, Ireland, and Flanders.[126]

Holmes was killed the same year at Delville Wood at the First Battle of the Somme. His younger brother, Fred, was also killed in 1918 during the Second Battle of the Somme. Smith greatly admired his romantic Uncle Horace's aggressive masculinity and open-heartedness, which he recreated in the congenial central character of Horace Gregson in his short story "King George's Idea." (see chapter 4)

The Silas Bradford character in "The Tongue-Tied Town" is a mysterious, grimmer sort. Many of Briardale's war veterans in 1922 had quickly left Rhode Island to volunteer in 1914 for service with the British and Canadian military. They are amused at naming the memorial square for Silas Bradford, a scamp, womanizer, and ruffian, but strongly object to the inclusion of another Briardale resident, Roger Bancroft, in the military parade at the war memorial dedication. Roger had waited for two years after the outbreak of war, caring for his beloved, dying Yankee stepmother, then joined the U.S. Navy as part of the American Expeditionary Force in 1917. "I wouldn't be wearing t' right sort of uniform. . . . Fact is, Aunt Emily, I'm a bloody outsider here—allus have been and allus will be. And you know why!" Aunt Emily reminds him that Roger's father, after the death of his first wife, did choose to wed a Yankee "outsider, . . . made an outsider of himself, and you and all, when he did."

Roger's loyalties to his family and his adopted country lead to his marginalization by the community. The war veterans who object to his American uniform distinguished themselves as Yorkshire Englishmen. Showing his stubborn Yorkshire nature, Roger is determined also to resist Briardale's condemnation of his choice of a sweetheart from among them and his decision to reject millwork and join the town police, a Yankee institution.[127] A decision by one Briardale lad to leave the worsted trade for a clerical job provoked a savage paternal beating and caused a change of mind.[128] Community disapproval was harsh.

To complicate matters, on the night before the dedication ceremonies for the war memorial and Silas Bradford Square, Silas, supposedly in his grave, is spotted in Briardale. The next day, which was Armistice Day 1922, George

Curtis, manager of Briardale's Binns-Cockcroft mill, overrules the older veterans. Roger Bancroft in the blue uniform of the U.S. Navy joins the British servicemen in their khaki and Highland kilts in the parade. The Union Jack and the American flags are both draped across the granite memorial with a bronze plaque bearing the names of Briardale's soldiers and sailors, all of them English. A sumptuous "knife and fork" Yorkshire tea of boiled ham and tongue, sausage rolls, and Cornish pasties waits at the Chapel.

The night after the dedication, Silas Bradford appears at Aunt Emily's door, "gaunt and disheveled," asking for lodging. He had disappeared for two years as part of the secretive British expeditionary force invading the Soviet Union in 1919 where "[w]e were thumped good and hard." His difficult escape led him to Sweden. He had had enough military hardship and migrates to Briardale. There he briefly flaunts his predatory sexuality and defiance of the village and ends up being shot and killed by persons unknown. His beaten and slashed body is dumped in the millpond.

After the inquest, "not more than a joke," Roger Bancroft, now a trained policeman, seeks to identify the killer, but no one in the village will talk to "outsiders" about a crime known to have been committed by one of their own. The police chief remarks,

> Your countrymen, Roger my lad, are running true to form, and not hiding their feelings. They're letting it be known very plainly, in more than words, that whatever had happened is all for the best, and is best ignored and forgotten. . . . In fact, about all we got out of any of them was that they knew him, and they could hardly deny that.

As one of the men at the Social Club bar puts it: "Custom's a funny thing 'at works in spite of the law and the prophets."[129] Their tongues are tied.

Migrants to Briardale, such as Miriam Ainsworth, who chooses to work in a Yankee-owned bank instead of clerking in a worsted mill, also become "outcasts," derided by their families as "casting in your lot with strangers and foreigners."[130] But not all Yankees are outsiders in Briardale village. The elderly bachelor Doctor Flower practices general medicine and treats whichever residents are willing to consult him. Dr. Flower early on indicates respect for and admiration of the qualities of the Yorkshire character. He practices many of them himself: gruff impatience with folly, the reluctance to express his feelings openly, and supreme practicality. As he comes to know his patients, he becomes an exquisite judge of their character. At times, he dismisses the Briardale folk with impatience. Summoned to examine a corpse that turns out to be Silas Bradford, he complains loudly:

These damned Yorkshire clowns. . . . If there's any way they can find o' making a nuisance of themselves and causing trouble to folk, find it they will. It isn't enough they'll die in their beds afore they'll grudge a couple o' dollars to a doctor to patch 'em up. I'm tired o' making out death certificates when I've never even been called in to look at 'em till the breath was out o' their bodies.

The tale of his outburst convulses the Social Club bar customers with hilarious laughter. "Briardale had an abiding, if surly affection for its 'stranger' doctor who had learned how to cope with them on their own terms. . . . For many years his grumpy sarcastic manner had been a rough cloak wrapped around a body of loving service and self-sacrifice."[131] He had even picked up some of their speech patterns.

Briardale's residents demonstrate their regard for Dr. Flower with a Yorkshire-style funeral. Female hands wash his body and place pennies on his eyes. The village carpenter fashions a beautiful solid-oak coffin with brass fittings. Although the doctor did not attend any church, most of his patients are Briardale Chapel members where the services are conducted. Even his old enemy, the village midwife and abortionist, attends the funeral.[132] And of course a splendid Yorkshire tea follows. He has become one of them. Hedley Smith was indicating that when given due respect on its own terms the community of Briardale was capable of both tolerance and affection, even to outsiders.

Stubborn and pervasive resistance to assimilation, an abiding transatlantic political perspective, and a fierce loyalty to Yorkshire cultural identity defined early twentieth-century life in fictional Briardale. In the late 1920s when times got hard in New England textiles, the skilled worsted workers of Briardale returned to Yorkshire with their savings. Others had already returned, such as stonemason Isaac Bond who stayed three years, then left after his wife died in childbirth.[133] Widows took their children home to Yorkshire, while other immigrants relocated to New Zealand or English Canada.

Thus many of these Yorkshire people are clearly migrants, forced to relocate and determined to return with their earnings to their homeland. In Smith's novella "Greedy Guts," part of a unpublished five-part collection titled "Outward Show," the Nicholson family of mill workers considers taking over a Yorkshire-style bakery whose elderly owners, the Shackletons, "loaded with profits, . . . had . . . scudded back to England . . . to live in luxury in their native town." Young Willie Nicholson, American-born, wants to stay and help run the bakery, insisting, "By Gow, mother, you're the best cook in all o' Briardale." His father agrees and sighs, "Aye, and in all Yorkshire for that matter. . . . I wish we were back there now."[134] They buy the bakery, but their difficult decision reflected the ambivalence of the first generation. On the other hand, Rhoda Denby's experiences in "The Mill Folk" with work, love, marriage, and widowhood led to sturdy independence and affectionate relationships, which bound her to Briardale village even after her dearest friends and disillusioned relatives had fled to England, Canada, and New Zealand. Smith's depiction of the complex and ambivalent feelings of the first generation of migrants reflected his own and his family's attitudes toward their new country.

3

Working, Writing, Loving, Enduring,
1923–1994

The mid-twentieth-century industrial economy of Rhode Island offered diminishing hopes to immigrants and their families. The cotton textile
industry in the Blackstone River Valley north of Providence began its official
decline in 1923, the year the Smiths landed in Boston. The worsted industry
followed. Both textile and textile machinery-making operations deteriorated
throughout the twentieth century. Factories closed, owners wrote off tax
losses, capital took flight, cutbacks hit workers, and businesses closed. In
Rhode Island factory centers, family income declined and per capita high
school graduation rates tumbled, while in small towns income stabilized and
housing improved.[1] Providence, the hub of machine tool-making, jewelry and
clothing production, higher education, and state government, attracted job
seekers. Commuter towns grew along new highways. Coastal areas relied on
tourism. Historic preservationists hoped to save and interpret the foundations of American industrial might at Old Slater Mill and in the Blackstone
River Corridor. In less well-known valleys, old industrial structures were
converted to other purposes or demolished. Such changes in the material
world and landscape of a state as small as Rhode Island altered everything.
Historic places either were celebrated or vanished.

The whole northeastern cotton textile industry fell to competition from
early twentieth-century southern mills and changing tastes in fabrics. By
the turn of the century, southern textiles posed threats to both the better
grades of cloth made in the Northeast and the export trade.[2] Southern mill
agents, many experienced managers of northern mills, used antilabor practices: the blacklist, the lockout, evictions from mill housing, and racial fears

to undermine any northern moves to organize unions. The southern mill worker was neither docile nor submissive to working conditions and low wages but accepted the cotton South's class and racial structure and rural values. Between 1880 and 1930, southern cotton workers earned about 60 percent of the wages paid in the North for a twelve-hour day. Rayon mills built by German firms in the 1920s for the U.S. market processed southern wood pulp into cellulose yarn. Within twenty years, the South, especially in Tennessee and Virginia, produced 70 percent of U.S. rayon, which became far more desirable than old-fashioned cotton cloth.

The industrial Depression of the 1930s hit textiles very hard, North and South. Strikers in Fall River and New Bedford, Massachusetts, joined others in Rhode Island, New Hampshire, and Maine or wherever textile mills continued operations. Violently repressive state governments in Rhode Island, Georgia, and the Piedmont area in the Carolinas disrupted picketing and intimidated or killed strikers, while recalcitrant mill owners gladly sold off their inventories. World War II returned prosperity briefly but did not halt the overall trends.

By 1970 North Carolina represented the premier textile state, producing near one-third of American fabrics and employing 280,000 workers.[3] But after 1980 many Southern textile mills began to close, giving up 500,000 jobs, a decline accelerated by the North American Free Trade Agreement and the elimination of tariff protection against Mexican and Canadian textiles. By 1995 all-black production workers and white supervisors dominated southern factories.[4] Textile capitalists restructured to meet late twentieth-century foreign competition worsened by a strong dollar, but as the U.S. economy shifted away from industrial production toward financial, technology, and service jobs, American consumers bought cheap, foreign-made garments, merchandised in large discount stores or through mail order and Internet catalogues.[5] The long slow process of deindustrialization of northern textile production and its subsidiary industries provided the background for the adult working years of Hedley Smith.

The political climate in twentieth-century Rhode Island shifted as decisively as the economy. Conservative Republicanism, grounded in the denial of the franchise or any other rights to the newly arrived or the property-less, had shaped nineteenth-century Rhode Island government until the emergence of Providence's first foreign-born Democratic mayor, Patrick J. McCarthy, in 1906. During interwar years, the Catholic parishes throughout the state became organizational bases for naturalized citizens and newly enfranchised Catholic women. These changes altered presidential voting patterns and who sat in Congressional seats, won gubernatorial races, and controlled munici-pal government offices. Republican voters with backgrounds associated with Yankee and English culture or who recoiled from Catholicism retreated from formal political power, as battles among Americans of French Canadian, Italian, and Irish descent transformed Rhode Island politics.[6]

Immigrant groups in textile work faced the disastrous economic decline, but Judith Smith's study of Italian and Jewish immigrants living in relatively prosperous Providence in the early twentieth century provides a compara-tive perspective centered on the cushioning bonds of family and kin. Hedley Smith's Yorkshire relatives, in-laws, and fictional folk represent a spectrum of the admirable, complaisant, self-sacrificial, malicious, and much in-between. The material Hedley Smith used in his Briardale fiction was partly autobio-graphical, drawing on people he had known or had heard of and places he had been. He had excellent recall: his trip from Liverpool to Boston on the *Winifredian* in 1923, although unrecorded, provided one detailed fictional setting in an important work: "The Lion and the Eagle." An investigation of his life after emigration and of his fiction provides a context for analyzing not only the experiences of emigration, acculturation, aging, and regret but, in this chapter and the next, of transatlantic political perspectives, sexual-ity, and the complex relationships between men and women. This analysis suggests that persistent feelings of personal loss including grief and rage, deeply concealed from family and friends, probably mark the emotional life of most emigrants and migrants. Certainly other groups had their own expressions of ongoing endurance similar to the Yorkshire commonplace: "We mun thoil it." Outwardly, however, they became citizens and partici-pated in both bicultural and ethnic community experiences. As did Hedley Smith, many succeeded in the material world. But emotionally they lived ambivalent, bifurcated lives unless and until a particularly intense experi-ence bound them to the new culture. Hedley Smith apparently did not have such an experience, even as a husband and father. Emigration remained the key emotional moment in his life.

Working and Writing

Beginning on December 31, 1923, when he was fourteen, Hedley Smith worked for the New England District of the National Jewelers Board of Trade in Providence for ten years. His parents Ernest and Alice shifted from job to job and rented furnished tenements in Johnston and in Centredale, both near Greystone village in the town of North Providence. Hedley and his brother, Sam, lived with their parents until they married, contributing to the family economy and tiding each other over through times of unemployment and dislocation. This unsettled life was decidedly a step down from their cozy situation in Lidget Green, Bradford. Although other immigrants in the early twentieth century from less favored areas than England and many contemporary migrants to the United States faced downward mobility, English immigrants at the turn of the century usually did not and certainly did not expect it.

Hedley and Sam developed a circle of friends among the English-born in the mill villages of North Providence and, once established in their jobs, took short vacations on the Rhode Island shore together. In 1928 the Smiths managed to buy on mortgage a small house or bungalow in Warwick, just south of Providence, where all the Smith men worked. Ernest, Alice, and Hedley became naturalized citizens as a family in 1929. Sam became a citizen as an individual. He applied for and was issued his American passport. His brother never did so. Both young men began to advance at their positions. After six years as a file clerk, Hedley at twenty became a trade investigator, reporting on the credit and prospects of jewelry retailers. This involved judgment as well as travel around New England. Every New England town had its library crammed with English classics, which Hedley greatly relished.

His transatlantic correspondence with schoolmates Horace Sharp and Tom Cromwell continued between 1923 and 1939. As David Gerber argued, this type of correspondence maintained relationships with "particular others" significant to the immigrant's understanding of himself and was often powerfully charged with emotions.[7] Unlike his own letters, which were not preserved and in which he apparently revealed little, his friends' lives became filled with exams and academic life at the University of Edinburgh and at Christ College, Cambridge. They also sent word about local football and cricket teams. Hedley continued to write, and instead of details about his life he mailed off manuscript after manuscript.[8] Tom was the severest of critics and the more respected. They teased each other about girls and sex. Although deeply disappointed at his stunted formal education, Smith was working at a job he performed well and spent as much time as possible reading and writing. He is pictured at the firm's Christmas party in his mid-twenties as well dressed, robust, jolly, and full of himself.

On January 31, 1933, Smith lost his job. During the worst four years of the Great Depression he was without regular employment. This greatly embarrassed him and strained his correspondence with his friends. Information about what he did during four long years between gainful employment is difficult to reconstruct. For a striver such as Smith, bitterness and defeat added to his other disappointments. He thoiled it.

His cultural background and his experience told him that education, at this juncture *practical* education, was the best use of his energies. Drawing on whatever savings he had, Hedley took night courses at Bryant Stratton Business School, accessible by trolley. He excelled in courses in writing, English literature for which he won an award of books, and typewriting. His children, Duncan and Portia, regarded his working-class parents as unusually literate. Ernest and Alice Smith belonged to the late nineteenth- and early twentieth-century working-class urban culture of traditional "labour aristocrats" who loved classic English literature and believed in self-improvement.[9] While Ernest served his apprenticeship to become a brushmaker between 1897 and 1903 in Bradford, the three elderly master craftsmen would send him out on errands including trips to the city library for literature to read and discuss. Bring back "what you want," they said, "as long as it[']s Dickens or Thackeray or Bronte or Lytton."[10] Ernest read them all. Alice read when she had the time, and Ernest read aloud to the family. When the Smith family sold their household furniture in 1923, they refused to abandon other treasured goods, including a complete set of Charles Dickens and the works of the Brontë sisters, purchased one book at a time.[11] Hedley intensified their literary devotions, but his brother loved the mechanical, becoming passionate about cameras and automobiles. Sam was never shown manuscripts. He returned once to Bradford in 1938 on his American passport to look up an old girlfriend he could not forget but returned without her. He always kept a picture of his old flame in his wallet.[12]

Like Ernest, Sam, and Hedley Smith, many Jewish and Italian male immigrants to Providence also faced abrupt changes in their work lives that contradicted both their training and experience. Italian artisan shoemakers tried to hang on to their craft, but many entered factories and repaired shoes only when unemployed. They would have understood the loss of status Ernest experienced when his plans to work as a master brushmaker upon arrival in 1923 collapsed. When an immigrant teacher of Hebrew in Providence was advised by his rabbi to be practical, he became a peddler. He would have sympathized with Hedley's disappointment. Sam was a born engineer but had no further formal education except that offered by his firm. He refused to become a manager at Brown and Sharpe, loving the activity on the shop floor. Among many of those whom he supervised in the machine tool industry of Providence were Italian immigrants, formerly unskilled laborers and agricultural workers. According to Judith Smith, few Italian and Jewish women entered factories and textile mills in Providence, but Alice Smith tried, possessing long years of experience and skills. English, Jewish, and Italian immigrants also shared the close-knit family connections and "family culture of work" that allowed the first generation to settle in and survive, even more so during the Depression years.[13] The Smith family understood that necessity.

By the early 1930s Hedley and his Yorkshire friends Horace and Tom became increasingly separated by ideology and educational and professional opportunity. Horace's family was Socialist, Labour Party, pacifist, and missionary Methodist. He took a degree in theology, failed to get on in a southern parish, and returned to the West Riding, relying on terrible earnestness to overcome his religious doubts and physical breakdowns. He agonized over Hitler's rise to power, choosing to support the Conservatives and the appeaser Neville Chamberlain in hopes of peace. In his letters to Hedley, probably received rather coldly and sometimes with no reply, he worried over how far he could stretch his moral conscience if England was invaded.

Tom's letters, which became fewer, reflected the new world he had entered at Cambridge. After taking a second-class degree in English literature and his BA in 1930, he was recruited by the British consular service. Buoyantly adventuresome, he ended up in Fukien Province, China, sending letters, which often went astray, about the threat of Japanese aggression and his enchantment with the Far East. His gift of a lacquered box was one of Hedley's treasures. Tom had a Chinese lover whom he wanted to marry and was working on a grammar/dictionary of the Fukien dialect when he was murdered by the invading Japanese in 1939. Reflecting on the fate of his friends forty years later, Smith wrote in a letter that for all their university degrees his intimate friends had been wiped out in "the holocaust of World War II." And those that survived scrambled to earn their "bread and cheese" in the bleak postwar years.[14] He denied that he had missed anything really important. Perhaps by then he had come to believe it.

While he struggled to gain additional business skills, Hedley cultivated acquaintance in Warwick, where his family had moved. Although Hedley had been baptized at St. Alban's Anglican Church in Bradford and confirmed in 1928 at an Episcopal church in Centredale, one of his favorite places became the Asbury Methodist Church's Men's Club in Warwick. This proved a far cry from the Greystone Social Club's Yorkshire conviviality and plentiful alcohol, but useful to make contacts for an unemployed, aspiring young man who had fallen in love. In Greystone Hedley and Sam had met, among others, Marshall Fowler, whose Yankee family from Maine lived in the village. When Marshall and Hedley took a boisterous trip together to Canada, Smith's citizenship as an American was challenged at the border. They talked his way in.[15] He was developing a reputation socially as something of a drinker, preferably scotch, and as a young man who could easily defend himself with his fists. His manly model undoubtedly was his Uncle Horace of the Kings' Royal Rifles Regiment, who had been known around Bradford for his capacities to drink and fight.[16] Over pints of bitter and pork pies, Hedley found out that Marshall had an interesting sister, Carmen.[17]

Loving, Enduring

By 1936 Smith was courting twenty-four-year-old Carmen Fowler, who taught high school English and shared his love of literature. In contrast with the Yorkshire ideal of female beauty, she was dark and slim, the prototype for Laura Richmond-Halliday Barraclough described in Smith's "The Lion and the Eagle."

> Her figure was good but nothing special: in fact, a bit too much on the skinny side by Yorkshire standards, calling attention to her more than average height. Yorkshire folk, who tend to be on the stubby side themselves though sturdy as oak trees, aren't over fond of tall, gawky women. They like their lasses to make a comfortably plump, soft armful.
>
> Her way of dress and her face were both Quaker plain, as was the demurely simple arrangement of her thick, dark hair. She had true Yankee features, all austere flat planes, with a high forehead and cheekbones, and a sallow tinge to her smooth complexion. Her eyes, with their bewildering capacity to flicker between violet and hazel and deep blue, never lost the wide, unflinching steadiness of their expression. Briardale folk had been known to condemn this long, deliberate look and the little frown that often accompanied it, as Yankee stuck-uppishness. Actually, it was mostly near sightedness. Sometimes, and always unexpectedly, a lively spark exploded in its depths, hinting at anger, or sympathy, or curiosity, or defiance, or any one of a dozen moods but no hint of uncertainty ever clouded it.[18]

Carmen's parents had been encouraged to move out of Auburn, Maine, where she had been born, by Donald Fowler's father, a successful, wealthy lawyer in Calais who judged his adopted son an irresponsible failure and negligent husband and father. His father-in-law, Marshall McKusick, agreed. Indeed, according to relatives, Donald regularly abandoned his wife, Ethel, and his four children but just as regularly returned.[19] Still, family money was available to tide them over until the next crisis. Among his various jobs, Donald Fowler had picked up the trade of a dyer in a Maine textile mill. In 1921 the Fowlers of Maine had had enough and sent Donald and his family to Rhode Island, where they rented a cheap apartment in Providence. From there they moved to Greystone, where presumably Donald Fowler got work in the Benn mills dye house, while family funds subsequently allowed the purchase of a small house. As Yankees, they found themselves surrounded by Yorkshire immigrants, but skilled dyers were always needed and Fowler always needed a good job. His situation didn't last; he got a job in the nearby Esmond blanket mill. When he disappeared periodically, his wife took in boarders.[20]

Carmen Fowler lived in Greystone beginning at the age of nine; she married in Greystone at twenty-five. Trained at the Rhode Island Normal School, she was intensely proud of her Yankee heritage and disdainful of Yorkshire mill people and their habits. As a boardinghouse mistress, her mother was forced to cook and wash for them. Isolated and frequently estranged from her husband, Ethel clung to her daughter as her closest friend. Carmen and her mother had no easy time getting on with the people of Greystone and ended up disliking them intensely. Hedley Smith describes the tensions in "The Lion and the Eagle," disguising himself as Eric Sutcliffe and Carmen as Minna-Louisa.

> No matter which way you went, you had to run the gauntlet of Briardale village . . . knowing eyes would follow the two "outsiders" marching together down the sidewalk. Eyes would roll upward under eloquent eyebrow-twitchings, looks of frank or grotesque curiosity or suggestiveness would clash like weapons crossing from one side of the narrow street to the other. . . .
>
> "How do you do, Mester Sutcliffe. Lovely day today, isn't it? An' how's your health? You're looking as if nowt ailed you. Back on your feet, I see. And looking as bright as bottled beer this morning." With greetings similar in degree to Minna-Louisa, in hearty Yorkshire voices that recognized no reason for muting themselves in tone or show reticence in language.
>
> "You shouldn't mind them," Eric said one morning, after the two had run this gauntlet and won their way to the tranquil solitudes beyond. Painful embarrassment, not unmixed with anger and shame, painted itself in the warm flush of the girl's downcast cheeks.
>
> "It's only their way, you know, of being friendly and showing they want to like you and hope you'll like them. They're generous and warm-hearted when you get to know them. And their frankness and plain speaking is not bad manners—just their nature."
>
> "It's like being made to walk naked before them all," she retorted with an angry little shudder. "I don't think they like me or want to like me, either.

They're just curious, like so many heartless boys gathered around to watch a sick animal, studying its pains."[21]

Nonetheless, Carmen if she wished could provide Hedley with detailed information about the people and the place. Indeed Greystone provided the setting for their courtship.

In "The Lion and the Eagle," Smith captures a scene familiar to courting couples in the village. As a young man living for several years in nearby Centredale, Hedley Smith knew the skating pond and its crowds well, but courtship lent special interest. "[A] man in love is only too ready to shape his life to anything that brings himself and his sweetheart together in any intimately shared experience, even though he had a lukewarm opinion of cavorting on ice and snow."[22] As an admirer of nineteenth-century German novellas and of the Brontës, one of the hallmarks of Smith's fiction was landscape.

> Above the bridge, the big milldam was penned behind a high barrier with narrow cascades of water at its proper level. In this sharp weather the slow pond was frozen hard and thick, and the overflow of the weirs hissed and seethed under clouds of white fog and spray. The Briardale folk used this broad area as a skating rink. Brushwood-covered islets upstream shut off the sharpest blasts of the northwesterly wind; the frozen surface was as smooth as glass; and the little pavilion of the cricket field was a convenient spot for changing shoes and skates, for donning and doffing warm clothes, and for resting in comfort between bursts of violent exercise.
>
> . . . The grind and sweep of skate blades, the warm full-throated shout of Yorkshire voices, blended with the barking of dogs, the shrieks of the timid and inexpert, the innocent bawdiness of the warm guffaws that throbbed out when occasionally a lass would lose her balance and go down in a whirl of petticoats that showed more of herself than she cared to have seen; and it all wove a pattern of sound and warmth, amusement and emotion as intricate and as manifold in texture and color as was ever a piece of cloth woven on the looms inside the great brick building overshadowing them all.
>
> . . . Briardale was out in full force and making merry—young and old and everything in-between. The ice cracked and groaned and shuddered as long trains of hand-linked skaters swept up and down in writhing serpent lines of bodies, roaring and shouting in the ecstasy of their sweeps and twists and the mock terror of imminent collision with struggling groups and individuals trapped in their path. All the dogs of Briardale—and in Briardale the dog population is no less abundant nor highly regarded than its children—had turned out in force to share the family enjoyment, and swelled with their barking and yelping the bedlam of voice and action. . . . Nobody paid much attention to a simple couple with skates in their hands as Eric and Minna-

Louisa crossed the ice to the little islet and sat on a fallen log before the fire. Here Eric helped his companion to fasten on her skates.

The scene also distills the reactions of the mill villagers to outsiders violating their community. Both in Briardale and in Bradford, marriage to an American was marriage with a "foreigner." Hedley Smith would become like Roger Bancroft in "The Tongue-tied Town," an outsider by association with Yankees. Smith also understood well Carmen's fearful anxiety about sex and her virginity. This depiction of public mocking of chastity in this scene conveys her raw humiliation.

> A very old man sat at the extreme end of the log with a mere slit of gray face showing between the rim of a knitted woolen cap pulled down over his ears and a bulky woolen muffler high around his throat. His hardened gums were crunching into a hot pork pie. . . . "I reckon that's it," Eric said, after a final check of their feet. "Are you ready?"
>
> The old man was so still they didn't think he had even noticed their arrival, and he had paid no attention to what they did, but at Eric's last words his body stirred, his head shifted among its swathings. Though they could not see, they could feel sharp eyes boring towards them.
>
> A crazed and ragged cackle, like the rattle of a decrepit old handloom, struggled from his chest up to and through his lips.
>
> "Are you ready! Hee, hee, hee!" His voice was high and thin; the whinnying of an old horse. "Aye, shooo's ready, I'll bet you. Shoo's ready enow. They're all ready!"
>
> A young couple, arms intertwined, skimmed dizzily around the thin point of the islet and diminished in the tricky moonlight. The old man waved his arm in a spacious gesture after them and whinnied again.
>
> "*They're* ready, choose how. An' why not? Go on! Mak' hay while the sun shines, that's what *I* say. Have your good time while you can. *I* did. It doesn't last that long!"
>
> . . . The old man's chuckle became a rattle of obscene mirth.[23]

Living among the Yorkshire people in the village, Carmen was likely to have noticed and disdained the sexual experimentation among the "vulgar" young mill workers. Her own impeccable morals constituted a license to teach. Intense animosity would come to mark the relationships between the Yankee Fowlers and the Yorkshire Smiths.

Among Hedley Smith's contacts at Warwick's Asbury Methodist Men's Club, where he had volunteered to become secretary, was a popular, rising Republican politician and lay leader in the church who appreciated his qualities and abilities. Albert P. Ruerat had moved from Providence to Warwick in 1930 and served on the city council with his eye on the mayor's office. The Rhode Island Republican Party remained deeply conservative and anti-New Deal, alarmed by the general textile strike in 1934 that involved violent upheavals in Rhode Island.[24] The landslide victory of the Democratic Party in the national elections in 1936 had confirmed the high tide of Franklin Roosevelt's New Deal, but statewide the Republicans regrouped. Among them Albert Ruerat gathered a body of supporters and promised jobs. Hedley Smith chose the Republicans as the party of the well-educated and the established Protestants over the Democrats who for Smith represented the "great unwashed": Irish and the Italian Catholics.[25] Not sharing his background or tastes, Smith dismissed them and their interests. When Ruerat was elected mayor of Warwick in 1937, Hedley Smith became his executive secretary, a post he held for twelve years. On the strength of this connection, Hedley and Carmen married in late August 1937 (see fig. 3).

The atmosphere of the wedding appeared tense. Hedley tried to persuade the rector of the Episcopal Church in Centredale to officiate, but Carmen

Figure 3. From the wedding of Hedley Smith and Carmen Fowler, August 28, 1937, Greystone, R.I.: (*left to right, bottom row, second through fourth from left*) Ethel Fowler, Hedley Smith, Carmen Fowler; (*middle row, first through third from left*) Alice Smith, Mrs. Ruerat, Mayor Albert Ruerat; (*back row, second from left*) Ernest Smith, (*fourth and fifth from left*) Berneice Greenway, Sam Smith. Courtesy of Portia Thompson.

had not been baptized. The religious backgrounds of both families were traditional if unenthusiastic: Congregational for the Fowlers and Methodist for the Smiths, except for Hedley. No matter: there was little money for a church wedding. A local pastor agreed to perform the ceremony at the Fowlers' house in Greystone. The wedding picture taken on the front porch shows the family party with a few friends, most dressed in dark colors on the late August day with the bride herself in "mahogany" crepe with a corsage. Her bridesmaid, also in a dark dress, beams a bright smile. The bride's mother looks reserved, even suspicious, the bride herself watchful. Hedley is proud and hopeful. Behind the bride and groom stand Mayor Ruerat and his wife in white, light summer clothes. Among the family members, Alice Smith smiles with delight. Her favorite son Hedley has a wife. She has no idea what is coming.

The Hedley Smiths rented a house within easy reach of Warwick City Hall and Hedley's parents and brother. The morning after the wedding, Hedley tried to tease his bride. As she offered him his orange juice, he announced, "I don't drink orange juice; I drink scotch." She gazed at him, thinking "we'll see about that."[26] Teasing was forbidden, along with any use of dialect. Whether or not Carmen intended to teach that fall, her quick pregnancy made that impossible. Hedley's job in the Ruerat administration became absolutely essential and quite successful. His skills in judging people and practical values learned in the jewelry trade proved just as important in municipal politics. Their daughter, Portia, was born in May 1938, named to celebrate her parents' mutual enthusiasm for Shakespeare. A son, Duncan, followed in July 1940. His weary, witty father suggested one night they rename him Macbeth: he who "doth murder sleep."[27]

As her children were born, Carmen stubbornly insisted that Alice and Ernest, who also lived in Warwick, not be allowed to see their grandchildren. How to fathom this cruel denial? A good deal of family lore among the Smith children and their acquaintances attributes Carmen's motives to a desire to protect her children against an impossible, screaming mother-in-law. A photograph taken early in the marriage shows Alice stiffly facing toward the camera held by her son Sam, while Carmen's body writhes away from Alice in revulsion. If body language speaks truly, profound distaste has overwhelmed the daughter-in-law. It is possible that when the family was told about the pregnancy in 1937, Alice confided to Carmen that she too had been pregnant before she married. Similar circumstances had been acceptable, even commonplace, among Yorkshire families. Whatever Alice's friendly intentions, Carmen would have received this approach as a deadly insult by an interfering, nosy, lower-class woman who, given any encouragement, would presume anything. Alice had to be exiled, and her husband must agree.[28] Alice's name was never spoken again in the Smith home.

Alice Smith had an angry confrontation with Carmen over seeing her grandchildren. With the help of her son Sam, who locked the two women into a room together, they had it out. This confrontation, during which Carmen apparently said little, only fueled her hatred and determination.[29] She never changed her mind. Hedley acquiesced and openly collaborated. On one occasion Alice presented herself at the Smiths' front door when her granddaughter Portia was about five, asking for Hedley. Portia had no idea who this lady was but awakened her father, who firmly removed her from the scene.[30] This denial was even harder to bear when Sam made it clear after his marriage in 1940 that he intended to have no children, a decision made against the wishes of his wife Berneice. When Alice died in 1952, Carmen had prevailed. Still, on the afternoon of her funeral, which Hedley did not attend, Sam brought his father Ernest to see his grandchildren, now in their early teens. They would see each other more and come to love and enjoy each other's company, but Sam was never forgiven.[31] Ernest died in 1959.

Hedley's children, Portia and Duncan, wondered how their father could have allowed such a separation, denying them the knowledge of their Yorkshire grandparents. Their abiding interest in the Yorkshire past, their ancestors, and their relatives springs from this denial, an interest Carmen deeply resented. Indeed, Hedley had his hands full. He probably harbored some conscious resentment over the emigration from Bradford that he felt cost him dearly, perhaps even ruined his life. Marrying a Yankee wife, according to his fiction, had made him an outsider, but his actions confirmed his alienation from his family. Certainly the family, including his brother, blamed him in return for not controlling his wife, but Carmen's life had put her on a path from which she could not return. Hedley came to understand this. A Yorkshireman knew how to be stoical; a lover of Thomas Hardy's novels understood that life's cruelties must be accepted and endured. Perhaps the old Yorkshire phrase of perseverance comforted him a bit: "We mun thoil it." He would need it.

Judith Smith's handling of the dynamics of immigrant family life allowed room for generational and gender conflict but cannot help explain the personal dimension in this breakup of the Smith family. Hedley Smith was a collection of character traits, talents, aspirations, feelings, experiences, and disappointments, a man with choices that carried repercussions and regrets. Because Portia Smith Thompson and Duncan Smith did not know their grandparents, they could not reconstruct their "bonds of kinship" or their friends and neighbors.[32] Alice's brother Arthur Collins, a machinist, had emigrated in 1906 and helped them relocate to Johnston in 1923, but his later connections with Ernest and his sister Alice are vague. Carmen and her brothers depended on their kin for support over the years and as adults actively worked together. Sam Smith took in his father Ernest after Alice's death and was close to Arthur Collins's only child, but Hedley would not involve himself.[33] The breakup of the family was one casualty of the Smiths' emigration.

Historians of immigration, especially those interested in community or neighborhood studies, can take warning from the tangled tale of Hedley, Carmen, Alice, and the grandchildren. Usually relying on census data, as I have done in chapter 2, geographical propinquity is assumed to mean family networks of support, vibrancy, and closeness. The tension built into mother-in-law and daughter-in-law relations is a given in most cultures, but other equally intense emotional reactions based on deep resentments as well as cultural and class differences are distinct possibilities. Tempers strained or even unhinged by the unknown difficulties of migration can overwhelm custom and intended niceness or restraint. Derangement can accompany movement. How is one to know that an intended gesture of kindness in one culture can be received as a mortal class insult and trigger bitter revenge?

During Carmen's formative years, she had developed an obsession with stability and control to counter her mother's intimate dependency on a feck-less, uncaring husband. School teaching gave Carmen some measure of in-dependence, but just as important to her was remaining on the closest terms possible with her mother. Cutting the Smith family out of her children's lives could not have happened without the tacit approval and support of her mother who enjoyed the company of all her grandchildren. The Fowlers had left Greystone in 1945 and moved to rural North Scituate, about twenty miles northwest of Warwick. Ethel's brother had bought the land and built his sister a small house, putting the property in the name of McKusick family members. Furthermore, Carmen was determined to rid her daughter Portia of any traces of "the Alice temperament" by treating her childish tantrums with cold showers. Duncan, two years younger, watched and, using the time-honored weapon of young children against controlling mothers, refused to eat. Duncan later described his mother as "she who must be obeyed."[34]

In 1952, the year Alice Smith died, Ethel Fowler was diagnosed with bladder cancer. The diagnosis traumatized Carmen. She took her mother to Boston hospitals repeatedly, oversaw her nursing care, and watched over her agonies until she died in 1953. She could dream of doing nothing less. Donald Fowler then sold the loam off the North Scituate property, rented the house, and resumed his wandering ways.[35] Her children remembered that Carmen's resulting deep depressions, unassuagable grief, and deteriorating physical health "ruled" family life. As a mature man, Duncan reflected,

> She tried so hard to deal with a lifetime sadness that was greater than anyone should have to bear and thank goodness she had my father as a companion because I cannot think of another person who could have managed to preserve his humor and his devotion in the face of all that blackness—no one but a Yorkshireman.[36]

Yet her children also recalled their mother as a dedicated, happy teacher who loved her work and provided them with access to a private school education by working without pay at the institution. She enjoyed a lively, independent intelligence and read widely, loved to garden and cook, and was devoted to her children and to her cats. Carmen maintained a few close friendships with women from her college days and from the various teaching jobs she had until her retirement.[37]

Hedley, although busy with his job and the frequent night-time meetings of municipal government, took time to lavish on his children the care of a devoted father. He lived as much as possible as if he still was in the West Riding. That included especially his taste in food and his talents in cooking. In his fiction, his characters express his own profound distaste for Yankee cooking, most explicitly in "The Lion and the Eagle," which included:

> all those subtle combinations of seafoods which their taste, as well as the proximity of the village fishmarkets encrusting the coastline beyond the Pier, found congenial to their palates. These reflected their American tastes, with their preference for snakelike, writhing and shell-encased varieties of marine life; all exotic specimens in their way no doubt, but to Eric Sutcliffe's beef-conditioned Yorkshire palate, to which fish was just fish, all too much alike in flavor and all reduced to a democratic principle of equality of oversaltedness.[38]

In one novella, an elderly Yankee woman expressed a longing for "creamed salt pork," a dish Smith described in detail to nauseate his prospective readers.[39] To him, drinking iced tea was the same as eating boiled ice cream.[40]

As a Yorkshireman-born, Smith prided himself on his Sunday beef roast, well done with an egg, flour, and milk mix expertly poured into the smoking-hot drippings to make puffy Yorkshire pudding. Carmen sometimes used the rest of the beef prepared with smothered potatoes and onions in white sauce, a Yankee dish. Hedley and his children preferred combining the beef and gravy with onions and potatoes in a frying pan with no white sauce. Smith was a regular at Sam Pickles' Yorkshire bakery in Apponaug, the Warwick neighborhood where the family lived, where he bought custard tarts, bread, and pastries. He did the marketing for the household, while his wife did the housework. He cooked the big meals, made bread, beef sausages, and baked beans for Saturday nights, and sometimes to delight the children made chocolate bread. For his finicky young son, he cut out of the mildest cheese an entire train including a locomotive and three cars. He also made up stories about a boy who lived only on peanut butter to coax Duncan to eat other foods.[41] Of course it worked. From local butchers, he bought kippers, tripe, and kidneys. Occasionally he made his own pork pies and cinnamon buns. Carmen loved good food, and her husband was an excellent cook. She told her children that food had been scarce in Bradford during World War I, explaining Hedley's inclination to eat pats of butter as well as the entire piece of salt pork from the bottom of baked beans. He became portly but steadfastly refused to drive a car and walked everywhere he could. In the most specific sense, Hedley Smith was what he ate.[42]

Working and Writing

On those walks, especially to and from his job at Warwick City Hall and at his routine work as administrative secretary, Smith's mind filled with stories that he wrote by hand at night and on weekends. He used his office typewriter to prepare the final draft of his manuscripts. In the early 1940s he plotted mysteries and short stories, hoping to become a published author. Carmen, who was a fan of the English mystery classics, read the drafts. Smith visited his New York agent who repeatedly discouraged him, insisting that the stories needed more sex scenes to sell. In Smith's "Hussy in the Well," his amateur detective Benedict Arnold signs a contract to write a generic mystery for a New York publisher who has just purchased an expensive dust jacket featuring a naked girl. It was the only one he refused to burn. Still he was continuing his lifelong dedication to writing, subscribing to at least one journal for professional writers and sending off finished manuscripts marked with word counts.[43]

Meanwhile, Duncan and Portia benefited from private school education, but both parents intended only their son for university training. Duncan was sent to Providence Classical High School, Portia to Warwick High School. She understood there would be no money for further education. At eighteen in 1956 she became the wife of Leslie Thompson, and the young couple lived in Warwick. Duncan attended Brown University and also earned his graduate degree there, keeping close ties with his parents.

This relatively settled life in Warwick rested on the political career of Republican politician Albert Ruerat. It came to an end when after six terms as mayor he decided to run for governor in 1948. This was the year when Harry Truman's upset victory led the Democratic Party to a national sweep, including the governor of Rhode Island, John O. Pastore. In 1950 Pastore became Rhode Island's first Democratic, Italian American, and Catholic U.S. senator. The powerful tide of Democratic support among Catholics and working-class voters in Rhode Island, running against conservative Republicanism since the Alfred Smith victory in Providence during the presidential campaign of 1928, had prevailed.[44] Hedley Smith's fortunes were tied up with the losers. He used his contacts to search for a job, ending up working for a gold refinery firm in Providence on a complicated commuting schedule, which included his exhausted school-teaching wife who did drive a car. Despite marital friction, Smith had little choice until Warwick elected in 1952 another Republican, Darius Goff, allowing him to return briefly to his old post as administrative secretary. The world of politics offered him only a brief illusion of security and the reality of routine, tedious work from which he regularly escaped by climbing into the dome of the city hall tower as a refuge to think or read.[45] After raising taxes, Mayor Goff failed to be reelected in 1954. Municipal politics were now a dead end.

Out of work at forty-six, Smith used his political contacts to find work as an accountant as well as a "dogsbody," expected also to do menial jobs at a bowling alley in Warwick owned by the former Republican mayor. He wore a shirt and tie every day. Carmen became openly scornful. But as in the early thirties, he took courses in advanced accounting at a local branch of the University of Rhode Island, hoping that someone might recognize his hard work and merit. While he waited, he consoled himself by writing and rereading his favorites, including Greek tragedies. The auditing firm at the bowling alley just happened to do the same work for the payroll department at Brown University. When a position opened up, Smith was encouraged to apply and was appointed in 1960. Any job at Brown in the City of Providence seemed full of promise. He could browse the bookstores, stay on after work to take extension courses in German, or have dinner with his son, now a graduate student. Furthermore, Carmen had been encouraging him to make something out of his digging around in the old documents in Warwick City Hall. He painstakingly wrote a historical novel of colonial Rhode Island, *The*

Gift of Armor: A Romance of Warwick, published locally in 1968 by Vantage Press and used in the public schools. He rewrote this tale of colonist Samuel Gorton acquiring the land for Warwick town by bestowing a suit of armor on the local Indian chief for adult readers but failed to sell it.[46] Still he had his first publication.

His work in the payroll department eventually led to Hedley Smith's idea of a dream job in the bookstore at Brown University. But at the same time, Carmen insisted on moving into her mother's old house in North Scituate, eventually stirring up her old depression. In 1968 she sold the house in Warwick to Portia and Leslie, bought out her brothers' interests in the property, and moved in. Hedley acquiesced. It was Carmen's house; his name was not on the deed. His son surmised: "My father thought he was in a Greek tragedy in any case and this move must have seemed to him just another act or scene as my mother descended into the madness of mourning."[47]

The house had been rented to careless tenants for years, and the land was piled with dumps in the rural New England fashion. With great energy Carmen cleaned up, organized, and planted in her mother's memory but, once finished, became seriously depressed although she continued to teach. She also became interested in spiritualism. On work days, Carmen dropped her husband at the bus stop to Providence before driving to Warwick. Smith may have briefly considered his son's wish for him to take a small apartment in Providence. But no; he was "t' husband."[48] Moving into a house not legally his own into a rural area was another forced relocation and probably stirred up buried memories of his exile in 1923. Smith understood it all in Yorkshire terms: he was t' husband and she was the powerful wife/mother. He had no choice that did not involve rupture and separation. He could not choose that, but the move took its toll.

In the Scituate house, tensions between wife and husband became more open. Whenever Carmen or Duncan dared to make an innocent but incorrect reference to English literature, Smith, who had memorized his favorites, would pursue the culprit through the small house, chanting the right lines, quoting them exactly and at length, louder and louder, until the fleeing victim cried out for mercy, throwing the cats into an uproar, and reducing his wife to weeping exasperation. His daughter remembers him, however, as a man who never raised his voice, yelled, or swore. When angry, he rubbed his face with his large hands until he had regained his composure. Self-control of emotions played a large part of the male persona in Yorkshire culture.[49] Hedley Smith had a lot of anger to control.

After spending a number of years in the payroll department, Smith who regularly browsed the university bookstore, met the new man in charge,

Dayton "Doc" Henson. This affable guy had the idea of creating a space in the bookstore where faculty could gather, talk, and buy books. He saw that Hedley Smith knew books, could deal with salesmen, and discuss literature with the academics. In 1967 Smith was put in charge of trade books. He loved his new job and bought himself a custom-made three-piece worsted suit with appropriate shirts and ties. Smith also lectured on Charles Dickens in several English courses, the results of interaction with the faculty. Hedley Smith probably consciously utilized the Anglophilia of many Brown faculty members and administrators to enhance his status.[50] Duncan, a member of the Department of Germanic Studies approaching tenure, remembered him as "a very happy and successful man" who developed a following among the faculty in the College of Arts and Sciences. But not all faculty members were charmed by Smith. Some treated him with condescension; others dismissed him rudely as just another clerk.[51]

Encouraged by his earlier *Gift of Armor,* Smith wrote intensely during these years, turning out at least six historical novels, which he sent off to New York literary agents.[52] The novels' themes included Puritan intolerance in early New England, the Roger Williams settlement story, and the Narragansett Indians, about which he had read a great deal. One of his literary agents, Scott Meredith, gave Smith a detailed critique in 1966 for "Stubborn Saint." Praising him as a professional writer and encouraging him to send more manuscripts, Morrow criticized Smith's failures to plot the story adequately, develop characters, provide action, and generally hold the reader's interest.[53] This review, which did not encourage a rewrite, must have been a hard blow, although the reviewer asked Smith to send his next effort. Hedley Smith digested it silently, moved on, and sent other manuscripts. He desperately wished to become a recognized author. He also began to sketch out his first "Yankee Yorkshireman" short stories, which were privately published as a collection in 1970.

After a few years, Doc Henson wanted to move on to another job and take Smith with him, but Carmen, as on other occasions when her husband had received offers of better jobs outside the state, refused to leave her mother's house and threatened to divorce him. He acquiesced. A new university president in 1970 brought his own assistants and an agenda for belt-tightening, including new standards for granting tenure. Henson's replacement as bookstore manager was an ex-naval officer and political appointee who regarded books as commodities. Duncan Smith, who would be up for tenure in the spring of 1971, and his father would "thoil it" together at Brown University. Hedley Smith received an abrupt letter of dismissal in April. One of many shocked faculty members protested to the *Brown Daily Herald:* "Mr. Smith could discuss intelligently any conceivable subject. He would always have suggestions or comments in any area of enquiry."[54] But his competence was not the issue; the prerogatives of the new book manager prevailed.

Meanwhile Duncan Smith and all other candidates for tenure in early 1971 were promised, in time-honored fashion, that if no one made trouble, all would be awarded tenure in due time. Duncan urged his colleagues to resist, only to be threatened personally and his department collectively with retaliation. He received a telephone call from a senior faculty member suggesting that his father's situation was also involved. If Hedley Smith did not resign immediately, charges would be brought against him for petty theft. When Duncan called the speaker's bluff, all threats collapsed. Hedley Smith was sixty-two years old, three years short of a minimal pension. Intervention with the administration on his behalf by a prestigious scientist plus Smith's threat of a public lawsuit resulted in a pension settlement.[55] It was a trifle. Duncan subsequently received his tenure, but his father's most rewarding job had lasted less than four years. His future was dismal.

Writing and Enduring

Hedley Smith was now stuck alone in a small four-room house filled with cats in a rural community without sidewalks that offered no solace of friendly neighbors, shops, bookstores, or nearby marketplaces. The woods and pasturelands of North Scituate in the spring and summer were full of poison ivy and insects, and Hedley's sensitive skin kept him indoors.[56] Long walks were out of the question. Now all he had was time on his hands. Carmen continued to teach. Occasionally he took the bus to Providence to make contact with old friends, such as his long-time literary correspondent, former Brown University physicist Bruce Lindsay.[57] Isolated and unhappy, he threw himself into the consolation of his memories, fantasies, and idealizations of Yorkshire people and their ways. In doing so he wrote and published one additional collection of short stories, *More Yankee Yorkshiremen* (1974), *Yankee Yorkshire Women*, with sketches by his daughter, Portia (1978), and *The History of Scituate, R.I.* (Scituate: Bicentennial Committee of the Town, 1976).

Smith used Harlo Press in Detroit, Michigan, a press that often accepted subsidies to publish ethnic literature, to bring out his stories in decent little books at minimal cost.[58] He had no editor and few reviews. He produced and privately published a charming little book illustrated by his granddaughter, *There WAS a Cat in Bethlehem* (1979).[59] He also wrote during the 1970s and 1980s the Briardale trilogy and fifteen other Briardale novels or novellas. It was a magnificent burst of creativity. He defied fate.

Smith still hoped to be commercially published, sent off manuscripts to agents, and received letters of criticism and rejection. He showed his manuscripts to no one who could give him a critical eye. Smith submitted novels set in seventeenth-century colonial Rhode Island: "One Escaped," formerly titled "Checkmate in Providence," to the Broome Agency of Sarasota, Florida. Receiving on May 20, 1976, a letter of condescending criticism and a contract to be executed when the author had paid for all editorial work, he asked for the return of his manuscript.[60] Smith submitted "Mr. Verein's Women" to the Richard Curtis Agency, of New York, in 1980, apparently rejected. However, the Curtis Agency also considered the first part of the trilogy "The Millmaster" in 1982 but did not make him an offer. Smith then sent "The Mill Folk," a variant of "The Millmaster," which he regarded as "perhaps a more effective piece of work," to the formerly sympathetic New York agent Scott Meredith, but it was rejected.[61] The other two parts of the trilogy were presumably written in between 1982 and 1986, the latter year during which he prepared his canon, a personally approved list of his works.

These manuscripts remained in Smith's hands. He showed his work only to Duncan and only if asked, but his son was careful to avoid offering any criticism. He confined his curiosity to questions about details and general situations.[62] Except for his involvement in the ongoing process, Smith kept his work private from most of his family and from his friends. At some point he may have simply given up trying to interest literary agents. Nonetheless he seemed to remember and benefit from the 1966 advice of Scott Meredith and from his own growing maturity as a writer in the last two parts of the trilogy and "Sinners Corner." They were his best work, but none were mailed off.

In a private letter to his friend Bruce Lindsay in 1976, Smith had sketched his biography before he began to write the Briardale trilogy.[63] He presented himself as well educated in "the hardest and best schools in the world" and his family as having "middle class roots in Yorkshire." He remained unwilling to acknowledge his working-class background, although pointing out that both of his parents worked in textile "plants." Smith confessed to a lifelong sympathy for the British Labour Party but only as a result of his many brilliant and ardently devoted Socialist teachers. The greatest events during his youth, he insisted, were World War I and the ensuing decline of the Bradford worsted industry which prompted his family to emigrate. The New England textile depression of the 1920s forced him into "a business discipline." He spoke little of his wife and nothing about his alienation from his parents or brother. His father, represented as both athletic and an avid reader, Smith insisted, had greatly influenced him by taking the family into the Yorkshire landscape and to its literary scenes, thus encouraging him to read widely and voraciously. He kept up his reading throughout his life. Perhaps most notably, he said little to his friend Lindsay about his plans to write, except that he was working on a history of the town of Scituate for the bicentennial.

Smith also lectured, reviewed books, read constantly, and corresponded with friends. He mourned the decline and the passing of the "Briardale" villages of Rhode Island, marked by the 1920s depression in New England's textile trades and the departure of many Yorkshire immigrants for home or into new occupations. In the introduction to *The Yankee Yorkshireman* (1970), he sourly described the decay that was swallowing up the mill villages of North Providence into "an unlovely urban pustule" with factory buildings "leprous with the nameboards of the second-rate little businesses" that had come to occupy their premises.[64] This became the particular theme of the novella, "The Spinster of Paradise Row." For him, a beloved landscape was gone, choose how.

Occasionally life offered him some satisfactions. He had eight grandchildren and saw them frequently. He corresponded with Yorkshire novelist Phyllis Bentley, sent her his books, and received her praise. In one of his letters, he described himself to her as "an involuntary exile at an early age."[65] An old, old contact, Alfred Balderson, the taxi driver who had taken the family to catch the Bradford train to Liverpool in 1923, read *Yankee Yorkshirewomen* and recognized his name.[66] Balderson wrote to Smith in 1979, and they began a correspondence full of reminiscence. Smith's work was becoming known in Yorkshire, and the Bradford Public Library collected all three of Smith's published volumes. The contact with Balderson culminated in a telephone call arranged by Duncan during one of his many visits to Bradford. Balderson had never owned a telephone and hardly knew what to say but was deeply gratified. Duncan became a member of the family. Hedley often had to offer excuses for why Duncan didn't spend all his time when in England with his adopted grandparents.[67]

As a "transplanted Yorkshireman," Smith had the pleasure during the bicentennial year of 1976 of informing Scituate residents about the history of their Yankee town, reassuring them that the original settlers were "not a lot of vagabonds and bums." In 1978 the Rhode Island Department of State Library Services recorded Smith's first short-story collection for the blind. In his seventies, an amused Smith turned down the offer of a trip to Moscow from Professor of Literature Dmitri Urnov, a colleague of his son, to read his "proletarian" writings, but one story, "Uprooted," appeared in the official journal of the Writers' Union of the USSR in 1980.[68]

Hedley and Carmen grew old together in North Scituate. They gardened as much as possible and occasionally entertained. He read aloud to her, and they reread their own favorites. For Smith, they remained nineteenth- and turn-of-the-twentieth-century British and European writers such as Hardy, George Moore, Balzac, Turgenev, and Frederich Spielhagen. They watched *Masterpiece Theater* on PBS, especially the mysteries and the English classics, on their small black-and-white television set. They listened to classical music on the radio and on recordings; she preferred Mozart, he Bach and Purcell. The number of cats grew to forty-four. Hedley's warm lap drew them; he preferred the battered tomcats.[69] Dust and cat hair collected. Hedley moved his pile of manuscripts to the attic out of harm's way and gave to Portia Tom Cromwell's lacquered Chinese box that one of the cats had damaged. They did not travel. Smith never returned to Yorkshire, although Duncan and Portia went there frequently and visited their relatives. Late in life, he admitted that he wanted to retain his memories intact and avoid feeling like a "ghost" wandering around a changed Bradford.[70] His brother Sam died in 1991.

Bruce Lindsay, with whom Smith had maintained a fifteen-year correspondence delving into literature, biography, and science by meeting, socializing, discussing, exchanging, and giving each other books, died in 1985. When Smith lost this precious friend, he prepared the canon of his writings. He also began to lose his eyesight. An operable brain tumor was diagnosed and successfully dealt with. His euphoria during recovery led him to consider seriously the possibility of a trip back to Yorkshire, but Carmen could not be left behind. Regardless, Smith never applied for a passport.

In his old age, burdening his wife with cares beyond her physical abilities was Hedley Smith's great fear. Carmen, always a slight figure, grew even slimmer, eating little and fasting one day a week, apparently to sharpen her spiritualist perceptions. Hedley was a big man with a large chest and shoulders; his calves and thighs were strong from years of walking. By the time his final illness came, he judged his wife too frail and his bulk too much for her to take care of. In a nursing home among the failing and the foolish, he would thoil it. His children visited him often and found him popular with the nurses, quoting Shakespeare and singing old songs with them. Quite a character, as he intended. Occasionally, fantasy brought Charlotte and Emily Brontë to dine with him. He died in January 1994 at the age of eighty-five. Portia and Duncan carried his ashes back to the various spots in Bradford that he remembered as his favorites.[71] That was how one beloved father returned to his homeland. Carmen died at eighty-two with her two children by her side.

Our lives overlapped, but Hedley Smith and I did not know each other. Culturally we were a generation apart. I was more like the son than the father. As much as I was interested in him, I suspect that he would have had little interest in me. There are many questions that I might have put to Hedley

Smith had we met. I have serious doubts, however, that he would have been willing to answer or take the project very seriously. But it would have been interesting for both of us.

There is much about this man that I have not learned or understood, much that remains elusive. He had never been a worker in a textile mill. His conservative Republican politics opposed granting any rights to labor unions; he distrusted most of those on the Left and those groups who were drawn to its class appeal. Yet he professed a sympathy for the Labour Party and referred with some empathy to the Yorkshire past of labor activism. But what do I know about the personal politics in and outside that Providence office where Smith worked from 1923 to 1933? According to his son, Hedley Smith in his younger days was known to use his well-shaped hands in fists to floor antagonists on Saturday nights. What was this all about? How did he fill those years of unemployment, 1933 to 1937? I cannot be certain. Smith used municipal government jobs for his own personal advancement. He attended Episcopal services for the music and the language of the King James Bible and the Book of Common Prayer. Smith was a nineteenth-century man who wrote off the twentieth century, the American Century, as unacceptable and vulgar, except when its technology brought him access to performances of Shakespeare or Bach. In the end, he seemed to me immensely talented but profoundly, grievously disappointed in life, extremely hard-working, resilient, dutiful, cruel to some, tenderly affectionate to others, difficult, genuinely creative, stubbornly isolated, and admirable to the end.

The Uneven Grip of Culture: The Second and Third Generations

Historians describe a general pattern of assimilation by the second generation and rediscovery of cultural ties by the third. Based partly on oral interviews, a 1968 study of three generations within the Jewish community in twentieth-century Providence, Rhode Island, reaffirmed this pattern of adjustment, Americanization, and the development of new forms of Jewish American identity.[72] In another study, the reaction of the second generation against the homeland culture, for example a reconstruction at one moment of southern Italy as an exemplary tradition by immigrant parents, can be inherently conflictual.[73] Variables accounting for different class and cultural experiences need to be factored into generalizations based on studies such as these. The family of Hedley Smith provides an example.

The cultural effects of migration by parents or grandparents on the second and third generations can be shaped by circumstances, personal and emotional situations, and family relations. Outwardly Hedley Smith appeared to have adjusted to Rhode Island society. He had not. Influenced by the repressive silence about their grandparents, his children, Portia and Duncan, seemed to act both the parts of second and third generations. They embraced New England society and explored their Yorkshire background. As Duncan Smith put it in early 2007, "It [Bradford] is as familiar to me as Providence."[74]

Hedley Smith's children and grandchildren provide the only examples for this particular Yankee Yorkshire family group, since his brother Sam and his wife had no offspring. Smith's daughter and son avidly sought contact with their Yorkshire relatives and culture. Members of the third generation, except for one child, seem relatively indifferent to their Yorkshire roots.[75] In this way as in many others, Hedley Smith's situation suggests that migrants find themselves shaped by their own peculiarities of time, place, and human personality. The results indicate a highly textured, unpredictable, individuated, and rich variation in migrant experience, for which words, such as patterns, floods, tides, or streams, seem inappropriate.

THE SECOND GENERATION

Interest in late twentieth-century immigration by "Hispanic" and "Asian" populations into the United States has revived interest in the concept of the second generation. Rubén Rumbaut argued that the United States will be reshaped by the second generation of turn of the twenty-first century migration. First-generation immigrants are usually defined as those who were born and socialized in another country and immigrate as adults. The second generation generally represents American-born and socialized children of foreign-born parents.[76]

Comparing late twentieth-century immigration with the immigration of Eastern European Jews and southern Italians at the turn of the twentieth century reveals historic and parallel examples of exclusion and prejudice for the second generation.[77] Regardless of chronological age, various historic circumstances and contexts may limit or open opportunity to second-generation immigrants or thrust maturity upon first-generation children. Novelists, such as Melania Mazzucco, best capture the latter situation and the toll it exacts.[78] Contemporary novelists have probed a far more conflictual situation for the second generation of migrants based on the longings for the society of departure in tension with the pull of modern culture and the ease of communication and transportation. Hedley Smith's children realized they had first-generation grandparents only when they were in their teens. For them, being second generation was unusually emotionally conflicted. But neither Duncan nor Portia Smith faced the constricted class and social situation of second-generation children in a southern Italian family of Providence.[79]

DUNCAN SMITH The career and writings of Hedley Smith's son, Duncan, both reflected and realized the aspirations of his father but translated those ideals into his own late twentieth-century concerns. His educational achievements at Providence Classical High School and Brown University gratified his father's thwarted ambitions. But they were also hard won in a battle between a resisting son and an authoritarian father. Duncan became physically ill each morning before departing for high school classes and dragged his feet before applying to Brown for admission as an undergraduate so much so that a local Episcopal priest and Brown alumnus was forced to intervene.[80]

In 1960 Duncan began to visit Bradford on both brief and longer visits, developing friends and staying in contact with special family friends. Duncan's choice of German studies as his major and graduate program reflected—perhaps in part, perhaps not—his father's affinity for certain German writers. But in the 1970s Professor Smith helped organize a bold transnational cultural program between Brown University and Rostock University (later Wilhelm Pieck University) in the German Democratic Republic during the bleakest years of the Cold War. Duncan's developing cultural links with communist East Germany must have disconcerted his father, who loathed all politics especially on the Left.

The Rostock Program, which operated between 1979 and 1990, constituted exchanges of faculty, administrators, and graduate and undergraduate students in literature and in scientific research attempting to bridge the opposing systems of capitalism and communism with cultural contacts. German humanist Johann Gottfried Herder provided the definition of the project as the ongoing task of "rememberance" of the past through literature in the western academic classical tradition. Duncan Smith believed that the credo of the endeavor was "steadfast optimism" in the face of world crisis and the threat of nuclear winter. He might have been drawing upon the Yorkshire phrase, "we mun thoil it." Research development, personal growth, cultural contact, and increasing trust between alienated peoples were steps toward the goal of a "peaceful and just world."[81]

These Rostock endeavors confirmed Duncan Smith's political radicalism begun in the 1960s and underscored his father's political skepticism. As Duncan put it, his father's role lay in mobilizing his son's Yorkshire "perversity" or determination. Throughout, Hedley Smith remained detached, supportive but "above the fray," proud but pragmatic. Brown University president Howard Swearer, an internationalist scholar from the Ford Foundation, overcame the deeply conservative forces on the Brown campus to encourage the development of the Rostock idea. Opposition from the West German government and from domestic surveillance agencies both in the United States and in West Germany raised formidable obstacles. President Swearer, with the backing of Rhode Island's Sen. Claiborne Pell, chair of the Senate Foreign Relations Committee, and funding from the U.S. Information Agency, reassured his young associate professor and helped alleviate political and bureaucratic difficulties. Smith was appointed to several administrative posts helpful to the program.[82] The University of Bradford, Yorkshire, also became associated with the Rostock program and put Duncan Smith into contact with Bradford University faculty. New friends intensified his visits in Bradford, sometimes as often as two or three times a year. This is how he came to know Bradford intimately.

Duncan Smith's commitment to the use of literature as a bridge to human contact between cultures and even as a catalyst for political change greatly extended his father's love of literature for its own sake. It is possible that Hedley Smith's writing of translocal fiction helped in formulating Duncan Smith's vision of transnational literary and cultural contact. He and his colleagues at Brown and at Rostock/Wilhelm Pieck enlisted academic and governmental agencies to support cultural exchange at a time of dangerous world political stalemate. If Duncan's father failed to grasp this, it was his loss. Duncan Smith also enjoyed several years in the 1980s as visiting professor at the Gorki Institute of World Literature in Moscow. Copies of Hedley Smith's short stories went with him and were received with interest. Duncan Smith believed in the power of literature to probe, reveal, and communicate the complexities of human experience in ways that bound people together in their joys and their miseries regardless of the state. His travels served his father as proxy journeys, and Hedley Smith proved a good correspondent.[83] Still, even after the conclusion of the Rostock program and the unification of the two Germanies in 1990, Duncan Smith faced stubborn anticommunist suspicions on the Brown campus for years before he retired. And like his father, he wrote and published fiction.[84] He also trained as a clinical psychologist. As conflicted as his relationship with his father might have been, Duncan Smith carried his Yorkshire heritage in his bones.

PORTIA SMITH THOMPSON Raised as a New England Yankee, Portia Smith was first introduced to her Yorkshire background in 1952 when at fourteen she met her grandfather Ernest. For a while, she could not understand his dialect at all. But her initial contacts with this charming, soft-spoken man piqued a lifetime curiosity. While Duncan traveled to Yorkshire and looked up family kin during his college summers, Portia and her husband, Leslie Thompson, a man of Scottish background via Nova Scotia, raised their children. Unlike her parents, Portia's Uncle Sam encouraged travel of all sorts and had driven both Smith children around investigating Rhode Island. As soon as she could, Portia Thompson made her first Yorkshire trip. In 1985 she and Leslie did London, Stratford-Upon-Avon, and then visited their son Andrew, enrolled in Bradford University. They investigated all of Hedley Smith's remembered spots around Bradford and, when joined by Duncan, all walked Hedley Smith's favorite moor. Then the Thompsons drove around Scotland, where Leslie's forebears had been born. Two additional Bradford trips followed.[85]

Portia educated herself despite the lack of interest from either parent. Neither expected her to attend a university or encouraged her. In this, she mused, her Yankee mother was more "Yorkshire" than she realized. In 1977 with a husband at work and her four children in school, Portia earned a bachelor of arts degree from the University of Rhode Island, majoring in psychology with a minor in art. She drew the illustrations for her father's novella, *Yankee Yorkshirewomen*. Her own children became well educated and her first granddaughter has her own college fund as an infant. Portia is active in historical societies, genealogical research, and cultural and historic preservation. When her father died, she became the keeper of the family records: pictures, all of her father's manuscripts, his correspondence, newspaper clippings, documents, and memorabilia of all kinds. Notably, she and her son John keep a variety of brushes hand-made by Ernest Smith, some of horsehair and some of hog's bristles. Portia has Alice's simple weaver's repair kit consisting of needles, scissors, and a hook. Her Uncle Sam gave it to her. His Triumph TR-4 roadster went to Leslie. Portia's New England heritage, perhaps because of proximity, seems as important to her ongoing activities as her Yorkshire roots. She has contemplated writing her memoirs as a Yankee Yorkshirewoman.[86]

THE THIRD GENERATION

Marcus Lee Hansen regarded the renewed interest of the third generation as a marker of the resurgence of ethnic culture.[87] How many among the siblings might respond; would they be sons or daughters? Portia's son John is very appreciative of his New England background and the region's history, inspired by his grandparents to develop an interest in nature and in Native Americans. Hedley Smith once told him an amazing story about a huge Indian skeleton with long black hair unearthed in Warwick from a gravesite being carelessly excavated for a municipal tennis court. As an environmental consultant with a private engineering company, John A. Thompson recently became aware of the impact of English influences at Lowell, Massachusetts, the first large industrial site in New England.[88]

Duncan A. Smith, his father's oldest child, also regularly saw his maternal grandparents, enjoys Yorkshire-style food, and accompanied his father on visits to London and Bradford. He loves reading English authors, especially Charles Dickens, "one of my grandfather's favorites."[89] His relationship to his family's cultural background appears to add richness to his life, talents, and tastes, but his identity—like that of his friends, regardless of their ethnic or religious background—is middle-class American.

Among his three siblings and four cousins of the third generation, only Andrew Leslie Thompson actively responded to the call of Yorkshire.[90] Born in 1964 Andrew is well aware of his mother's Yorkshire heritage, describing her as "first generation." As he put it, having a grandfather from a "European" country allowed him to be accepted by school friends whose grandparents came from Italy or Portugal. Andrew saw his maternal grandparents on a regular basis. He apparently picked up enough of his grandfather's English pronunciation to be able to understand the lyrics to the music of the "Second English invasion" of pop music: "the Police, The Clash, Modern English, the Thompson Twins, Eurythmics, Duran, Duran . . . were the biggest things going . . . It was in vogue to be English." Feeling a connection with the music and the culture, he took his junior year at Bradford University, where he became at ease.

> I thought it would be great to see the places that my grandfather and great uncle had run around when they were growing up. It would be just different enough, I thought, from what I was so used to that it would seem exotic, but at the same time familiar. And it did. . . . I felt I really blended in and in a way even belonged.[91]

Andrew enjoyed being mistaken for an English undergraduate and showing his mother and father around Bradford. But back he came after a year, attended law school, married, and intends to raise his children with an awareness of their cultural background. As a practical man, he admits, "We'll see!" What the fourth generation may think of their grandparents and great-grandparents is yet to be seen.

4

Transatlantic Perspectives, Strong Women, and Sexual Politics in Fiction

Ethnic fiction, whether published in the original language that subsequently fell into obscurity or, as in the case of much of Hedley Smith's work, remained unpublished, represents new possibilities for understanding emigration and immigrant experience. Smith's fiction illuminates early twentieth-century Yorkshire immigrant/migrant communities in specific ways. The reach of transatlantic politics into the lives and culture of Yorkshire people during the coming and aftermath of the first World War became a major component of the Briardale locale and the resulting political and social tensions with local Yankees. World War I is a recurring theme in Hedley Smith's fiction and acts as a metaphor of cultural and political identity.

Historians who study emigration as state policy argue that citizenship is defined through exit as well as entry and return.[1] Smith, however, shrewdly guessed that behind the outbursts of patriotism among Briardale residents lay some ambivalence and reservation by migrant Yorkshiremen less willing than others to join in the English cause in 1914. His own father had been threatened by the specter of the Western Front. To the despair of his family, Ernest Smith had been conscripted at the age of thirty-five in 1918 and trained to be sent into the trenches, when to their delight the Armistice saved him.[2] Nonetheless, beloved relatives died on the battlefields of the Great War. The imprint of World War I on the Smith family was profound but was shared by the whole generation of peoples who suffered and survived the war years.

In addition to these transatlantic political and cultural experiences and connections, Smith's interest in sexual rituals and customs, intercultural marriages, and his profound awe of female power and respect for strong women constitute other major themes. They reflect the key emotional experiences of his life and the abiding concerns of his mature years. Of his eighteen unpublished novels and novellas, part 2 of the Briardale trilogy, "The Lion and the Eagle," and several of his short stories best illustrate these concepts in the Briardale fiction.

Hedley Smith's narratives differ from the purposes of fiction written by Polish immigrant writers in early twentieth-century America, recently studied by Karen Majewski. These Polish language novels, their plots, and characters collectively helped model an identity for their readers that connected them with the homeland yet "articulated Polish-American perspectives and experiences."[3] Polish immigrant writers and Hedley Smith shared transatlantic political perspectives and an interest in the way personalities and sexual politics shaped social and cultural patterns. Hedley Smith did not, however, advocate any political agenda for the homeland, in contrast to that on the minds of many Polish writers of popular literature. Instead, Smith described a lost social and cultural Yorkshire, the values of which he believed worth preserving, while probing the character of its inhabitants. At best, he hoped to capture and celebrate the early twentieth-century Yorkshire culture in New England. Smith's sense of Yorkshire ethnicity in New England was distinctly defensive in a hostile, deteriorating setting. He had felt it to be so. Still homeland connections powerfully shaped the identity of Yankee Yorkshiremen and -women.

Transatlantic Perspectives in the Briardale Fiction

In all of his Briardale fiction, Hedley Smith wrote to preserve the Yorkshire dialect. In "The Lion and The Eagle," he used dialect as a foil to explore cultural contacts and conflicts between regions and nations. For this purpose, he created Yorkshire-born Enoch Thorpe, a naturalized American citizen, a member of the transatlantic West Riding Dyers' Association, and a canny capitalist with worldwide experiences and multiple investments. People such as Enoch Thorpe, caught up in these multiple layers of superficial loyalties and connections, risk the loss of the genuine cultural values cherished in the Briardale short stories. Smith's imaginative vision is persistently transatlantic and severely critical of industrial and finance capitalism, epitomized by Thorpe's activities. In this novel and in others, he is also interested in the impact of world war for migration and on migrants. His vision thus edges toward the historical settings of old societies in crisis, a theme crucial to two of his favorite writers, Balzac and Turgenev. His choice to situate his well-developed characters and their conflicts in the historic time frame of England's early twentieth-century decline makes this novel one of Smith's best unpublished work. He probably modeled three of his novels on Phyllis

Bentley's own Yorkshire trilogy. Tiny Briardale, the focus of most of his fiction, became his "Wessex," Thomas Hardy's sweeping make-believe county in England's West Country, cut down to fit the dimensions of Rhode Island. Smith declared that what "applied to Hardy's countryfolk" was "just as true of Briardale's Yorkshire textile workers."[4]

Written during the later years of his retirement, "The Lion and the Eagle" reveals Smith's deep attachments politically and emotionally to his homeland. Although he quickly became a naturalized American citizen along with his family in 1929, he remained ardently attached to the West Riding. He lived as much as possible like a Yorkshire man in Yankeeland, cherishing Yorkshire cultural values against "slow attrition" throughout his creative life.[5] Hedley Smith's wife loved English classical literature, one of her qualities that first attracted him. They married in 1937 just as the issues of appeasement of Nazi Germany and isolationism began to emerge in American partisan politics, but Carmen's political leanings remain unclear. During World War II she became deeply distracted with two little children ages three and one, while in 1942 her husband, using his position in municipal government, organized local war relief for Warwick's sister city in England.[6] Life circumstances and stubbornness made it impossible for him to return physically to Yorkshire, even for a visit. How many others were like him but unable or unwilling to write about it, remaining inarticulate and unknown? The pull of World War I on Smith's fictional characters constitutes a metaphor for homeland longing, for the preservation of a way of life, for self-sacrifice on behalf of a nation, if only as known through a beloved region.

"The Lion and the Eagle" begins on a voyage in early 1914 from Liverpool to Boston. On the *Winifredian,* the ship that the Smith family had actually taken from Liverpool to Boston in 1923, Enoch Thorpe meets Yorkshire lawyer Eric Sutcliffe. Sutcliffe has been dispatched by the Bradford relatives of wool buyer Walter Barraclough working in Briardale to assess the influence of Walter's new American wife on his business decisions. Thorpe, like Hedley Smith and his family, had already decided to become an American citizen for very practical reasons, as he explains to Sutcliffe. The contrasts in Enoch and Eric's speech patterns are marked, but Smith uses Enoch's words to open Eric's eyes to the character of Americans and the ways of American economic life. Ironically, for men like Enoch Thorpe, the lack of a formal education becomes a positive advantage.

> "You know, lad," he cautioned. "There's one thing you've got to get straight, you and all your bloody countrymen. A sort of a blind spot that afflicts all of you in your degree, from your lah-di-dah upper class down through t'

businessmen and professional like yourself, all the way down to the common working fowk that comes here with their bare arses showing through t' rents in their breeches, seeking for jobs to fill their bellies afore they clems [starves] to death at home."

Enoch describes the differences between English and American society.

"Now, you listen to me. You all come to this country, as I did in my time, full o' your own self-conceit and knowing it all, as though time had stood still for better or for worse in t' last hundred years; thinking nowt's changed and you're coming to a bloody, half-civilized colony of inferior Englishmen, country yokels settled in a lot o' little Wilsdens lost in a far land.

"But it's not that way: this isn't an English colony nor even an English civilization. Americans is Americans, and they're as big a mixture with as many layers to it, as ever your own class society had or has. . . . But they're *themselves,* choose how; and you'll have to see that, and thoil it and meet 'em at least half way, if you want to get on wi' em.

"Take me, nowt I know I'm nobbut a tradesman myself, that never got beyond standard six and half-time, and has had to live by my wits ever sin', to get where I am. . . . Walter Barraclough were smart enough to go to t' school of experience, way I did. Bear that in mind when you come face to face wi' him and his American wife, if you know what's good for you."[7]

Indeed in Yorkshire terms, Walter Barraclough has wed a "foreigner" and thus distanced himself from his Bradford relatives as well as from the Yankee society which his wife Laura Richmond-Halliday Barraclough represents. Like Hedley Smith, he is a man situated in-between two cultures, a major refrain in the Briardale fiction. But then so is the more calculating Enoch Thorpe.

Later during the voyage, Thorpe continues his conversation with Eric Sutcliffe and describes his prospective business ventures in early 1914 and the international politics that influence them. Two German passengers, textile chemist Herr Hermann Schmieder from Frankfurt-am-Main and his daughter Minna-Louisa, represent England's great imperial antagonist in the early twentieth century. The coming of the Great War shapes the events in the novel and the fortunes of all: Walter and Laura Barraclough, Eric Sutcliffe, Enoch Thorpe, and the Schmieders. Thorpe describes his plans and the role of international politics in them. Here is the clash of national loyalty and profit.

"We all know what's happening in Europe and what sort of a bloody bust-up is shaping there. That's going to change things to such a tune they'll never change back again. I know, I know what you're saying; they're always fratching and killing one another in the Balkans, but this is different. Mester Schmieder

[Minna-Louisa's father] knows it, happen better than we do, 'cause he's had the advantage o' being able to watch it at first hand, right in the middle of where it's moving fastest. That's why he's over here with his lass, trying to cut loose afore it's too late and not get burned in the ruins. That's what Europe is going to be, you know, in a year or two. Nowt but a heap of ruins. . . .

"And then, you mark my words, this country'll be top dog: it'll take over everything and own everything and end up by buggering up everything in the whole damned world."

Enoch Thorpe wants to persuade Walter Barraclough to join in his investment schemes. Hedley Smith's themes of greed, pride, and lust distilled in the character of Enoch Thorpe create ample opportunities to explore both dialect and character difference as well as the workings of international capitalism in the context of the terrible World War beginning in August 1914. Off the ship and in Briardale, Enoch Thorpe explains his plans to Walter excitedly, dismissing all caution.

"Business of all sorts is humming like a top, and all these places we've put our money in are making money hand ower fist. Textiles! Machine Tools! Chemicals! Insurance! Fuels! And what we've lent out at interest'll double itself at least afore we see the end of it."

"It's easy to see you, yourself, believe what you're saying," Walter said good-naturedly. . . . "It mid not last as long as you think, according to what all the experts are saying. They don't believe this thing came go on beyond Christmas, at latest."

"The experts!" Enoch snorted his contempt. "Take no stock in experts, so-called, Walter lad, but listen to thy own commonsense and to me! What do the *experts* know? But *me,* I've been knocking up and down this world a long time, prying into every nook and corner of it, and mixing with them that knows what's what. *I* tell thee, this thing's been building up for years and years—for generations—and they've been getting ready for it. More than that, *they want it!* [B]ut take my word for it, all o' you, we're in for a long, hard, and bloody time. And we're going to make piles."

Enoch Thorpe means no less than to dominate textile production in the United States during the war. Profit-taking has tipped his political loyalties. Walter is persuaded to join a corporation to buy heavily into textile mill stock. Stock prices were low in 1913 and 1914. Enoch reassures Walter:

"They're down now, but they'll be up by and by. 'Cause when armies is mobilized and blowing one another to bits all up and down Europe, they'll turn here for supplies and materials as fast as they've used up their own. There'll be big orders: blankets, shirts, uniforms, waterproof cloth, hospital supplies, munitions, God knows what, and prices no object but millions to be made."

With the backing of these war profits from textiles, Thorpe and his associates will venture into new technologies, such as oil and rubber.

> "And we'll run 'em till we bankrupt 'em, some of 'em. And the brass we'll lose, we'll make up and more by not having to pay taxes. And we s'll be better off than ever." Thorpe spells out his projects to Barraclough for the postwar period, buying cheap and selling high. And when the war is over? "Why, then there's a bust," Enoch answered promptly, and as though he was talking to a bairn. "What of it? We salln't be there. We shall sell out on the crest and leave somebody else holding t' bag. That's business, that is!" . . . Well, then when values have gone down as far as we think they will, we'll buy back at a bargain."[8]

Enoch Thorpe, expansive, scheming, and optimistic, epitomized the bustling English bourgeoisie who fitted so well into the practical world of American capitalism. He meant to imitate but indeed top its investment strategies. He thus cast off the taciturn character and cautious nature of Yorkshiremen: all but his dialect and the Yorkshire love of "brass."

International politics of the Great War era deeply influenced New England society, Yankee and immigrant. Yankees and naturalized immigrants, Yorkshiremen and Germans, provide the major characters in "The Lion and the Eagle." German immigrants represented an important prewar German settlement in Providence that Smith had already recreated in part 1 of the Briardale trilogy "The Millmaster." His son Duncan's interests in local Germanic culture provided the details on the early twentieth-century German community in West Providence, which enjoyed two weekly newspapers and Turnvereine for exercise with numerous restaurants, shops, and social clubs.[9] With the outbreak of war between the United States and Germany in April 1917, however, the community dispersed. Walter Barraclough describes to his friend Eric the growing anti-German opinion in early 1914 Providence. "I understand a lot of families here have stopped doing business with Vogelsang, the big pork butcher in the Annex, and they were his best customers, just as he was the best of his trade anywhere. And some with t' other retail businesses. Even that grand German restaurant downtown I once took you to."[10]

Anti-German feeling is also stirring up Briardale village. Eric tells Walter about an unpleasant occurrence while he and Minna-Louisa were skating together on the millpond in Briardale. At first the crowd seems to enjoy their skills.

But as the applause surged up to its peak, the great swell of it suddenly collapsed and shattered into a stunned silence; then came the sharp, jeering stab
of an angry taunt. "Three cheer for t' bloody Germans? What you think you're
doing. Aye! That's what these is: bloody foreigners. Three cheers my backside!
Down with 'em, down with 'em and their Kaiser Bill, and down with all them
that creeps up the arseholes of these bloody Huns."[11]

Long before the outbreak of the fighting, Western European nations prepared for war by gathering in their citizens and cornering markets in military
supplies, such as the British cornering the raw wool market in 1914.[12] Migrants
to Rhode Island, German and English, felt the reach of their homeland governments. The Schmieders, father and daughter, try to negotiate the situation.
Enoch explains to Eric the impact of this on the fate of the Schmieders in early
1914. Meanwhile, Hermann Schmieder becomes Herman, buys a wardrobe
of good English "checks and tweeds, of serges and worsted, of bowler hats
and tightly rolled umbrellas." He finds a good job with a Rhode Island dyers'
association and is "a happy and contented man with just one fear that his Fa-
therland could, if it wished, still exert its authority over him and dictate his
future fate for some years to come in certain contingencies." Those contingencies occur when the Balkans erupt in battle in 1914. Enoch Thorpe observes:

> "He's in mortal terror, if owt broke out in Europe right now, they might think
> they needed his scientific skills back in his own land, and he's looking franti-
> cally for loopholes in the naturalization laws. . . .
>
> "[T]here'd be an easy road for her. In fact, it's summat her father and me
> has discussed." He knocked the ashes from his cigar. "Haven't you tumbled?
> You, wi' your lawyer's brain and all. Aye, now, I see you have. Suppose Minna-
> Louisa were to become Mrs. Enoch Thorpe, for example. By Gow, she'd be an
> American citizen as quick as leaping out o' bed or into it, ye mid say. No five
> years waiting period *then*."[13]

Indeed, Enoch Thorpe marries Minna-Louisa, while her father is forced to
return to Germany. Enoch understands it best and explains it all to Walter.

> "Why? What right or business had the German Consul or the German Kai-
> ser himself, for that matter, to go calling and ordering folk about in a foreign
> country?" Walter spluttered. "It's all a piece o' their bloody arrogance. . . ."
> [Enoch replies] "And my firm has been doing the same thing in our way,
> though happen for different reasons. The [dyers'] association has been bring-
> ing its men home from lots o' places up and down the world. Take the Balkans!
> There's two or three there, engineers and such, has been missing for months.
> Completely disappeared. Serbia, Montenegro, Albania, Austria, where fighting

is a natural state of affairs. Happen they've gotten in the way of it and been killed. Happen they're in jail. We s'll find out, sometime."[14]

In the meantime, Enoch Thorpe is safe as a naturalized American citizen. Much more troubling to Walter Barraclough is that the coming conflict between Germany and England "really is reaching right into our private lives, Laura and mine." Not that Laura is wavering about her loyalties. As he explains to Eric: "Dammit, Laura's more of a pig-headed Englishman than I am myself, and she always was. It's twixt her and her own kin that the soreness is beginning to hurt." Walter has always had his troubles with his stiff-necked female in-laws, the Richmond-Halliday sisters. "Finally, they're taking advantage of the European situation to stand up for t' Germans, saying it's all the fault of the corrupt British Empire that's been a blight on the world for a century or more, and it's time for a change, and everybody'll be better off when it's wiped out."[15]

Laura's uncle, Mansfield Richmond-Halliday (modeled on Henry James), lived the life of an expatriate writer in London. After his death, Laura sorts though his unpublished writings, seeing him as a family treasure, despite the disapproval of his sisters. Hedley Smith, regarded by his children in a similar light, also left a bulk of unpublished writing to be discovered by later generations. Smith describes Mansfield as criticized for his writing habits: "he never took time to think things over and revise and polish. Just poured it all out. . . . But he survives, if he's worth his salt; he rises and comes into his own." Hedley Smith often confided this hope to his children.

Laura becomes her uncle's champion at family gatherings.[16] One night at a dinner party hosted by the Barracloughs for their in-laws to memorialize the death of their expatriate brother, Laura makes a particularly defiant gesture. Pinned to her pale satin dinner gown and winking in the candle light is her uncle's gift of "a miniature Union Jack: a perfect replica of the flag itself done in red, white and blue enamels, the flagstaff an ingenious contrivance of gold pin and chain to fasten it firmly in place." Hedley Smith explores the conflicting emotions felt by Walter Barraclough in this situation.

> [Walter] was irritated with his wife for the deliberate provocation she had intended by wearing the bauble at all. At the same time, he was proud of her spirit and her strong sense of loyalty to her uncle, and even while he was deploring her aggressiveness, he was loving her for her love and loyalty to himself and to his country which she had made her own and a part of her love and pride in himself when she first came into his arms. She was sticking up for him and his own like a true wife at a time and place when love and comfort and understanding were things he needed.

Just as carefully Smith analyzes the cultural and class conflicts that underlay these emotions.

> For New England, in these days—this crabbed and artificial aristocracy that pretended it wasn't an aristocracy at all—was getting a bit of its own back, indulging its long-standing, sulky resentment against the rough, brisk Yorkshire invasion that had brought its people and its mills and factories and its blunt manners into these parts and taken over. Doing nothing active, of course, but showing as plain as it could that its sympathies were with whatever circumstances or developments or other antagonistic civilization might put a spoke in the wheel and bring these abrasive immigrants down a peg or two from the heights of their arrogant prosperity. And Laura's aunts, as true representatives of their class, were the very embodiment of this spirit of inherited grievance and chafed, long-suffering resentments.

Walter deepens the tensions by defending with spirit his country and his wife.

> When Walter at last sufficiently mastered himself to speak, his voice was reasonable and his outward appearance calm; though there was a deep, underlying thrill of emotion in the steady flow of his words, and in the quietness of his demeanor was the vibrating equilibrium of strong contesting feelings. It was the Yorkshire temperament asserting itself in him, as the accents and cadences and colloquialisms of its speech forms flowed in the current of his language with a dangerously quiet and yet a devastating power.
> " . . . [T]here couldn't be owt sillier than this fretting and fratching. Do you know what's going on in this crazy world these days, outside our own circles? It's on the point of tumbling into rack and ruin about our heads, and here we're sitting, like a bunch o' lambs cooped up in a pen, pushing and shoving and guzzling, and not an eye nor a thought to t' butcher standing sharpening his knife on t' grindstone t' other side of the hurdle."
> Defiant, Aunt Marion continued to scowl at the table, her hard jaw immovable.
> "That is *your* point of view," she said sulkily. "Not everybody shares it. What may be rack and ruin for a decadent empire built on greed and oppression and persecution, and the self-interests of a decayed aristocracy, could be a rebirth and a golden age for the rest of the world."
> "Wi' Saint William the Second at head of it and t' bloody Kingdom of Heaven in Berlin. Aunt Marion, with all due respect to you, you dunnot know what you're talking about."[17]

The coming war disrupts family and kin in Briardale. The mill villagers feel it too. The outbreak of war in August 1914 causes an intense political reaction and an outpouring of patriotic activities. "Union Jacks blossomed in the windows of Briardale houses without a single exception." Patriotic songs "rattled the windows of the Social Club" long after the legal closing time, along the clink of glasses. The Women's Clubs and Guilds in the Chapel turned out woolen socks and scarves and jerseys and gloves for shipment to the trenches in Flanders and the Naval depots. "On the front lawn of the chapel a broad notice board, quickly improvised as the preliminary to a more solid and permanent erection later on, memorialized the steadily-growing list of names of Briardale dwellers who had gone back to do their bit for their native land." The most active of all wasn't a Yorkshire native at all, but a foreigner: Walter Barraclough's Yankee wife, Laura.

As did village and family, Walter Barraclough and Eric Sutcliffe become deeply involved politically and emotionally in the European War.

> The [British Army defeat at] Mons, the retreat in Flanders, ship sinkings, and a whole assortment of mistakes and miseries wrapped up in untidy festoons of governmental red tape had been the order of the day since the nightmare [dinner party on the] Fourth of August. The national pride had taken many a hard knock, felt with an added keenness in this particular community, and with the exception of a lonely voice here and there like [the Australian editor] Rathom's in the *Providence Journal*, a national press and a national spirit [in the United States] could not hide the note of smug complacency and self-satisfied importance it felt in witnessing the humiliation of the proud and the set-backs of the mighty.

Walter worries about the physical and emotional toll that war work is taking on Laura. He convinces Eric to take her to South County, Rhode Island, for a few weeks. In turn Laura worries about Walter. Neither is very happy. These worries now disrupt their most intimate sexual relations.

> "He takes it to heart himself," she said [to Eric]. "You wouldn't think it, to go by his steady demeanour. . . . But he hurts so much underneath. Not at the jeers and the smug mock-condescension he meets with in his daily affairs, but at other things far worse. Do you realize how many lads and men from the Briardale area went back to England and volunteered for service overseas? Lads that he knew: their sayings and doings living, intimate memories to him. And now the casualty lists are coming back; it's appalling how big they are and how many homes and families here have been touched by them. He notices! He broods on it. He goes for long, solitary walks, and he won't let me or anybody talk to him about it. Even at night when we're in bed together, it gets between him and our lovemaking, and that's something we've always had that nothing has been able to touch or spoil till now."

One afternoon in November 1914 from a vantage point in a South County cottage overlooking glittering Long Island Sound, Eric and Laura observe the passing merchant ships. As if a magnet is pulling them, all of the ships are headed east toward the war zone, loaded with guns, munitions, food, and hospital supplies. Some of them are doomed never to arrive at their destination. Both recognize the haunting significance of the word "submarine." Eric announces his imminent departure for England; he cannot stay away any longer. Within a few months, Walter decides that he too must return to England with Laura. Life in Rhode Island has lost its meaning for him and for her. In early 1915 he sends Eric this letter.

> [I]t's come over me very strong of late. I want to see my own kith and kin back in England once more, afore it might be too late. Now, I'm not being lugubrious, or fearful, or superstitious. But it's just a feeling I have. And these *are* uncertain times and likely to be so for a long while to come.
>
> Don't you go fretting, now, about the dangers of ocean voyages and submarines and mines and raiders and all that. We s'll be all right. I have booked us passages on the *Lusitania*: the fastest and safest boat on the Atlantic, as well as the most comfortable and luxurious. It'll be a real holiday. . . .
>
> We sail in the beginning of May, and we'll be seeing you and you'll be seeing us in Bradford, talking over old times, as fast as we can get there.
>
> When Eric had finished his reading and folded up his letter and put it away, it was as if a cheery voice had just faded into the silence of the early morning.[18]

In "The Lion and the Eagle," Smith created the character Laura as an idealized version of what a Yankee wife might become if unlike Carmen she was willing to alienate her own kinfolk and deeply commit her allegiance to her husband's culture. Perhaps that is why Smith sent Laura to the bottom on the *Lusitania* in 1915: she was too good to be believed.[19] Walter and Laura Barraclough, the Yankee Yorkshire couple, tried to return to the homeland, but like Hedley Smith they never completed the journey.

Ernest Smith's escape from service in the trenches in France in 1918 and the deaths of his much admired uncles drew Hedley Smith to the classic literature on World War I, including the poetry and autobiography of Robert Graves. He preferred, however, Patrick MacGill's *The Great Push* (1916) as "more honest and realistic and less sentimental."[20] According to his son Duncan, Smith appreciated the dark humor in MacGill's grim depiction of and relentless realism about the situation, which he likened to the fatalism of the Greek tragedy.[21] He also admired MacGill's autobiographical novels about the terribly desperate lives of Irish youngsters and adults in the early twentieth century who migrated seasonally to Scotland to dig potatoes.[22] In Smith's fiction, the Great War became a metaphor for the decline of his homeland and the grief and disruptions of family life.

The reach of transatlantic politics into the lives and culture of Yorkshire migrants during World War I became a major component of the Briardale experience and the intensifying political tensions with local Yankees. It is also a recurring theme in Hedley Smith's other fiction. In Smith's novel, "The Mill Folk," young Rhoda Denby, who lives with her extended family from Wilsden, West Riding, describes the wildly celebratory scenes in Briardale at the outbreak of World War I, the singing of Army songs, celebrating imperial conquests: "The Girl I Left Behind Me," "The Road to Mandalay," and "Soldiers of the Queen," and the dismissive Yankee reaction to the jickeys in "thin and vinegar sharp voices." As in "The Lion and the Eagle," Smith includes the unrestrained sexuality expressed by the villagers as part of the passions of the celebrations.[23] Part 3 of the Briardale trilogy, "The Tongue-tied Town," centers entirely on the 1919 World War I memorial, the return of Silas Bradford to Briardale, and his murder (see chap. 2).

Smith, however, surmised that behind these outbursts of patriotism were some Yorkshiremen unwilling to join in the English cause. His own family had been threatened by the specter of the Western Front, and a few had immigrated to Canada. During World War I, some Briardale residents who supported the British war effort materially and politically were actually glad of the thousand miles of ocean they had crossed as they scanned the casualty lists and built the local war memorial. Smith's characters include Yorkshiremen who had served in the Boer War but did not respond to the tunes of glory that rang out during World War I. Alfred Petty, a character in *Yankee Yorkshirewomen*, had volunteered in 1901 for service in South Africa to his regret and decided to emigrate and farm wheat in Saskatchewan, Canada, before war broke out in Europe.

> "I had my eyes open when I was slogging up an' down Africa, an' if I could fight I can farm. And talk o' fighting, I've had enough of it, and more, to last me a lifetime and I'm none going to do no more. Let King George and Kaiser Bill do their own fighting."[24]

One such disillusioned army veteran provides a notably strong male character in the short stories. Based on Smith's adored uncle, Horace Holmes, the character of Horace Gregson in "King George's Idea," a story in *More Yankee Yorkshiremen*, had joined the British Army at fifteen and served the Empire for thirteen years, mostly as an unruly private. After duty in South Africa,

Malta, Gibraltar, and Egypt, he returns disillusioned to Yorkshire, "burnt brick red" and as tough as leather. After immigrating with his mother to Briardale, which he compares unfavorably with the African Veldt, he briefly rejoins the army but returns to Rhode Island a subdued man. His hard-gained maturity and varied experiences have made him into a resilient and thoroughly Yorkshire man in the best sense.

Gregson's tolerance and frankness serve him well. Selina Jenkins, a Yankee schoolteacher who boards with his mother, possesses true Yorkshire-type beauty: a "peaches and cream" complexion, full red lips, lively blue eyes, plentiful blonde hair, and a figure that would embellish any soldier's uniform.[25] When Selina becomes pregnant by an old boyfriend, Horace confronts her with his knowledge of her missed menstrual periods and threatens to beat the man "to a bloody pulp." Selina is aghast at his knowledge of her intimate physical life. "How did you know?" she asked.

> "Oh come on. Thee and me's lived in the same house for months. And the Army . . . has long trained me to keep my eyes open and miss nowt. You've missed your time twice running, I know. . . . Stop thy fussing. How, do [I know] you say? Because you're the lass I love, and shall allus love, and—by God—tha couldn't even get an ache in thy little finger without my knowing it."[26]

Selina, honestly shamefaced but no weepy hypocrite, wins herself a loving husband. Smith celebrates, as in many of his stories and novels, the frank sexual relations based on honest openness between men and women, however elusive in his own life.

Aside from Horace Gregson, Walter Barraclough, and Stephen Draper, the Yorkshire-born Rhode Island colonist and rebel in "Sinners Corner," admirable male characters are few, compared with the forceful, positive female characters in Smith's fiction. Simon Hardacre, the hard-driven protagonist in "The Millmaster," part 1 of the Briardale trilogy, is a Yorkshire lad with few prospects who immigrates to Briardale and works his way up in the local mill with the help and blessing of the superintendent. But Hardacre's real passion is to unite the mills of Briardale and of neighboring Middleton (Centredale) under his own domineering command. Once that goal is achieved, he is immediately struck down by a fatal stroke, as if in a Greek tragedy by his own hubris. Sam Knowles, a character who pops up in both stories and novels, plays the part of a shrewd, salacious observer of Briardale folk in all conditions and situations. As a weaving room overlooker, he knows the workings of the mill and the village inside and out but primarily casts his observations in vulgar cynicism. In this he is topped only by the predatory Grandfather Denby in "The Mill Folk." Combining greed and sexual seduction, Royal Tudor of the Arachne Corporation, aided by her unscrupulous lawyer Josh Boothby, cheats Miss Janet Thorne, the only surviving heir to the Thorne mill properties at Indian Hill, Rhode Island, out of her inheritance as well as her hopes for an attachment befitting an aging Yorkshire lass.[27] Yorkshire men at their worst are bold scoundrels and seducers.

The Strong Women of Yorkshire

In comparison with many of his male characters, Smith displayed a deep sympathy and admiration for Yorkshire women. Novelist Phyllis Bentley praised Smith for his perceptive understanding of the character of Yorkshire women. Although several middle-class female characters in "The Mill Folk" and in "The Lion and the Eagle" become sharp antagonists over international politics and over men they mutually desire, the collected short stories, such as "The Wise Child" in *More Yankee Yorkshiremen* and the 1978 novella *Yankee Yorkshirewomen* explore the deeply loyal attachments and the proud independence of working-class women. Smith seems to offer belated homage to the women in his family who worked as weavers in worsted mills, his mother and both of his grandmothers.

In "The Wise Child," Sally Greaves and her son David, born of a "slip" she makes in Yorkshire, immigrate early to Briardale with a friend when skilled weavers are desperately needed. Sally has defied village custom by refusing to identify or marry Luke Spencer, the boy's father. She works full-time for Binns-Cockcroft, lives on "Mill Row," and labors as a charwoman at night, "nipping and scratting" to send her boy to Providence High School. Joth Boothby, a Briardale lawyer, who has briefly been Sally's lover, gets his start in New England by cheating Luke Spencer out of a patent on a new shuttle. Lawyer Boothby becomes convinced from their physical resemblance that David is in fact his own natural son. He and his Yankee wife have no children, while Luke Spencer dies in World War I. When Joth insists on providing something for the boy, Sally settles for a job for David in Boothby's law office but takes nothing herself. "I'm content as I am, and I'm bound I'll take nowt from nobody as long as I can fend for myse'n. . . . A millworker I was born and a millworker I'll die."[28] Although it costs her a great deal, Mrs. Boothby persuades Sally to let Joth acknowledge David as his own son and heir. When both Boothbys are gone, David Greaves Spencer Boothby, the wise child, inherits the property generated from his real father's invention. The key to the resolution of this tale is Sally Greaves's self-reliance, patience, and shrewd generosity on behalf of her son.

The novella *Yankee Yorkshirewomen* explores a similar pattern of dignity, self-sacrifice, and devotion between two sisters, Clara and Cissie Croft. They immigrate to Briardale just before World War I to avoid the risk of hard feelings when both fall in love with Rupert Preston in Yorkshire. Accompanied by their well-to-do Aunt Rhoda, they lead contented lives until the aunt so exhausts herself with war relief work and her grief over the terrible war casualties among local residents that she dies "in harness" during the flu epidemic of 1918. She leaves them all her money held jointly in a savings account. Alfred Petty, who had earlier escaped war service by farming in Canada, sends the two sisters a letter, proposing marriage first to Clara, and if she refuses, to Cissie. Cissie, the second choice, scathingly remarks that Alfred's offer to wed Clara means she would become "his skivvy.... He wants your brass, not you."[29] But Clara, having sacrificed a chance to marry in Yorkshire, travels to Saskatchewan and decides to marry Alfred, leaving her money safely in Cissie's hands with instructions to send sums to her when requested. With falling postwar wheat prices, bad weather, endless work, and increasing ill health, Clara, who has had her first child, exhausts her portion of the inheritance, while Cissie dips into her own to help her.

Desperately lonely, Cissie in Briardale falls into a deep depression while constantly worrying over what is really happening on that Canadian farm. Rupert Preston, once beloved by both sisters, arrives in Briardale from Yorkshire, seeking Clara after having lost his entire family. After he learns Clara is married, Rupert becomes attached to Cissie and offers to wed, but Cissie puts off a decision. Rupert is galvanized into action when word comes that Clara is dangerously ill with tuberculosis. He personally takes some of the Croft sisters' money to Canada and sees that she is placed in a convalescent home. Then in a rush of events, Alfred Petty dies in a railroad accident, while Rupert and Clara find themselves in love again, leaving Cissie with no one. A life of disappointment and bitterness shapes her "standoffish, close-mouthed ways." Clara's illness prevents her from reentering the United States, and after Rupert and Clara both die tragically, Cissie becomes mother to Clara's child, "Little Cissie." Hedley Smith was familiar with the sentimental Victorian novel in which death inspires the best in the survivors. After Cissie's own death, no one except the Briardale Chapel minister and the little girl appreciate how good a mother she was and how much she loved Clara and her child. The story ends with the minister's stoical but appreciative words: "She hath done what she could."[30]

Martha Hobson is a far more active and attractive example of the strong Yorkshire female in "Squire Widdop's Wooing." Martha straightens everything and everyone out. Well-to-do Squire Widdop, the chief cashier at Binns-Cockcroft, slips on wet leaves in front of Martha Hobson's house, badly spraining his back. Blaming her, he allows himself to be coaxed into the house for a rest and a generous toddy of excellent brandy. As he looks around, he notices how much Martha values solid quality, befitting a partner for his declining years. But Martha, formerly a weaver, runs a successful small business and is in no hurry to wed, for she has "had her fun" in her time.[31] Still, Widdop suddenly makes up his mind and offers marriage on the spot. Martha decides to think it over and agrees to keep it quiet.

In looking to dispose of her variety shop, Martha uncovers many a secret. Emily Binns, her best friend, has a daughter Ruth who her mother insisted upon sending to college. Emily, a widow and a weaver, denies herself only to find the educated girl rejected by the villagers. Martha offers Emily the shop, spilling the beans about Widdop's marriage offer. She feels obliged to tell Squire but still finds him in great pain from his back injury, doctors him, and moves in to run his household despite his protests about "appearances." But then with a great smile, he gives in, praising Martha as "Just champion."[32] Within the week, a pregnant Ruth Binns arrives in Briardale. Her mother Emily wails, but Martha is unsurprised, suggesting that college life is no different from mill life in that respect. Ruth insists: "I'm no common mill girl." This provokes Martha's eloquent defense of mill lasses:

> "Now listen to me. . . . Don't look down your proud nose at any mill girls. There isn't a pin o' difference between them and you wi' your clothes off. They're hard-working, sensible and modest lasses and they make good wives for the most part, and it doesn't hurt 'em one bit 'cause they're forced to learn early and hard what's good and what's bad about life. I misdoubt we can say as much for your lot, with all their fancy education. Never scorn a mill lass in my presence, Miss Nancy!"[33]

Ruth, as it turns out, is Squire Widdop's own child, but Emily at the time preferred another man for her husband. Widdop has paid for his daughter's education and had offered marriage again to Emily when she is widowed. He finances both Ruth's marriage and further study with her new husband in Europe despite his deep misgivings. Martha Hobson now knows Squire

Widdop is indeed flesh and blood and foolish, even at times with money, when it comes to love and attachment. That very much suits her.[34]

To maintain a human balance in his Briardale fiction, Smith also portrays Yorkshire immigrant women in Rhode Island as controlling mothers and dominating sisters, while the unsavory character of the village gossip and abortionist Marth' Ann Bell suggests the worst. Still, homage is paid to women of resilient independence, of devoted yet publicly concealed affection, and of uncomplaining acceptance of what life offers. He was no feminist, far from it; these were essentialist virtues. And to Smith, they were the prime virtues of Yorkshire culture. They sustained him. He may have hoped that they sustained his mother and father. Smith portrays Yorkshire women as both strong and powerful as individuals and in the family, in the mill villages, and in society. He may have felt a profound if belated sense of guilt at his treatment of his mother, for he had been her favorite child.[35] Baptized at St. Alban's Church in Bradford and confirmed in a Centredale Episcopal church, Smith knew and loved Cranmer's *Book of Common Prayer* and enjoyed the rituals of St. Barabas's Episcopal Church in Warwick with his son Duncan.[36] Perhaps his portrayal of Yorkshire women was a literary act of contrition.

Awe, Fear, and Sexual Politics

Hedley Smith represents groups of workingwomen in other roles, participating in Yorkshire customs steeped in sexual politics. In these scenes, his awe and fear of female sexual power becomes dramatic and graphic. As Kevin Kenny recently argued, a transregional, comparative approach can offer corroborative evidence to illuminate some of the most elusive historical experiences, in this case female sexual customs.[37] Smith's stories, bolstered by Yorkshire memoirs, reveal immigrant workingwomen, especially weavers, organizing and thus preserving Yorkshire mill village customs that mocked and challenged male patriarchy. Here is depicted in detail Patricia Pessar and Sarah Mahler's transnational gendered geographies of power.[38] Furthermore, historians of immigration to the United States have debated whether or not female immigrants represented the "arch-conservators of tradition."[39] If so, these Yorkshire immigrant weavers were actively choosing which traditions to conserve and use for their own purposes.

One custom among female mill workers, meant to turn the tables on male sexual patriarchy, was to choose a young mill lad to be "sunned," as described by Rhoda Denby in "The Mill Folk." Sunning was performed within the context of a new lad being "fair game" to his older mates, both lads and lasses (see fig. 4). Indeed the women weavers did appear to give out the worst treatment. These women thus sent a message of female power to the whole working-class community—lads, lovers, husbands, co-workers, and overseers—to consider and remember.

> The first thing he'd [a new lad] be doing would be tending the bobbins winding on the frames, reaching up to tie a breakage when it came in one of the threads, then pegging the filled bobbins on square boards and delivering them to the women at the looms in the weave shed. . . . The chief trouble would be getting through the first week or two. A young beginner was always fair game to his older mates, lads and lasses alike, and the women were the worse of the two. There were some old traditions and customs that he'd have to go through before he was accepted as one of them, that would hurt him in body and spirit alike—things I'd only known by hearsay because some of them weren't fit for me [a young lass] to hear, like being "sunned." . . .

Figure 4. Some of the mill lads. Unknown group portrait of workers at the Greystone Mill, North Providence, R.I. n.d. Courtesy of the Rhode Island Historical Society. Thanks to Bruce Lepore.

A whole crowd of women and lasses same as a pack of fox hounds in full scent, only noisier, was galloping across the field, their skirts flying and their hair tossing and their scarves streaming in back of them. And in front, like the fox at its last gasp, Mike [the new lad] was toiling along and you could see his terror in every movement of every limb.

There was nothing I could have done to help him, even if I'd been able to reach him before they caught up. . . . Almost at my feet he collapsed and I was pushed aside in the rush and tumble of the women following him. They shrieked with laughter as they gathered round, and one of them, a big buxom lass I knew was only just recently wed, flung herself across his chest. She held his arms tight and her big bosoms pinned him down to the ground while others caught hold of his legs, which were thrashing about and held them still so that others could get his trousers down. Whatever he might have tried to say was drowned out in their yellings.

"Aye, let's see what he's gotten," they screamed, and "Nay, he's nobbut half a man at that," and "Reach us the oil can here." They had a long spouted oil can with 'em and they emptied it onto his privates and rubbed it well in with hard hands and fingers and knuckles that were used to kneading a bowl o' dough and did the same thing now with his wincing flesh. Then, when they'd had their fun, they broke and scattered same as a flock of crows, and went galloping off across the fields, screeching and laughing like demons, but good natured at bottom of it all.[40]

The oil in the can itself was relatively clean, but smearing lubrication for machinery on the human body is ritual pollution. The oil seeps through the lad's pants; he cannot return unwashed to the mill. He is soiled. Once he is well oiled, the women rub his genitals with hard hands and rough movements until they judge the job well done. Unmanly tears streak his face, his flesh wincing from the pain and the public humiliation by females. Some of these lads may have had uncontrollable partial erections during the sunning ritual, another measure of being "nobbut half a man."[41] Satisfied, the screeching women romp off, finished with their prey and having "had their fun."[42] Bewildered by the cruelty and wanton mistreatment, the lad will never forget what ordinary women in his mill village are capable of. He will carry this lesson into the mill and the union where he will face those same female weavers on new grounds of respect tinged with fear.

J. B. Priestley's 1962 memoirs of growing up in Bradford, Yorkshire, confirm the Bradford origins of Smith's fictional account of the sunning ritual in Briardale and thus the transatlantic connection. Priestley's paternal family and grandparents were all mill workers: "both men and women," a "solid steady sort." His father was a schoolteacher, but "he had plucked my mother, my real mother, about whom I know nothing except she was high-spirited and witty, from the clogs and shawls 'back o't mill,' a free and easy, rather raffish kind of working-class life, where in the grim little back-to-back houses they shouted and screamed, laughed and cried, and sent out a jug for more beer."[43]

At sixteen, Priestley became a junior clerk with a yarn-exporting firm, observing with fascination the budding sexual life among the youth in the streets of Bradford.[44] His treatment one late afternoon by a group of female weavers led him to discover the sunning custom.

It is true that the women and girls who worked in the mills then were no models of feminine refinement. Sometimes, when I finished earlier that usual at the office and walked home, the route I preferred took me past one of the largest mills in the district, often just when the women were coming out. I would find myself breasting a tide of shawls, and something about my in-nocent dandyism would set them screaming at me, and what I heard then, though I was never a prudish lad, made by cheeks burn. And it was still the custom, in some mills if not in that particular one, for the women to seize a newly-arrived lad and "sun" him, that is, pull his trousers down and reveal his genitals. But all this not unwholesome and perhaps traditional female bawdiness—there was a suggestions of mythology, ancient worship, folklore, about that queer "sunning" ritual—was far removed from cynical whoring. There was nothing sly, nothing hypocritical, about these coarse dames and screaming lasses, who were devoted to their own men, generally working in the same mill, and kept on "courting," though the actual courtship stage was over early, for years and years until a baby was due, when they married. They may not have lived happily afterwards, but they saved themselves from some unpleasant surprises.[45]

Smith certainly read Priestley's memoirs and much of his other work and may have absorbed accounts of the "sunning" ritual over pork pies and pints of bitter at the Greystone Social Club. Female weavers in Belgian cotton textile factories developed more individual acts of sexual humiliation, which their young male victims called rape.[46]

Smith's version in "The Mill Folk" imagines collective female action over-powering a new lad, displaying, denigrating, handling, and dirtying his geni-talia. The symbolism of the "sunning" ritual as reconstructed by Smith is richly sexual and deeply abusive. The young victim is dragged away from other men by a group of women workers, the mature and newly married teaching the younger how to proceed. In a flash the lad is alone, bewildered, and at their mercy. Even if forewarned by his more experienced mates, the young victim could scarcely believe the actuality of the ritual. The once-familiar faces of the weavers are now transformed by Smith's imagination into the Bacchic women of Euripides.[47] They chase the lad as if they were foxhounds and he the fox, to be torn apart when caught for sport. Galloping after him in a pack—hair tossing, skirts flying—they catch him with anticipatory shrieks of laughter knowing what is to come. This "disorderly" public behavior by ordinary working women turns them into demons and crows, merciless and rending. Throwing the terrified lad down and pinning his arms—one with her ample bosoms—and holding his legs, they can do with him as they like. As his trousers come down and his genitals are exposed, the laughing women gather around, evoking primal fears of castration. And their judgments denigrating the size of his penis are cutting indeed. Let's see what he's got; he's "nobbut" half a man. This judgment on his manhood is being made by half the community, the more powerful half to Smith's mind.

That lesson is passed on through the ritual. In "The Mill Folk," young Rhoda Denby, the witness to the ritual and the narrator, learns on the afternoon of the "sunning" the power of female sexuality over men folk and vows to use it on her own behalf.

> I'd learned a lesson unknown to myself. For to that moment I had always sort of looked up to Mike and bowed before the masterful ways he had with him, and done and thought as he wanted. But from now on I felt that somehow I was stronger than he was. And I was! For that is the way Nature plans it, making it up to women for all the spiteful things she heaps on them otherwise. For if they are *right* women they can always hold a man by that he has between his legs, and make him dance to their tune and follow to their leading for as long as they want.[48]

"Right" women in Yorkshire terms demonstrated agency, initiative, and imagination in their social "locations," as Pessar and Mahler argued, both "corporal and cognitive."[49] They knew exactly what they were doing.

Hedley Smith's relationship with his wife taught him about female power in marriage, but his sense of awe was universal. Duncan Smith understood his father's view of women well, and not only as the most powerful members of the family. Smith saw all men as hoodwinked by women who actually ran the world, although men thought *they* did. "[I]n them [the women] there is terrific strength especially in the face of domestic and even mill yard or mill floor discord and debate."[50] In the "sunning" ritual, an open threat to male sexuality helped to establish that power. Smith's rereading of Greek tragedies during the toughest times of his life prepared his imagination for these universal possibilities of interpreting the role of women in Yorkshire customs.

The Yankee Yorkshireman in Ethnic Fiction

Smith's two published collections of short stories, *The Yankee Yorkshireman* and *More Yankee Yorkshiremen,* can be compared with a favorite contemporary genre in ethnic fiction: the short-story cycle.[51] Hovering between the short story and the novel, a cycle of the short stories, organized around one or more themes, Rocio Davis argued, is a particularly apt way to capture the "enigma of ethnicity," the sense of being between two worlds.[52] The titles of Smith's published works, representing the doubled identity classic to the displaced person, serve as an organizing concept.[53] Other ethnic writers pivot their fiction and stories around a single place or an experience shared by many characters.[54] One of Smith's few references to Yorkshire immigrants as an "ethnic group" appeared on the book jacket blurb to *More Yankee Yorkshiremen* (1974), repeated almost verbatim for *Yankee Yorkshire Women* (1980), promoting his second book as a "timely contribution" to the approaching bicentennial celebration.[55] Hedley Smith remained uninterested in this sort of literature, including the classics of ethnic fiction and autobiography readily available to him. Had he picked up Mary Antin's *The Promised Land* (1912) with the opening lines in the introduction: "I was born, I have lived, and I was made over," he would have gone no further.[56] In addition, his son Duncan, a scholar of German literature, insists that his father disdained modern literary criticism.

Whatever Smith intended, those intentions are difficult to prove and almost as hard to figure out. Still Smith used place, character, and culture in the "Yankee Yorkshiremen" stories to illustrate some of the themes explored by other ethnic short-story cycle writers. On the whole, Yankee characters are few; they represent the world surrounding but seldom penetrating Briardale village. As Smith intended, Yorkshire culture remained resilient. Still, his refusal to be part of ethnic literature does not mean his fiction cannot be interpreted in relationship to it.

Ethnic fiction writers have used the short-story cycle to probe the various yet shared situations of place, displacement, and adjustment for the immigrant and migrant in the twentieth and twenty-first centuries. But living in Greystone/Briardale was quite a different experience from residing in Latino Chicago, in Chinatowns, or anywhere else in ethnic ghettos. The Benn Company decided in 1903 to build Greystone as a Yorkshire-style mill village. Smith's Yankee Yorkshire folk dwelt in a place conducive to transplanting in the short term their work skills, their dialect, and their habits, complete to a poultry fanciers' club. For over thirty years, the corporation stabilized the mill village. Thus Greystone/Briardale provided an idiosyncratic setting for immigrants and migrants. Furthermore, Hedley Smith wrote not about his own generation and their adjustments to a new culture but about the past. What did he have to say in his first collection of short stories about identity and community in Briardale?

Among the five stories in *The Yankee Yorkshireman*, "The Black Sheep," best encompasses the village inhabitants and explores the dominating role in the village of the transatlantic connections to the parent corporation in Bradford, Yorkshire.[57] Neglecting his comely wife Bertha, Elijah Stott, the acting manager of Binns-Cockcroft mill in Briardale, falls for the sex tease Maud Binns, who happens to own with her sister Martha considerable mill shares. Stott is after Maud and her shares, and during the pursuit his work suffers. The town gossips chatter, but Bertha seems indifferent. As she explains to Parson Denton of the Episcopal church, "if he thinks he can find summat better under another woman's petticoats, happen I can do likewise inside another man's breeches."[58] The parson groans.

The Binns-Cockcroft corporation back in Bradford sends Tom Wilson, a Cockcroft nephew, budding manager, and scoundrel, forced to leave England over yet another lass in trouble, to Briardale. If the black sheep Wilson can straighten things out and get control of the mill shares, he will have Stott's job. In a hilarious depiction of a Whitsuntide Feast sponsored by the Primitive Methodist church, Maud Binns trips during the single women's hundred-yard dash. With her long skirts up to her navel, she exposes her "bare bum," to the surprise of all and the delight of many. Only her prim sister Martha is really offended. Elijah Stott runs onto the field to help her cover up, but Maud smacks him on his head and nearly knocks him down. Later she enjoys much male attention at the Social Club bar.

In the story's resolution, Tom Wilson marries not the provocative Maud but her sister Martha and gains control of the mill shares. He dominates Maud by spanking her sadistically before the family and Elijah but also promises to take her home to a better life in England. He, too, has had it with Briardale. Meanwhile, Bertha Stott has arranged an assignation with Tom Wilson out of town to spite Elijah but finds in bed not the man but the mill shares. Elijah's job is safe, and their marriage is ready to be mended. Tom Wilson, after all, is only a sheep of the darkest grey.

The story reveals that the overwhelming influence in Briardale is the Binns-Cockcroft corporation in Bradford and the way it moves people and their relatives back and forth to Briardale. But this is not all. With the other stories, "The Black Sheep" underscores the strong currents of sexuality, religion, resilience, conscience above "brass," strong tolerant women, and wayward but conscientious men. Are these people bicultural Yankee Yorkshiremen and -women? Not in the first short-story collection. They are Yorkshire migrants working for a Yorkshire business in a Yorkshire-style village surrounded by an unseen Yankee-dominated society.

Evoking the spirit of "Dickensian fellowship" and family reunion at Yorkshire Christmases, the introduction to *More Yankee Yorkshiremen* raises questions asked by Yorkshire people about the fate of those emigrants who left Bradford.[59] Smith is focusing on the consequences of emigration. The unifying theme is intercultural marriage. Marriage becomes a metaphor for bridging cultures and other inter-personal difficulties. "Minnie Kettlewell's Husband" explores the reactions of Sam and Minnie when their son Bob marries Adeline "Silva," the daughter of an Italian immigrant stonecutter and his wife (see chap. 2). Love and forbearance conquers deep cultural divides. In "The Wise Child," an unfortunate intermarriage occurs between Joth Boothby, the Briardale lawyer, and Minetta Sweet, the daughter of "old Skinflint" Samuel Sweet, a grain and feed store owner with a lot of land. Minetta is the personification of Yankee female: "tall, thin, droopy . . . with a sad face . . . behind her big spectacles."[60] And she is barren. In "King George's Idea," ex-British Army soldier Horace Gregson weds pregnant Yankee schoolteacher Selina Jenkins lovingly and joyfully, the best outcome for both.[61] Most intercultural marriages work out for the best.

The most intricate story in the collection, "The Partnership," develops the theme of intermarriage with many twists in meaning. Also present, as in all the short stories, are the Yorkshire connections and the influence in Briardale of the parent corporation. But Smith introduces homeland tastes, unobtainable even in Briardale, which drive the story: a tasty, chewy malt bread called Velva made with a secret family recipe. Before leaving Bradford to inspect the delivery of new Belgian looms in Briardale, mill engineer Frank Naylor and his wife promise an elderly couple, the Higbys, to try to locate their long-lost daughter Emma and her husband Billy Wright. The Higbys had made the Velva bread and wish to pass on their savings to their only child. In Briardale, Frank and his wife stay with Sally Craven, his eldest sister and a weaver, who had taken in her orphan granddaughter, Barbara, now grown up and inclined to be stubborn and independent. She refuses to become a weaver and works for a big Providence confectionary and bakery firm.

Barbara falls in love with an odd sort in the eyes of the Naylors, little Johnny Winters, born he claims in Birmingham, England, and a traveling salesman for a Providence jewelry firm. Frank Naylor must travel to Worcester and New York about textile machinery, and during his absence his wife and sister

Sally discover a secret. "The Annex, a working-class district of Providence full of factories and tenements and markets and little specialty shops" was about forty-five minutes by trolley. There a man both tells fortunes and bakes bread and pastries. They persuade Frank to join them. When Frank tastes the bread, he declares: "That slice o' bread I just ate . . . it were Velva bread."[62] Also in the Annex, they discover Emma Higby Wright, a neglected, aging wife who had lent the secret recipe to the baker. When she shows Frank a picture of her absent husband, who should it be but Johnny Winters!

Racing back to Briardale, the Naylors are too late. Barbara is sporting a big wedding ring with her new "husband" in tow. When Barbara and Emma learn of Winters/Wright's deception, he takes off with the sample case of jewelry for parts unknown. Having been "had" by the same scamp evokes a characteristic response from these two resilient Yorkshire women. After a bit of sobbing and sighing, they decide to form a partnership. Barbara has the gumption and business sense, and Emma has great need and the secret recipe. Borrowing enough money from Uncle Frank for a start, they operate a successful bakery in Briardale that draws customers for their pastries, pork pies, and above all for the Velva bread. When Johnny/Billy drags himself back sick, shabby, and penniless, they agree to take him in. Barbara points out:

> "Emma, lass, I don't really know what to say, but I reckon that creature is your husband; and if he isn't mine and all[,] it's not for want o' trying. Now we're in partnership, lass, for good or for bad; and that means we're bound to share not only our assets but our liabilities as well. And that's what I call that thing that's sleeping upstairs."[63]

Briardale manages to take it all in stride, after lifting its eyebrows a bit. Indeed the partnership works as a marriage should and better, given that the husband was a "foreigner" from Birmingham.

Although Smith captured and preserved the Yorkshire immigrant and migrant experience in the North Providence enclave, his short stories also reveal how powerfully the homeland shaped the lives of Briardale folk living for the time being in Rhode Island. In "The Partnership," he concedes that this influence also included unforgettable tastes and smells, as in contemporary ethnic fiction. Here through the symbol of Velva bread, it becomes a major theme, but there are many hints throughout his fiction. He himself tried to duplicate Yorkshire-style bread, sausages, pork pies, buns, and pastries. In "The Spinster of Paradise View," Miss Janet's maid-of-all-work produces incomparable maids of honor: a delectable combination of pastry, raspberry jam, and cake topped with a frosted cross of pastry. Other favorites included eccles cakes, flaky pastry cases filled with currants, candied citrus peel, and spices slashed and sugared on the top.[64] There were Yorkshire teas and then there were special Yorkshire "knife and fork" teas. The teas with guests featured sandwiches of ham and beef tongue on well-buttered thin bread followed by jam tarts and currant tea cakes with brandy-spiked tea for the men. Knife and fork affairs usually solemnized feasts, funerals, and weddings and indicated sit-down meals of roasted meats and special pastries. With his emphasis on homeland attachments, whether through the metaphor of World War I or the taut connections between Briardale village and Bradford firm or the unforgettable tastes and smells of Yorkshire foods, Smith's fiction inadvertently provides links with other late twentieth-century fiction about contemporary immigrants and migrants from other cultures.[65]

Transatlantic perspectives, the depiction of strong women, interest in translocal sexual customs and behaviors, and a profound awe of female power are some of the major themes in Smith's fiction. Another is intercultural marriage, prominently in "The Lion and the Eagle." Such marriages for theorists of assimilation become a metaphor for bridging cultures, and in Smith's novel the Yankee wife becomes an enthusiastic Englishwoman. On the other hand, he also explores the theme of female sexual power and the intense conflicts of family life. He lived and imagined both. While exploring these themes, Smith described a lost social and cultural world in New England. He notes well the implications of world war for migration and migrants. The reach of transatlantic politics into the lives and culture of Yorkshire migrants during World War I becomes a major component of the Briardale experience. The results are increased political tensions with local Yankees and for those who returned as war veterans a new sense of identity as Yorkshire English.

The Ethnic Prose of the Yankee Yorkshireman and Regional Fiction

The short-story cycle has also been prominent in New England regional fiction. Using one place, Dunnet Landing, as a setting for *The Country of the Pointed Fir* (1896), Sarah Orne Jewett explored Yankee characters and their customs in late nineteenth-century coastal Maine. Hedley Smith, the Yankee Yorkshireman, has defined Yankee as a component of ethnicity in his tales. Recent debates over regionalist literature as re-emergent in a global economy have inspired a renewal of interest in contemporary regional and local colorist writers.[66] New England, especially Massachusetts, has a lively tradition of regional and ethnic writing.[67] Rhode Island has the Yankee Yorkshireman and his Briardale immigrants. When Smith is viewed as a regionalist writer—although I have argued that *translocal* is a more appropriate term—his work reflects the intense cultural isolation of Briardale's inhabitants and conveys a sense of time and place, which the author connects with the larger Atlantic world. His focus on urban industrial life and on an ethnically distinct but neither marginal nor dispossessed people and his exploration of tensions over sexuality and war, however, indicates considerable distance from the New England regionalist "canon," of which he was aware.[68]

The Yankee Yorkshireman's fiction reflects a mid-twentieth-century mixture of local-color fiction from the late nineteenth-century New England tradition with some elements of realist and naturalist fiction.[69] But Hedley Smith's stories give regionalism a twist that fits yet modifies Marjorie Pryse's definition of regionalist writers as including marginal or "nondominant" men who along with women regionalists focused on themes of resistance and difference.[70] As an author, Smith stretches the meaning of Pryse's nondominant men to include white males who wrote out of marginal ethnic cultures, stubbornly refusing in their fiction both New England and American values.

Contemporary reevaluations of regionalist literature regard both cultural pluralism and the relationship between ethnicity and "region" as significant themes.[71] Smith's ethnic narratives explore the corrosive tensions in early twentieth-century Rhode Island society resulting from migrant resistance in North Providence mill villages to Yankee economic, political, and culture dominance. For this he possessed what Pryse has termed "a deep structure of local knowledge," attitudes strongly resistant to the dominant culture, and a pervasive reliance on local customs and dialect to tell his stories.[72] The Yankee Yorkshireman also alters the relationship of regional writing to American national boundaries, giving another twist to the meanings of regionalism. Hedley Smith did not view himself as an American writer but as a conserver of one transatlantic culture within American society. His geographical setting includes the composite, "Briardale" and its "folk," the mill villages of the Blackstone Valley, and extends to Yankee-dominated "South County," bordering on Long Island Sound. Smith also reaches across the Atlantic to the working-class and middle-class society of Wilsden and Bradford in Yorkshire, calling forth popular memories about their forebears' role as early as the Napoleonic Wars in addition to personal adventures stretching from the Boer War to British military intervention in Soviet Russia after World War I. Smith redefines New England regional fiction by adding the dimensions of transatlantic history and memory.

Conclusion
The Inner World of Emigration and Migration

Historians study emigration as a process involving push and pull factors, transportation networks, agencies of assistance, ports of embarkation, passenger lists, state policies, and as seasonal or return migration.[1] The term *emigration* tends to be replaced by *immigration* once the person or the family lands in the port of debarkation. Off the boat and through the admittance process, they become immigrants. Whatever their intentions or their emotional reactions to the process of emigration and unless they return at some point, they seem to be where they want to be.

Concealing emotional upsets and distress eases the difficulties through the whole process. This was especially the case in an emotionally repressed culture such as Yorkshire. Resistance can persist on the level of emotions or personal identity, whatever the outward behavior or status. The emotions felt by emigrants and migrants are a dimension hard to know but are vital to understanding fully the migration process. Emigration involves many complex trails of physical movement. Emigration can also be an incomplete and resisted inner process, resolved neither by a return or seasonal migration nor by an acceptance of acculturation. Historians might well consider and question these ambiguities and wonder about the feelings behind those photographed faces.

Admitting that the waves of Spanish immigrants to Buenos Aires actually consisted of "drops" representing human beings, Jose Moya seemed to fear that attention paid to individuals rather than to useful patterns based on group analysis undermines scholarship.[2] My study of one individual and his family argues that emigration, the reluctant leaving of the homeland, to a degree unknown and unacknowledged by historians can be a transformatory process deeply felt. It can involve great personal loss, distress, and persistent if unexpressed rage. This anger is often experienced at the level of family relationships. Furthermore, in the case of Hedley Smith, the cycle of emigration, immigration, and acculturation can be refused. He believed himself—like the Briardale villagers—to be a migrant, an involuntary alien.

Hedley Smith's losses and anger fueled his creativity. Similar feelings were experienced by other members of the Smith family who accepted their emigration and became immigrants. The evidence is both direct and indirect. The disappointments, grief, and anger of Ernest, Alice, and Sam Smith were born in silence or expressed privately. At the end of his life, Ernest told Sam he wished he had never emigrated. Alice's deprivation of her grandchildren, she doubtless knew, would never have happened in Bradford. When Sam was rebuffed by his Bradford girlfriend in 1938, he settled against the wishes of his American wife for marriage without children. Sam took in his father in 1952 when his mother died but did not get along with this mild-mannered man. I suspect Sam had never forgiven him for botching the emigration arrangements in 1923. In an understood context, behaviors can reveal or at least suggest linkages to complex emotions. Family life and kin became the cauldron of bitterness and offered no refuge from the disappointments resulting from leaving the homeland.

Incomplete emigration and a refusal to acculturate is not just a twentieth- or twenty-first-century experience. Spoken or unspoken anger can flow from a situation of dependency and loss of status during the immigration process. And dependency varies by age and gender over time. David Gerber brings to life Mary Ann Wodrow Archbald.[3] She longed for her "Little Isle" off of western Scotland as an early nineteenth-century immigrant farmer's wife in central New York. This mature woman, who left behind in 1807 an aging mother and four children in their graves, experienced emigration as a dreadful loss of emotional ties, cultural contacts, social status from her family connections, and personal identity. No gain in material terms or security from indebtedness could ever balance those losses. She never gave up the dream of returning to Little Cumbrae. Archbald knew well that dependent upon her husband's decision to emigrate, she had no power in a situation that would reshape her life profoundly. As a cultured and well-read woman, especially fond of Scottish history and literature, she developed proto-feminist views and a critical aversion to American culture and society. Archbald, like Hedley Smith, created in her imagination an idealized myth of a historic and personal past. Unlike Smith, Archbald sustained her identity though her immediate family and personal correspondence.

Emigration at fourteen denied Smith any chance to use his hard-won scholarship earned at secondary school. This forestalled a future career that might have led to intellectual and social status in England and underscored his dependency on his family's choices. Ironically, he was the first to get a job in Rhode Island. When his family as a group became naturalized citizens in 1929 after the five-year waiting period, Hedley was twenty years old and a minor. His brother was naturalized as an adult and issued a passport. All of this was symbolic but reinforced Smith's inner image of his dependency. He directed his anger at both his family and at the society he was supposed to accept. Whatever happened to him in the United States would never make up for his separation from his desired path and his powerlessness. The ensuing misfortunes that transformed his life convinced him that he had been right all along. They became the basis of his refusal to accept the completion of the emigration. His Briardale literature and personal tastes sustained his identity while he lived a life as an apparently integrated American citizen. Like Archbald, success in the material world was irrelevant. The treasured world had been lost.

English immigrants to Canada, depending on their status and class, often refused to fit in the new society. Dirk Hoerder found that Canadians treated them as outsiders, ridiculed for their pretensions, conceit, and unwillingness to perform hard, practical work.[4] Leaning on family connections for employment really meant lack of qualification or experience. Retired British officialdom or young men dependent on family allowances offered little but expected deference. The English faced hostility from Canadian Welsh, Irish, and Scots. And known trade unionists had trouble finding jobs. The hostility of Canadian people and their own condescension made acculturation for many English immigrants long and complicated. Although letters, diaries, memoirs, and autobiographies served as sources for Hoerder's study, little is known about how they actually felt during this process.

In contrast, Hedley Smith, both an ambitious and cultured man, worked hard, educated himself, pursued any kind of job, and expected credit only for his hard-won abilities. His pursuit through his life of the best, in his opinion, of Western literary culture, his impressive, long-term endeavors to become a published author, and the use of his talents to preserve Yorkshire culture in Rhode Island were something more than the expression of middle-class aspiration or status-striving. He squeezed a pinched budget to see the Briardale stories in print and distributed them himself. Like the English in Canada, he did not acculturate.

Grief and loss and rage of varying intensities may be the central emotions of all participants in emigration and immigration and "re-migration" or

Hoerder's memorably blurred concept: "e/im-migration."[5] Without the revealing subjectivity of autobiography, poetry, memoir, letters, diaries, oral history, and fiction, intimate lives and deepest feelings remain hidden. Often they were intentionally hidden from families. Intentions and feelings are always complex and elusive. The more historians can identify the individual complexities of intent and response, the deeper and richer will be their analyses of structure, empirical data, and the patterns of migration.

What Smith and His Fiction Let Us See

Hedley Smith's depiction of the complex and ambivalent feelings of the first generation of immigrants reflected his own and his family's attitudes and what they had experienced. Human considerations and individual decisions overrode ongoing economic and political trends in migration patterns. Smith's family had a history of migration starts and stops. His paternal grandfather, Sam Smith, had seriously considered immigration both to the United States in the early 1870s and to South Africa in 1903, long before the Smith family left Bradford in 1923. Either plan—if carried through—would have changed the story dramatically. Ernest Smith would not have married Alice Collins, if Sam Smith's roving instincts had not been halted first by his sweetheart's reluctance and later by his own fatal illness. Political reprisal as well as personal misjudgment colored state intervention in 1923 and disrupted Ernest Smith's plans to pursue his promised job and retain his status as a skilled artisan. This profoundly altered the subsequent fortunes of his family. The consequences of migration included the uncontrollable and unforeseen, resulting in the family's downward social and economic mobility. Dashed hopes did not result in return migration to England and denied young Hedley his greatest desire for his life course. These circumstances shaped Hedley Smith's life and imagination.

The place in which the Smiths settled, North Providence, Rhode Island, was part of the Atlantic economy of European investment and global labor migration, creating a culturally complicated society. The implications of the mélange of migrants with transatlantic connections and multiple political perspectives shaped early twentieth-century New England worsted centers. Not even the transfer beginning in 1904 and 1905 of groups of Yorkshire worsted workers from West Riding factories to a small Bradford-style mill in Greystone village, North Providence, guaranteed protection from these complexities.

Hedley Smith was aware of but chose to avoid class politics and the multicultural connections within North Providence in order to build his culturally pure, nonassimilating Briardale in homage to the Bradford of his birth. Still his fiction in its portrayal of dialect and custom connects Briardale people living in a dominant Yankee culture with the larger Atlantic world. His stories, except for ones about Yorkshire intermarriage with other groups, reflect the intense cultural isolation of a migrant enclave and convey a sense of time and place, for which the author, as a late comer depended on the memories of others. For the same reasons of cultural purity, his depiction of the World War I memorial in Greystone expunged the Italian, French Canadian, and female names and added the Union Jack to the Stars and Stripes. His ambivalence about whether Yorkshire migrants and indeed he himself constituted an ethnic people in America reflects his unresolved feelings about his emigration.

But his ambivalence cannot override what he stood for. In the 1920s and early 1930s, both he and his brother associated with Yorkshire-born people in the mill villages of North Providence and in Providence and Warwick. The same assumption must be made for his parents. Smith's fondness for the Greystone Social Club where—he had remarked that he wished that he had a nickel for every pork pie he had eaten there—represented strong ethnic bonds.[6] His tastes, marriage, values, demeanor, attitudes, and habits marked him as a Yorkshireman living among Yankees. His writings defined an ethnic group in American society not eager to join in, critical of Yankee values, unwillingly to integrate, and thus distinct. Their presence enriches our understanding of the patterns of twentieth-century migration.

The Yankee Yorkshireman and Ethnicity

What did Smith mean by the terms *Yankee Yorkshireman, Yankee Yorkshiremen,* and *Yankee Yorkshirewomen*? Consciously or unconsciously for Smith, the terms seemed to have at least three meanings: one for the textile immigrants and migrants to Greystone, Rhode Island; another for the characters in the Briardale fiction; finally, and perhaps most complicated for Hedley Smith, himself and his family. Much as he tried to deny and avoid the ethnic label, all of these groups of English immigrants and migrants behaved and thought and felt like ethnic people.

Greystone village did not contain just Yorkshire mill workers as Harrison Benn intended. Yorkshire migrants who resided in Greystone felt the need to form social and political contacts with fellow textile workers in neighboring mill villages as quickly as they organized Yorkshire-style holidays, co-ops, and religious activities. Violations of customary work rules and standards underscored the distance between North Providence and Bradford. Some filed first papers; others became naturalized citizens. The worsted industry in the

American Northeast was developing fast. Internal migration may have been on the minds of many. In the meantime, intercultural cooperation with new immigrants just entering the mills made sense. The English had experience in labor activism and many grievances to address. The Great War brought huge orders for cloth but when it ended, 75 percent of the original Yorkshire residents of Greystone had left, some as return migrants. As internal migrants, they would behave as immigrant workers in the worsted mills of Lawrence or Philadelphia did: find their own ethnic group and join in their activities and associations.

In the Briardale fiction, Yorkshiremen and -women lived for a time in "Yankeeland," an old English term for that upstart colony across the pond that periodically required closer examination. These migrants lived in an enclave, the better to stay apart from the surrounding inferior and hostile culture and ultimately return to the homeland. The distinctiveness of this enclave preserved the best in Yorkshire values and behaviors. However, some of the conflicts that emerged in the stories came partly from the difficulties of remaining distinct: temptations of intermarriage out of the community, advancement in the Yankee world, unwelcome interference from the homeland corporation or kin, and the inability to maintain Yorkshire ways of life in a new setting however well arranged. The challenge to preserve homeland ways in a strange land is the classic dilemma for immigrants.

Hedley Smith also called himself a Yankee Yorkshireman, and he did not live in an enclave, work in a mill, or return to Yorkshire. He hated the emigration but lived as an ethnic English American. He married a Yankee and had, from the perspective of his own culture, become an outsider. Smith attached himself to the Yankee host culture for marriage and for social, cultural, and political reasons. Yet his writings revealed that he despised it. When in the end that Yankee culture failed him, he sought refuge and relief from aging and regret in the idealization of his homeland as he remembered it and in Rhode Island mill village life as told to him and as he imagined it. His isolation in North Scituate provided him with the opportunity to probe the meanings of living as a Yorkshire exile in Rhode Island. His efforts to make Briardale distinct produced fine ethnic fiction.

Grief and Loss

As a very private man, Hedley Smith would, I judge, have never spoken to me about his grief or his anger. His son, Duncan, is well aware of his father's sense of deep privacy and his stoicism in the face of terrible losses. "He loved travel, loved cities, never traveled save for the immigration, married a woman who hated going anywhere at all and lived in the country because she hated cities. Fate grinning at him and he just grinned back and wrote."[7]

As a clinical psychologist, Duncan Smith also understood but was unable to alleviate his mother's periodic black depressions. Hedley Smith's sense of loss and his grief about his disconnection with Yorkshire and thus his chance for a different life led him to acts of rage against his parents. How else to explain the cruel separation in the 1940s of grandparents and grandchildren who lived in the same community? Joining with his wife, Carmen, who hated Ernest and Alice for her own twisted reasons, was an act of revenge. The family stories about Alice dying in the midst of one of her screaming fits, told with humor by her grandchildren, are chilling in the context of her deprivation. Hedley Smith also separated himself from his brother Sam, who nonetheless developed a close relationship with Duncan and Portia. Sam was not welcome in the home of Carmen and Hedley, but offered his niece and nephew affection and a vision of travel beyond the confines of Warwick. Having accepted his place as an immigrant by revisiting Bradford on an American passport, Sam offered a way back to Yorkshire.

Hedley Smith's interior rage and passive acquiescence to his wife's demands in distancing himself from his relatives may have affected his novel writing. His most discerning literary agent argued that his major characters remained passive and undeveloped and his plots without convincing structure or action.[8] His suppressed anger over the most important change to his life and his indirection in confronting his parents with his loss and grief could have crippled his creativity by forestalling his own development. He had after all read the great novel writers of the nineteenth century with excellent plotting and memorable characters. But his most riveting, best conceived, and well-written novella, "Sinners Corner," was never in the hands of an agent.

Smith agreed with Thomas Hardy that migration in its many forms was fatal to the preservation of local custom, "inter-social relations, and eccentric individualism."[9] So Smith tried to capture custom and dialect in his Briardale fiction. Briardale's residents speak only a strong and positive affirmation of homeland culture, but Hedley Smith lived the grief and anger from his losses. John Bodnar has argued that "private history, the pursuit of the particular, has clearly deserved the charge of being history with the politics left out."[10] Hedley Smith's inner life and his fiction of isolation from the host society were outright rejections of an inferior society. He maintained this intensely political stance personally for a lifetime. Such writers and their literature carry significant political content. Literature has its own individual, historic, and political setting and purposes. Global migration and contemporary migration literature has its own as well.

A study of contemporary Bradford, West Riding, Yorkshire, analyzed the persistent but changing forms of homeland attachments by pioneer Pakistani immigrants and second- and third-generation British Pakistanis.[11] The first immigrants, traditionally called the "community of suffering," endured racism and labor exploitation in order to return with their earnings to Pakistan. Few did. Leaving no record, many of them doubtless suffered deep regret, grief, anger, and loss in silence or in private. If they did return, it was as corpses to be buried. Recent global and local politics of Mideastern war and Islamophobia recreated similar longings for a return to the idealized homeland of Pakistan among the second and third generations. Meanwhile, British Pakistanis ritually send escorted groups of children to the homeland to be grounded in village life and regional values. They return more mature and assured of their place in the British Pakistani community. Hedley Smith could have benefited from such a ritual, but then the Briardale stories might not have been written.

Refused emigration may be resolved over time. Positive experiences or emotional bonds forged in the new society bolster self-esteem and help to ease the loss and grief. These experiences can include a strong family life, meaningful work, a good marriage, a wise choice, a beloved, promising child, a valued role in the community, a sustaining friendship, and creative achievement. Hedley Smith had, or could have had, some of these. When Smith wrote his canon in 1986, had he made peace with his life? Perhaps.

Notes

Abbreviations

BO   *Bradford Observer*
CIS   *Rhode Island Commissioner of Industrial Statistics*
LA   *Labor Advocate* (Providence)
PJ   *Providence Daily Journal*
TM   *Textile Manufacturer* (Manchester)
YFT   *Yorkshire Factory Times* (Huddersfield)

Introduction

1. Hedley Smith to Phyllis Bentley, undated (c. 1970), courtesy Portia Thompson.

2. Elliott R. Barkan, "Race, Religion, and Nationality in American Society: A Model of Ethnicity from Contact to Assimilation," *Journal of American Ethnic History* 14 (Winter 1995): 38–76. On invisible immigrants, Charlotte Erickson, *Invisible Immigrants: The Adaptation of English and Scottish Immigrants in Nineteenth-Century America* (Ithaca, N.Y.: Cornell University Press, 1990).

3. In general, uprooted means the loss of culture in the process of movement, while transplanted opens the possibility of recreating homeland culture in a new location. We owe these concepts to Oscar Handlin and John Bodnar, cited below.

4. David A. Gerber argued similarly in his analysis of immigrant letters: *Authors of Their Lives: The Personal Correspondence of British Immigrants to North America in the Nineteenth Century* (New York: New York University Press, 2006).

5. Nancy L. Green and François Weil, eds., *Citizenship and Those Who Leave: The Politics of Emigration and Expatriation* (Urbana: University of Illinois Press, 2007).

6. Wilbur S. Shepperton probed the diverse experiences of seventy-five English

return migrants largely in the early nineteenth century through their published writings: *Emigration and Disenchantment: Portraits of Englishmen Repatriated from the United States* (Norman: Oklahoma University Press, 1965).

7. Oscar Handlin, *The Uprooted: The Epic Story of the Great Migrations That Made the American People* (New York: Grosset and Dunlap, 1951), 259–63, esp. 259.

8. "But America was the land of separated men"; ibid., 305.

9. John Bodnar, *The Transplanted: A History of Immigrants in Urban America* (Bloomington: Indiana University Press, 1985), xx–xxi.

10. *The Yankee Yorkshireman* (Detroit: Harlo Press, 1970); *More Yankee Yorkshiremen* (Detroit: Harlo Press, 1974); *Yankee Yorkshirewomen* (Detroit: Harlo Press, 1978). See the list of published works for three other privately published books.

11. Sigurdur Gylfi Magnusson, "The Singularization of History: Social History and Microhistory within the Post Modern State of Knowledge," *Journal of Social History* 36 (Spring 2003): 701–35.

12. Charles Tilly, "Transplanted Networks," in *Immigration Reconsidered: History, Sociology, and Politics,* ed. Virginia Yans-McLaughlin (New York: Oxford University Press, 1990), 79–95.

13. Dirk Hoerder, *Cultures in Contact: World Migrations in the Second Millennium* (Durham, N.C.: Duke University Press, 2002).

14. Ibid., 19–21.

15. Hoerder had studied letters, diaries, memoirs, and autobiographies of immigrants to Canada to understand their private lives: *Creating Societies: Immigrant Lives in Canada* (Montreal: McGill-Queen's University Press, 1999), 15–26.

16. See chap. 1. Dirk Hoerder, "Introduction," in *Distant Magnets: Expectations and Realities in the Immigrant Experience, 1840–1930,* ed. Hoerder and Horst Rössler (New York: Holmes and Meier, 1993), 12; Hoerder, "Segmented Macrosystems and Networking Individuals: The Balancing Functions of Migration Processes," in *Migration, Migration History, History: Old Paradigms and New Perspectives,* ed. Jan Lucassen and Leo Lucassen (Bern: Peter Land, 1999), 73–84; Hoerder, *Cultures in Contact,* 16–17; Dirk Hoerder, "An Introduction to Labor Migration in the Atlantic Economies," in *Labor Migration in the Atlantic Economies: The European and North American Working Classes During the Period of Industrialization,* ed. Hoerder (Westport, Conn.: Greenwood Press, 1985), 12.

17. James R. Barrett, "Americanization from the Bottom Up: Immigration and the Remaking of the Working Class in the United States, 1880–1930," *Journal of American History* 79 (December 1992): 996–1020; Gary Gerstle, "Liberty, Coercion, and the Making of Americans," *Journal of American History* 84 (September 1997): 524–58; Donna Gabaccia, "Liberty, Coercion, and the Making of Immigration Historians," *Journal of American History* 84 (September 1997): 570–75; James R. Barrett and David Roediger, "Inbetween Peoples: Race, Nationality and the 'New Immigrant' Working Class," *Journal of American Ethnic History* 16 (Spring 1997): 3–44; David Montgomery, "Racism, Immigrants, and Political Reform," *Journal of American History* 87 (March

2001): 1253–74; Donna Gabaccia and Fraser Ottanelli, eds., *Italian Workers of the World: Labor Migration and the Formation of Multiethnic States* (Urbana: University of Illinois Press, 2001); and Donna Gabaccia and Franca Iacovetta, eds., *Women, Gender, and Transnational Lives* (Toronto: University of Toronto Press, 2002).

18. Donna Gabaccia, "Is Everywhere Nowhere? Nomads, Nations, and the Immigrant Paradigm," *Journal of American History* 86 (December 1999): 1115–34; Dirk Hoerder, "Historians and Their Data: The Complex Shift from Nation-State Approaches to the Study of People's Transcultural Lives," *Journal of American Ethnic History* 25 (Summer 2006): 85–96, esp. 91–92; Elliott R. Barkan, "America in the Hand, Homeland in the Heart: Transnational and Translocal Immigrant Experiences in the American West," *Western Historical Quarterly* 35 (Autumn 2004): 331–54; Sherron P. Schwartz, "Bridging 'The Great Divide': The Evolution and Impact of Cornish Translocalism in Britain and the USA," *Journal of American Ethic History* 26 (Winter/Spring 2006): 171–89.

19. Loretta Baldassar, *Visits Home: Migration Experiences Between Italy and Australia* (Melbourne: Melbourne University Press, 2003), 1–4, 13. Donna Gabaccia makes a similar argument in "Weighing 'Diaspora' on the Scales of History," unpublished paper, cited courtesy of the author.

20. See the transnational correspondence of Elise Amalie Wærenskjold as cited in Barkan, "America in the Hand," 13.

21. Wendy Webster, "Transnational Journeys and Domestic Histories," *Journal of Social History* 39 (Spring 2006): 651–66.

22. Nancy L. Green, "The Comparative Method and Poststructural Structuralism—New Perspectives for Migration Studies," *Journal of American Ethnic History* 13 (Summer 1994): 3–22.

23. Jose C. Moya, *Cousins and Strangers: Spanish Immigrants in Buenos Aires, 1850–1930* (Berkeley: University of California Press, 1998), 404, 117–20, 128–30.

24. Ibid., 394.

25. Matthew Frye Jacobson, "More 'Trans-, Less National," *Journal of American Ethnic History* 25 (Summer 2006): 74–84, esp. 83.

26. Frank Thistlewaite's 1960 essay, "Migration from Europe Overseas in the Nineteenth and Twentieth Centuries," *Emigration and Immigration: The Old World Confronts the New,* ed. George E. Pozetta (New York: Garland, 1991), 630–58, is widely regarded as the precursor of global migration studies. Also see Thistlewaite, "The Atlantic Migration of the Pottery Industry," in *Emigration and Immigration,* ed. Pozetta, 614–29.

27. Marcel van der Linden, "Transnationalizing American Labor History," *Journal of American History* 86 (December 1999): 1078–92; "What Is the Problem? And How Can We Be Part of Its Solution?" *Labor History* 47 (November 2006): 566–70.

28. Jan Lucassen and Leo Lucassen, "Migration, Migration History, History: Old Paradigms and New Perspectives," in *Migration, Migration History, History,* ed. Lucassen and Lucassen, 9–20.

29. Barkan, "America in the Hand," 7.

30. Hedley Smith used broad West Yorkshire dialect, which included the term "fowk" throughout his fiction; Duncan Smith, emails to author, July 13, 14, 15, 2000.

31. Robin Cohen, *Global Diasporas: An Introduction* (Seattle: University of Washington Press, 1997), ix–xii and chap. 6, and Steven Vertovec and Robin Cohen, eds., *Migration, Disaporas and Transnationalism* (Cheltenham: Edward Elgar Publishing, 1999), xiii–xxvi, esp. xxi.

32. David H. Fischer, *Albion's Seed: Four British Folkways in America* (Cambridge: Cambridge University Press, 1989).

33. Charlotte Erickson, *Invisible Immigrants,* Erickson, *Leaving England: Essays on British Emigration in the Nineteenth Century* (Ithaca, N.Y.: Cornell University Press, 1994), and Rowland T. Berthoff, *British Immigrants in Industrial America, 1790–1950* (Cambridge: Harvard University Press, 1953), represented English immigrants as easily acculturated and thus "invisible." Berthoff's handling of Yorkshire immigrants in the textile industry is brief, 37–39, as is William E. Van Vugt's in *Britain to America: Mid-Nineteenth-Century Immigrants to the United States* (Urbana: University of Illinois Press, 1999), 63–66.

34. For British migration to the United States, see chap. 1.

35. Alejandro Portes and Rubén G. Rumbaut, *Immigrant American: A Portrait* (Berkeley: University of California Press, 1990), 106–7.

36. William E. Van Vugt, "British (English, Welsh, Scots, Scotch-Irish)," in *A Nation of Peoples: A Sourcebook on American's Multicultural Heritage,* ed. Elliott R. Barkan (Westport, Conn.: Greenwood Press, 1999), 75–95.

37. A. William Hoglund, "Celebrating Five Ethnic Groups in Rhode Island History," *Journal of American Ethnic History* 11 (Fall 1991): 81–86. Those five groups include the Irish, Germans, Portuguese, Jews, and Armenians but absent are English, Italians, Franco-Belgians, and French Canadians.

38. Paul Spickard, *Almost All Aliens: Immigration, Race, and Colonialism in American History and Identity* (London: Routledge, 2007), 176–80. Much labor history on British immigrants is unfortunately thus ignored.

39. Kathleen Neils Conzen, David A. Gerber, Ewa Morawska, George E. Pozetta, and Rudolph J. Vecoli, "The Invention of Ethnicity: A Perspective from the USA," *Journal of American Ethnic History* 12 (Fall 1992): 18–19; Bruno Ramirez, "Canada in the United States: Perspectives on Migration and Continental History," *Journal of American Ethnic History* 20 (Spring 2001): 50–71.

40. Gerber, *Authors of Their Lives,* 13–14, 24, pt. 2, esp. sections 8, 9.

41. On English immigrant conflicts with American culture, Richard Stott, "British Immigrants and the American Work Ethic in the Mid-Nineteenth Century," *Labor History* 26 (1985): 86–102; Mary H. Blewett, *Constant Turmoil: The Politics of Industrial Life in Nineteenth-Century New England* (Amherst: University of Massachusetts Press, 2000); Priscilla Long, *Where the Sun Never Shines: A History of America's Bloody Coal*

Industry (New York: Paragon House, 1991); and John H. M. Laslett, *Colliers Across the Sea: A Comparative Study of Class Formation in Scotland and the American Midwest, 1830–1924* (Urbana: University of Illinois Press, 2000).

42. R. W. Widdis, *With Scarcely a Ripple: Anglo-Canadian Migration into the US and Western Canada, 1880–1920* (Montreal: McGill-Queen's University Press, 1998), and "With Scarcely a Ripple: English Canadians in Northern New York State at the Beginning of the Twentieth Century," *Journal of Historical Geography* 13 (1987): 169–92, esp. 190.

43. Hoerder, *Creating Societies,* 284.

44. David Feldman and M. Page Baldwin, "Emigration and the British State, ca. 1815–1925," in *Citizenship and Those Who Leave,* ed. Green and Weil, 135–55, esp. 148.

45. Ethnic archives contain vast numbers of collections of unpublished immigrant memoirs and letters, but apparently little unpublished fiction in manuscript. The published and unpublished work remain the property of Portia S. Thompson, Wakefield, R.I., and of Duncan Smith, Department of German Studies, Brown University, Providence, R.I., and are quoted with their permission, as is the typescript of taped 1997 interview (hereafter 1997 interview) with Portia Thompson and Duncan Smith, Nov. 8, 1997, Wakefield, R.I. All form the collection of Hedley Smith at URI.

46. Donna Gabaccia, *From the Other Side: Women, Gender, and Immigrant Life in the U.S., 1820–1990* (Bloomington: Indiana University Press, 1994), 72–74; Donna Gabaccia and Franca Iacovetta, "Introduction," in *Women, Gender, and Transnational Lives,* ed. Gabaccia and Iacovetta, 30–33; Donna Gabaccia, "Immigrant Women: Nowhere At Home?" *Journal of American Ethnic History* 10 (Summer 1991): 68–71; Dirk Hoerder, "International Labor Markets and Community Building by Migrant Workers in the Atlantic Economies," in *A Century of European Migrations, 1830–1930,* ed. Rudolph Vecoli and Suzanne Sinke (Urbana: University of Illinois Press, 1991),107 n. 76.

47. Judith E. Smith, *Family Connections: A History of Italian and Jewish Immigrant Lives in Providence, Rhode Island, 1900–1940* (Albany: State University of New York: 1985), chap. 1.

48. Patricia R. Pessar and Sarah J. Mahler, "Transnational Migration: Bringing Gender In," *International Migration Review* 37 (Fall 2003): 812–47.

49. Hedley Smith, "Introduction," *The Yankee Yorkshireman* (Detroit: Harlo Press, 1970), 7.

50. Hedley Smith, interview, *Scituate [Rhode Island] Observer,* June 21, 1973.

51. Katharine W. Jones analyzed English identities as socially constructed and contested although often perceived as natural, in *Accent on Privilege: English Identities and Anglophilia in the United States* (Philadelphia: Temple University Press, 2001).

52. Rudolph Vecoli, "Comment: We Study the Present to Understand the Past," *Journal of American Ethnic History* 18 (Summer 1999): 115–25.

53. For example, Thomas Dublin, ed., *Immigrant Voices: New Lives in America,*

1773–1986 (Urbana: University of Illinois Press, 1993); Jon Gjerde, ed., *Major Problems in American Immigration and Ethnic History* (Boston: Houghton Mifflin, 1998); Roger Daniels, ed., *Coming to America: A History of Immigration and Ethnicity in American Life* (New York: Harper Perennial, 1991). For absence of English experience, Philip Butcher, ed., *The Ethnic Image in Modern American Literature, 1900–1950* (Washington, D.C.: Howard University Press, 1984), and Maria Mozziotti Gillan and Jennifer Gillan, eds., *Growing Up Ethnic in America: Contemporary Fiction about Learning to Be American* (New York: Penguin, 1999). The exception is Gabaccia, *From the Other Side*, 99–100.

54. Interview, *Scituate Observer*, June 21, 1973.

55. Baldassar, *Visits Home*, 3.

56. Russell A. Kazal, "Revisiting Assimilation: The Rise, Fall, and Reappraisal of a Concept in American Ethnic History," *American Historical Review* 100 (April 1995): 437–71, esp. 458–59.

57. Richard Alba and Victor Nee, *Remaking the American Mainstream: Assimilation and Contemporary Immigration* (Cambridge: Harvard University Press, 2003), 1–5, esp. 4.

58. Fischer, *Albion's Seed*, 35, 438–39, 809; Hedley Smith, "Sinner's Corner," undated, Smith Collection.

59. Rudolph J. Vecoli, "Comment," *Journal of American Ethnic History* 14 (Winter 1995): 76–81.

60. Blewett, *Constant Turmoil*, chaps. 4, 6, 7.

61. Conzen et al., "The Invention of Ethnicity," 3–41, esp. 17–19; David A. Gerber, *Making of an American Pluralism: Buffalo, New York, 1825–60* (Urbana: University of Illinois Press, 1989), 96–109.

62. Conzen et al., "The Invention of Ethnicity," passim.

63. Kazal, "Revisiting Assimilation," 457. Kazal, however, is critical of Bodnar's anticapitalist analysis as not distinctly American.

64. Kazal, "Assimilation Revisited," 458–61; Conzen et al., "The Invention of Ethnicity," on English invisibility, 6–8, 31–32. Elliott R. Barkan expressed similar concerns in "Race, Religion, and Nationality in American Society: A Model of Ethnicity from Contact to Assimilation," *Journal of American Ethnic History* 14 (Winter 1995): 38–76.

65. Eric Hobsbawn, "Introduction," in *The Invention of Tradition* (Cambridge: Cambridge University Press, 1983), 14; Benedict Anderson, *Imagined Communities: Reflections on the Origins and Spread of Nationalism*, rev. ed. (London: Verso, 1991), 192–93.

66. Barkan, "Race, Religion, and Nationality," 38–76. See a critique of this concept of core culture, Vecoli, "Comment," (1995), 76–81.

67. Elliott R. Barkan, "Introduction: Immigration, Incorporation, Assimilation and the Limits of Transnationalism," *Journal of American Ethnic History* 26 (Winter/Spring 2006): 7–32, esp. 8–12.

68. Ibid., on voting with the heart, 13.

69. Jones, *Accent on Privilege,* 45.

70. Jones saw this sense of superiority as a social construction in response to the undiscriminating Anglophilia of American society; ibid., 61–107.

71. Hoerder, *Cultures in Contact,* 9–10.

72. Werner Sollors, "Introduction," in *The Invention of Ethnicity,* ed. Sollors (New York: Oxford University Press, 1989), xiv; Karen Majewski, *Traitors and True Poles: Narrating a Polish-American Identity, 1880–1939* (Athens: Ohio University Press, 2003).

73. Interview, *Scituate Observer,* June 21, 1973.

74. Among these groups were German migrants who however for political reasons began to emphasize their status as "old stock" Americans after World War I; Russell A. Kazal, *Becoming Old Stock: The Paradox of German-American Identity* (Princeton, N.J.: Princeton University Press, 2004).

75. On Western and Northern European immigrants as defying the "new" and "old" categories, Maldwyn Jones, "The Background to Emigration from Great Britain in the Nineteenth Century," in *Perspectives in American History,* vol. 3, *Dislocations and Emigrations: The Social Background of American Immigration,* ed. Donald Fleming and Bernard Bailyn (Cambridge: Charles Warren Center, Harvard University, 1974), 53–54, 90–91, and Hoerder, "Migrant Workers in the Atlantic Economies," 79–80.

76. Bodnar, *The Transplanted,* 206–16, esp. 208–12.

77. Jon Gjerde, "New Growth on Old Vines, the State of the Field: The Social History of Immigration to and Ethnicity in the United States," *Journal of American Ethnic History* 18 (Summer 1999): 40–66.

Chapter 1. A Region of Movement and Change, 1650–1923

1. Peter Clark and Paul Slack, *English Towns in Transition, 1500–1700* (Oxford: Oxford University Press, 1976), 38–39, 46–49, 92.

2. Hoerder, "Introduction to Labor Migration," 4; Leslie Page Moch, *Moving Europeans: Migrations in Western Europe since 1650* (Bloomington: Indiana University Press, 1992), chap. 2; Steve Hochstadt, *Mobility and Modernity: Migration in Germany, 1820–1989* (Ann Arbor: University of Michigan Press, 1999), 35–46.

3. Family reconstitution research using seventeenth- and eighteenth-century ecclesiastical records in sixteen English parishes studied geographical mobility among married adults between 1550 and 1812; David Souden, "Movers and Stayers in Family Reconstitution Populations," *Local Population Studies* 33 (1984): 11–28, esp. 23.

4. Stephen King, "Migrants on the Margin? Mobility, Integration and Occupations in the West Riding, 1650–1820," *Journal of Historical Geography* 23 (July 1997): 284–303; Christine S. Hallas, "Migration in Nineteenth-Century Wensleydale and Swaledale," *Northern History* 27 (1991): 139–61.

5. Riding is the Yorkshire name for an administrative district. There is no South

Riding. John Langton, "The Industrial Revolution and the Regional Geography of England," *Transactions of the Institute of British Geography* 9 (1984): 145–67.

6. Pat Hudson, *The Genesis of Industrial Capital: A Study of the West Riding Wool Textile Industry c. 1750–1850* (Cambridge: Cambridge University Press, 1986), 259–62.

7. Eric M. Sigsworth, *The Black Dyke Mills: A History* (Liverpool: Liverpool University Press, 1958), 1–10, 63. Norwich mills paid both transport and import duties for coal from Newcastle (14–15).

8. A. G. Walker, "Migration into a South Yorkshire Colliery District, 1861–81," *Northern History* 29 (1993): 165–84; Moch, *Moving Europeans,* 142–43; Hoerder, "Introduction to Labor Migration," 4–7; Sigsworth, *Black Dyke Mills,* 60–62.

9. Phyllis Bentley, *The Rise of Henry Morcar* (London: Pan Books, 1968), 207.

10. Gary Firth, "The Bradford Trade in the Nineteenth Century," in *Victorian Bradford: Essays in Honour of Jack Reynolds,* ed. D. G. Wright and J. A. Jowitt (Bradford: City of Bradford Metropolitan Council, 1982), 8; Sigsworth, *Black Dyke Mills,* 34, 62–68.

11. Jack Reynolds, *The Great Paternalist: Titus Salt and the Growth of Nineteenth-Century Bradford* (New York: St. Martin's Press, 1983), 50–54; "The Affairs of Sir Titus Salt, Bart., Sons and Co. Limited," *TM,* Sept. 15, 1892, 397; Firth, "The Bradford Trade," 15.

12. "A West Riding Love Story (1766)," in Phyllis Bentley, *Love and Money: Seven Tales of the West Riding* (New York: Macmillan, 1957), 89–116.

13. Jonathan Smith, "The Strike of 1825," in *Victorian Bradford,* ed. Wright and Jowitt, 63–66.

14. Leslie Page Moch in *Moving Europeans* cited the examples of early nineteenth-century deindustrialization in English and Scottish handloom cotton and in Irish and Flemish handloom linen production as well as in the woolen cities of Auffray and Roubaix in France, 115–36, esp. 115–20.

15. Smith, "The Strike of 1825," 66–67, 72–73.

16. Phyllis Bentley, *Inheritance* (London: Victor Gollancz Ltd., 1932), 29, 44.

17. Theodore Koditschek, *Class Formation and Urban Industrial Society: Bradford, 1750–1850* (Cambridge: Cambridge University Press, 1990), 85, 471–75, esp. 471; Smith, "The Strike of 1825," passim; Firth, "The Bradford Trade," 69–76, 12–13.

18. Koditschek, *Class Formation and Urban Industrial Society,* 475–82, esp. 482.

19. Karl Ittmann, *Work, Gender and Family* (New York: New York University Press 1995), 44–45; Koditschek, *Class Formation and Urban Industrial Society,* 85; Tony Jowitt, "The Retardation of Trade Unionism in the Yorkshire Worsted Textile Industry," in *Employers and Labour in the English Textile Industries, 1850–1939,* ed. J. A. Jowitt and A. J. McIvor (London: Routledge, 1988), 95; Sigsworth, *Black Dyke Mills,* 41–43; Ittmann, *Work, Gender and Family,* 55–56.

20. J. W. Jowett, "Bradford Seventy Years Ago," foreword to Fenner Brockway, *Socialism Over Sixty Years: The Life of Jowett of Bradford (1864–1944)* (London: George

Allen and Unwin, 1946), 17; Koditschek, *Class Formation and Urban Industrial Society,* 353–63.

21. Amy Bainbridge, letter to Portia Thompson, c. 1980, courtesy Portia Thompson.

22. Ittmann, *Work, Gender and Family,* 19, 54, 113.

23. Portia Thompson, email to author, Feb. 22, 2005.

24. John Hartley, *Yorkshire Lyrics* (London: W. Nicholson, 1898), 43–45.

25. All figures from Table 1.1 in Ittmann, *Work, Gender and Family,* 19 and 17–20; see also 54. Tony Jowitt, "Late Victorian and Edwardian Bradford," in *The Centennial History of the Independent Labour Party,* ed. David James, Tony Jowitt, and Keith Laybourn (Halifax: Ryburn Academic Publishing, 1992), 97; Jowitt, "Retardation," in *Employers and Labour,* ed. Jowitt and McIvor, 102, 87, and 90–91, Table 5.4.

26. Dracupp, with the double *p,* is the seventeenth-century spelling of this name.

27. Portia Thompson, emails to author, Oct. 18 and 30, 2005.

28. Hudson, *Genesis of Industrial Capital,* table 3.7 and p. 82.

29. C. Richardson, "Irish Settlement in Mid-Nineteenth-Century Bradford," *Yorkshire Bulletin of Economic and Social Research* 20 (May 1968): 40–57; Jowett, "Bradford Seventy Years Ago," 13, quoted in Brockway, *Socialism Over Sixty Years,* 26.

30. Sigsworth, *Black Dyke Mills,* 63–64, 73; Ittmann, *Work, Gender and Family,* 102–3. Bradford Parish then included the townships of Horton, Manningham, and Bowling. Firth, "The Bradford Trade," 14; Ittmann, *Work, Gender and Family,* 14.

31. Moch, *Moving Europeans,* 133; Sigsworth, *Black Dyke Mills,* 67–68; Richardson, "Irish Settlement," 41, 43, 46–47, 49, 53, 55–56. For patterns of reactions to labor migrants, see Hoerder, "Introduction to Labor Migration," 12.

32. Family tree provided by Portia Thompson in the author's possession. Portia Thompson, email to author, Jan. 12, 2006; Bainbridge, letter to Thompson, c. 1980.

33. J. B. Priestley, "Preface" to Brockway, *Socialism Over Sixty Years,* 10.

34. Roger Davis Simon, "The Birds of Passage in America, 1865–1914," M.A. thesis, University of Wisconsin, 1966, 4–5; Thompson, emails to author, Oct. 18 and 30, 2005.

35. Hudson, *Genesis of Industrial Capital,* table 3.8, 83; Ittmann, *Work, Gender and Family,* 149–52; Hoerder, "Introduction to Labor Migration," 9, 19.

36. R. Rollins, "The Jewish Contribution to the British Textile Industry: Builders of Bradford," *Transactions of the Jewish Historical Society of England* 42 (1951–52): 45–51; Adam McKeown, "Global Migration, 1846–1940," *Journal of World History* 15 (June 2004): 155–89, esp. 163; Sigsworth, *Black Dyke Mills,* 65–66; David Russell, "The Pursuit of Leisure," in *Victorian Bradford,* ed. Wright and Jowitt, 216–17; J. B. Priestley, *English Journey* (New York: Harper and Brothers, 1934), 126.

37. Rollins, "Jewish Contribution to British Textile Industry," 47–48.

38. Clare Delius, *Frederick Delius: Memories of My Brother* (London: Ivor Nicholson and Watson, 1935), 13–69, 196–97.

39. Priestley, *English Journey,* 126–27.

40. "The Tongue-Tied Town," and "The Lion and the Eagle," unpublished novels. Duncan Smith had personal memories of connections between Bradford and Halle; email to author, Jan. 3, 2006.

41. Hoerder, "Introduction to Labor Migration," 22.

42. By then Great Horton had become a section of the city of Bradford. Obituaries, Joseph Benn, *BO,* Aug. 23, 1897; Harrison Benn, *Bradford Telegraph, Yorkshire Observer,* July 25, 1921.

43. "The History of Beck Mill, Clayton, 1845–1926," typescript, Bradford Public Library, 1985.

44. *TM,* March 15, 1896, 109.

45. Sigsworth, *Black Dyke Mills,* 72–73.

46. Jowitt, "Retardation of Trade Unionism," 96–97.

47. Compared with other West Riding towns, Bradford in 1851 had few domestic servants; Adrian Elliott, "Social Structure in the Mid-Nineteenth Century," in *Victorian Bradford,* ed. Wright and Jowitt, 104–7.

48. On middle-class formation in Bradford, see Koditschek, *Class Formation and Urban Industrial Society,* pt. 2.

49. Eric Ford, "Phyllis Bentley: Novelist of Yorkshire Life," *Contemporary Review* 270 (February 1997): 89–94.

50. Phyllis Bentley, *A Modern Tragedy* (New York: Macmillan, 1934), and *Ring in the New* (London: Victor Gollancz, 1969).

51. Phyllis Bentley, *O Dreams, O Destinations* (New York: Macmillan, 1962), 34, 79, 83, 134, 141–55, 213–14.

52. Deirdre Busfield, "Skill and the Sexual Division of Labour in the West Riding Textile Industry, 1850–1914," in *Employers and Labour,* ed. Jowitt and McIvor, 154–56.

53. Joanna Bornat, "Lost Leaders: Women, Trade Unionism and the Case of the General Union of Textile Workers, 1875–1914," in *Unequal Opportunities: Women's Employment in England, 1800–1918,* ed. Angela V. John (Oxford: Basil Blackwell: 1986), 211; on opposition to working wives, 222–27.

54. Ittmann, *Work, Gender, and Family,* 141–64. For the quote and the general acceptance of paternalism along the lines of Saltaire in the West Riding, D. James, "Paternalism in Mid-Nineteenth Century Keighley," 104–19, esp. 107, and R. Reynolds, "Reflections on Saltaire," 43–72, in *Model Industrial Communities in Mid-Nineteenth Century Yorkshire,* ed. J. A. Jowitt (Bradford: University of Bradford, 1986).

55. James Lawson, *Letters to the Young on Progress in Pudsey During the Last Sixty Years* (Stanningley: J. W. Birdsall, Yorkshire Printing and Publishing Works, 1887), 35–36; Reynolds, "Reflections on Saltaire," 46–50, 55; Reynolds, *The Great Paternalist,* 276–77; Patrick Joyce, *Work, Society and Politics: The Culture of the Factory in Later Victorian England* (Brighton: Harvester Press, 1980).

56. Sian Moore, "Women, Industrialization and Protest in Bradford, West Yorkshire, 1780–1845," Ph.D. diss., University of Essex, 1986, 61; Frank Mott, *Dangerous*

Sexualities: Medico-Moral Politics in England since 1830 (London: Routledge and Kegan Paul, 1987), 47–49; Bainbridge, letter to Thompson, c. 1980.

57. Hedley Smith, "The Mill Folk," unpublished novel, 28–37. See chap. 4, and Mary Blewett, "Yorkshire Lasses and Their Lads: Sexuality, Sexual Customs, and Gender Antagonisms in an Anglo-American Working-Class Culture," *Journal of Social History* 40 (Winter 2006): 317–36.

58. Patricia Knight, "Women and Abortion in Victorian and Edwardian England," *History Workshop* 4 (Autumn 1977): 57–70; Bornat, "Lost Leaders," 211, 222–27. James Hammerton's *Cruelty and Companionship: Conflict in Nineteenth-Century Married Life* (London: Routledge, 1992) questioned the relevance of women's status as wage earners to the recurrent patterns of sexual antagonism in marriage (17–22).

59. Busfield, "Skill and the Sexual Division of Labour," 154–56.

60. Ittmann, *Work, Gender and Family*, 152 n. 56, 230–35. Also see Diana Gittins, *The Fair Sex: Family Size and Structure in Britain, 1900–1939* (New York: St. Martin's, 1982), 87–94, 158–65.

61. Elizabeth K. Blackburn, *In and Out the Windows: A Story of the Changes in Working Class Life 1902–1977 in a Small East Lancashire Community* (Burnley: privately published, 1978), 21; Portia Thompson, email to Duncan Smith, June 30, 2005.

62. Ittmann, *Work, Gender and Family*, 202–22, 234–35; Wally Seccombe, "Starting to Stop: Working-Class Fertility Decline in Britain," *Past and Present* 126 (1990): 151–88.

63. Jowitt, "Retardation of Trade Unionism," 102.

64. Sigsworth, *Black Dyke Mills*, 73–88, 93, 325; Firth, "The Bradford Trade," 13, 24; Portia Thompson, email to author, Aug. 13, 2000.

65. Sigsworth, *Black Dyke Mills*, 240–43; William Cudworth, *Rambles Round Horton* (Bradford: Thomas Brear, 1886), 1–2.

66. *TM*, Jan. 15, 1891, 38; Firth, "The Bradford Trade," 27; Jowitt, "Late Victorian and Edwardian Bradford," 98; Sigsworth, *Black Dyke Mills*, 100 and 102–10.

67. Carl Strikwerda, "Tides of Migration, Currents of History: The State, Economy, and the Transatlantic Movement of Labor in the Nineteenth and Twentieth Centuries," *International Review of Social History* 44 (1999): 367–94.

68. For the tariff schedules, *BO*, Dec. 15, 1890; *TM*, vol. 16 (January to December 1890), Oct. 15, 1890, 470, 491–92, 498.

69. The exact percentages of the wage reductions were much debated; *YFT*, Dec. 19, 1891.

70. Bornat, "Lost Leaders," 216–18; Mary H. Blewett, "Diversities of Class and Gender Experience and the Shaping of Labor Politics: Yorkshire's Manningham Mills Strike, 1890–1891 and the Independent Labour Party," *Labor History* 47 (November 2006): 511–35; Blewett, *Constant Turmoil*, chaps. 3, 4; Donald B. Cole, *Immigrant City: Lawrence Massachusetts, 1845–1921* (Chapel Hill: University of North Carolina Press, 1963), 43.

71. *YFT*, Feb. 6, 20, 27, March 6, 20, 27, April 3, 1891; *BO*, April 28, 1891.

72. *YFT*, June 5, 1891.

73. *TM*, Sept. 15, 1892, 397; Titus Salt, Bart, Sons & Co, Ltd., *Saltaire, Yorkshire England: A Sketch History* (Saltaire: Sr. Titus Salt, Sons and Co. Ltd., 1895), 19–20.

74. *TM*, Sept. 15, 1892, 411.

75. *TM*, March 15, 1892, 124; April 15, 1892, 173, 154–56; Jan. 15, 1893, 21; Dec. 15, 1893, 551; Jan. 15, 1894, 22–23; May 15, 1894, 215; Sept. 15, 1894, 373; Jan. 15, 1895, 2; Aug. 15, 1897, 309–10; Nov. 15, 1897, 425–27; July 15, 1898, 242; July 15, 1901, 218.

76. Sigsworth, *Black Dyke Mills*, 109–12, esp. 109–10, 321–23, 235–40, 124–29, 133; J. B. Priestley, *Margin Released: Reminiscences and Reflections* (London: Reprint Society Ltd., 1963), 14.

77. For example, Daniels, *Coming to America*.

78. Marcus Lee Hansen, *The Immigrant in American History* (New York: Harper and Row, 1964), 168–72.

79. Jones, "Background to Emigration," 3–94, esp. 53–54, 90–91. For the data used by Jones, which excluded Scottish emigration and Irish residents in England, Stanley C. Johnson, *A History of Emigration from the United Kingdom to North America, 1763–1912* (London: George Routledge and Sons, 1913), 344–48.

80. Blewett, *Constant Turmoil*, 357.

81. Jones, "The Background to Emigration," 53–54, 90–91; Dudley Baines, *Migration in a Mature Economy: Emigration and Internal Migration in England and Wales, 1861–1900* (Cambridge: Cambridge University Press, 1985); Walter Nugent, *Crossings: The Great Transatlantic Migrations, 1870–1914* (Bloomington: Indiana University Press, 1992), 48; Simon, "The Birds of Passage in America," 4–5. Hoerder relied on Nugent's work for *Cultures in Contact*, 336–38; see also 339.

82. Johnson, *A History of Emigration*, 346.

83. Baines, *Migration in a Mature Economy*, 2–3, 45–52, 59, 77, 88–89; Nugent, *Crossings*, 44–48.

84. Baines, *Migration in a Mature Economy*, 80, 134, 139, 205–6, 263–64, 280, 282; on Charlotte Erickson's work on American ship lists, 82–83. Baines viewed these decisions as "economically rational behavior" (139, emphasis his). On the scarcity of literary evidence for women migrants, see Charlotte Erickson, *English Women Immigrants in America in the Nineteenth Century: Expectations and Reality* (London: LLRS Publications, 1983).

85. Baines, *Migration in a Mature Economy*, 87; Erickson, *Leaving England*, 32; Stott, "British Immigrants and the American Work Ethic," 86–102.

86. Brinley Thomas, *Migration and Economic Growth: A Study of Great Britain and the Atlantic Economy* (Cambridge: Cambridge University Press, 1954), 30–31, 35–55, 92–113, 118–22.

87. Thomas cited the findings of the 1911 Immigration Commission on the "racial" shift in the U.S. textile workforce in *Migration and Economic Growth*, 146–47; see also 68–72.

88. Duncan Smith, email to author, April 3, 2007. Duncan Smith recalled letters written by Alice to her husband, Ernest, as "rather tender especially for a Yorkshire-women."

89. Copy of photograph of Ernest, Alice and Hedley Smith, Aberdeen Place, Bradford, c. 1922–23, courtesy Portia Thompson.

90. H Smith to "Dear Tom," Jan. 20, 1921, copy in the hands of the author. The first diary was destroyed.

91. "Isle of Man Diary," 1922 manuscript copy in possession of author.

92. Felicity Harrison, email to author, Dec. 19, 2005.

93. The whole story was revealed decades later in Hedley Smith to Bruce Lindsay (hereafter Hedley Smith to Lindsay), April 5, 1979.

94. Ship's Manifest, SS *Winifredian,* Liverpool, Sept. 26, 1923, 276, copy courtesy of Portia Thompson.

95. Hoerder, *Cultures in Contact,* 21.

96. Feldman and Baldwin, "Emigration and the British State," 135, 148–51.

97. The highest rates of illiteracy were among migrants from southeastern Europe; Robert A. Divine, *American Immigration Policy, 1924–1952* (New York: Da Capo Press, 1972), 5.

98. Darrell Hevenor Smith and H. Guy Herring, *The Bureau of Immigration: Its History, Activities, and Organization* (Baltimore: Johns Hopkins University Press, 1974). This volume contains a compilation of immigration legislation from 1882 to 1923.

99. Keith Fitzgerald in *The Face of the Nation: Immigration, the State, and the National Identity* (Stanford, Calif.: Stanford University Press, 1996), argued that the legislation in 1917 "formalized a new national state sector" (128–29). Daniel J. Tichenor regarded the restrictions in the legislation as a "crucial breakthrough for nativists": *Dividing Lines: The Politics of Immigration Control in America* (Princeton, N.J.: Princeton University Press, 2002), 21.

100. Maldwyn Jones, *American Immigration* (Chicago: University of Chicago Press, 1960), 268–77; George M. Stephenson, *A History of American Immigration, 1820–1924* (New York: Russell and Russell, 1964), 175–88; Divine, *American Immigration Policy,* 5–18.

101. The exact number of aliens to be admitted to the United States annually was determined jointly by the State Department, the Secretary of Commerce, and the Secretary of Labor; Smith and Herring, *Bureau of Immigration,* 209.

102. Thomas, *Migration and Economic Growth,* 191–93.

103. Hedley Smith, "Sinners Corner," unpublished novel, 3.

104. Citing Erickson, Berthoff, and Vugt's work, Gerber, *Authors of Their Lives,* 16.

105. Hedley Smith to Lindsay, April 5, 1979.

106. These procedures are listed in section 3 of the 1917 Immigration Act; Smith and Herring, *Bureau of Immigration,* 181. In part, "persons hereinafter called contract

laborers, who have been induced, assisted, encouraged, or solicited to migrate to this country by offers or promises of employment, whether such offers or promises are true or false, or in consequence of agreements, oral, written, or printed, express or implied, to perform labor in this country of any kind, skilled or unskilled." For fines, 103–4, and sec. 6 of the extension of the 1921 act, 210–11.

107. McKeown, "Global Migration," 173.

108. Hedley Smith, "The Millmaster," unpublished novel, 180–81.

109. The contract labor law, the Foran Act, had been in place since 1885, but apparently no one tipped Ernest Smith off to conceal the agreement with his friend. My thanks to Walter Hickey, National Archives, Waltham, Massachusetts.

110. Hedley Smith to Lindsay, April 5, 1979.

111. 1997 interview; Portia Thompson, emails to author, Feb. 2, 2002, and Nov. 19, 2005.

112. Duncan Smith, email to author, Nov. 2, 2006.

113. Hedley Smith to Lindsay, Aug. 7, 1979.

114. Mary H. Blewett, *The Last Generation: Work and Life in the Textile Mills of Lowell, Massachusetts, 1910–1960* (Amherst: University of Massachusetts Press, 1990).

115. Duncan Smith to author, Nov. 2, 2006.

116. Copies of photograph of Hedley Smith, December 1923, and letter of recommendation, M. Denby, Headmaster, Grange Road Secondary School, City of Bradford Education Committee, Sept. 24, 1923, courtesy Portia Thompson.

117. 1997 interview.

118. Strikwerda, "Tides of Migration," 367–94, esp. 371.

119. Berthoff, *British Immigrants in Industrial America,* 37–39, 73, 95.

Chapter 2. Migrations of Capital, Industry, and People

1. *William Smith, A Yorkshireman's Trip to the United States and Canada* (London: Longmans, Green and Co., 1892), 5, 129–32, 169–71; TM, Feb. 15, 1891, 81; March 15, 1891, 134; May 15, 1892, 194.

2. Moch, *Moving Europeans,* 132–36.

3. For Sigsworth, Derek Aldcroft, *The Development of British Industry and Foreign Competition, 1875–1914* (Toronto: Toronto University Press, 1968), 134–39.

4. Gary Gerstle, *Working-Class Americanism: The Politics of Labor in a Textile City, 1914–1960* (Cambridge: Cambridge University Press, 1989); Richard Dobson Margrave, *The Emigration of Silk Workers from England to the United States in the Nineteenth Century* (New York: Garland, 1986); Sven Beckart, "Migration, Ethnicity, and Working-Class Formation: Passaic, New Jersey, 1889–1926," in *People in Transit: German Migrations in Comparative Perspective, 1820–1930,* ed. Dirk Hoerder and Jorg Nagler (Cambridge: Cambridge University Press, 1995), 347–77.

5. Gerstle, *Working-Class Americanism,* 61–78; Ken Fones-Wolf, "Transatlantic Craft Migrations and Transnational Spaces: Belgian Window Glass Workers in America, 1880–1920," *Labor History* 45 (August 2004): 299–321.

6. *Providence Board of Trade Journal,* March 1907, 27–28; *American Wool and Cotton Reporter,* July 31, 1911, 31.

7. Interview, *Scituate Observer,* June 21, 1973; *Providence Board of Trade Journal,* June 1911, 285–99.

8. John S. Gilkeson, *Middle-Class Providence, 1820–1940* (Princeton: Princeton University Press, 1986), 109–11; Blewett, *Constant Turmoil,* 225–38, 312; William Kirk, ed., *A Modern City: Providence, Rhode Island, and Its Activities* (Chicago: University of Chicago Press, 1909), 84–85. For an overview of Providence and its growing immigrant population, 1870–1940, see Smith, *Family Connections,* chap. 1.

9. *Wool and Cotton Reporter,* June 29, 1905, 16–17; *Wade's Fibre and Fabric,* Jan. 7, 1905, 5.

10. On the American Woolen Company's presence in Rhode Island, *Fibre and Fabric,* Dec. 10 and 23, 1905, 9 and 8, respectively, and *Providence Board of Trade Journal* 23 (June 1911): 285–92.

11. Little is known about the competing market strategies of the German-owned Botany and Forstmann and Huffmann Companies in Passaic and the American Woolen Company in Lawrence.

12. Those states in the 1903 Census of Manufacturing were in rank order New York, Connecticut, Maine, New Jersey, New Hampshire, and Vermont; see *Immigrants in Industries,* pt. 4: *Woolen and Worsted Goods Manufacturing* (1911; reprint, New York: Arno Press, 1970), 639–40.

13. Ibid., 640–41. No English families appeared in the detailed analysis of 440 households with woolen or worsted mill operatives, but in the study of 24.4 percent of the total U.S. workforce, English-born male and female employees appeared in significant numbers (641–47).

14. The report listed 623, 402, and 10 Italian migrants in Providence, Lawrence, and Philadelphia respectively; *Immigrants in Industry,* 649–52.

15. Ibid., 660, 665–66.

16. "Racial Displacements," in ibid., 745–46; *Immigrants in Industry,* 749–50, 752–53; Ardis Cameron, *Radicals of the Worst Sort: Laboring Women in Lawrence, Massachusetts, 1860–1912* (Urbana: University of Illinois Press, 1993), 120.

17. For quotes, Cole, *Immigrant City,* 43.

18. Cole did not have access to this newspaper, which was recently found in the Essex Institute, Salem, Mass.; Blewett, *Constant Turmoil,* 129–30.

19. Rare Books, Concord Public Library, Concord, Mass.; Blewett, *Constant Turmoil,* 128–30; Cole, *Immigrant City,* 43, 140–46.

20. "An English Village in Rhode Island," *Providence Sunday Tribune,* Dec. 15, 1912. For comparative data on capital assets, *The Blue Book, United States and Canada* (New York: Davison Publishing Co.), annual volumes for 1905–39. The Benn Company closed its Rhode Island operations in 1939 and left no business records except for those in the trust documents of William Harrison Benn, Bradford Archives. During World War II English business paper was often recycled for other uses.

21. *Fibre and Fabric,* June 18, 1904, 6–7; Nov. 19, 1904, 12; Feb. 25, 1905, 12; March 15, 1905, 12; *Wool and Cotton Reporter,* Feb. 18, 1904, 17; Oct. 27, 1904, 15; Gary Kulik and Julia C. Bonham, *Rhode Island: An Inventory of Historic Engineering and Industrial Sites* (Washington, D.C.: U.S. Department of the Interior, 1978), 130. On the construction of the Greystone mill, *Fibre and Fabric,* June 18, 1904, 6–7, and Nov. 19, 1904, 12; *Yorkshire Daily Observer,* Nov. 4, 1904.

22. Hedley Smith sketched a verbal landscape of Briardale village in "Yankee Yorkshire Yesterdays," unpublished introduction, 1–10.

23. On the use of streetcar lines for commuting from the Italian enclave of Federal Hill in Providence, see Smith, *Family Connections,* 38.

24. Smith, "Yankee Yorkshire Yesterdays," 2; *Providence Sunday Tribune,* Dec. 15, 1912.

25. *Yorkshire Daily Observer,* Nov. 4, 1904. This practice is depicted in Smith's "The Mill Folk."

26. Manuscript on microfilm, U.S. Census of Population, 1910 Greystone Village in the town of North Providence, R.I., households 151 and 134.

27. Thomas, *Migration and Economic Growth,* 64–67; *Wool and Cotton Reporter,* July 6, 1905, 30–31.

28. U.S. Census of 1910, household 157; Evelyn Savidge Sterne, *Ballots and Bibles: Ethnic Politics and the Catholic Church in Providence* (Ithaca, N.Y.: Cornell University Press, 2004), 195–201.

29. Smith, "King George's Idea," in *More Yankee Yorkshiremen,* 86.

30. Smith, "The Mill Folk," 22–23.

31. Ibid., 26.

32. Smith, "The Tongue-Tied Town," unpublished novel, 14–15. Smith's novel "Pea Wally" listed in his 1986 canon has been lost.

33. "An English Village in Rhode Island"; obituary, *Wool and Cotton Reporter,* July 1921, 39. Many of the structures in Greystone are still standing: the Social Club, the Greystone Primitive Methodist chapel, mill row houses, the war memorial, and the mill itself; photographs taken in 2006, courtesy of Portia Thompson.

34. *Providence Sunday Tribune,* Dec. 15, 1912. Also see Thomas Dobson, "Life in Greystone as Recalled by Rebecca (Grimshaw) Bullough's Son," posted February 2005, James and Rebecca Grimshaw Bullough, www.grimshaworigin.org.

35. *Providence Board of Trade Journal,* June 1911, 285. The feature story in the *Providence Sunday Tribune* on Dec. 15, 1912, includes (among others) photographs of the Whitehall Building, site of the Greystone Social Club, and the Workingmen's Club, and of school pupils and their teacher. The village was governed by the town of North Providence.

36. Frank C. Angell, *Annals of Centredale, 1636–1909* (Central Falls, R.I.: E. L. Freeman Co., 1909), 62–65; *Providence Sunday Tribune,* Dec. 15, 1912.

37. *Providence Sunday Tribune,* Dec. 15, 1912; Dobson, "Life in Greystone."

38. Smith, "The Millmaster," 7; "The Conscience of Mr. King," in *The Yankee Yorkshireman,* 13–30.

39. Smith, "Miriam Ainsworth," unpublished novella, 12–13; "The Black Sheep," in *The Yankee Yorkshireman,* 72–73.

40. Moya, *Cousins and Strangers,* 401, 404, 327–31.

41. Table on the Census of 1910. These are in District 105 which lists part of Greystone village and part of Centredale; District 112 also lists part of Greystone village and part of Centredale.

42. *Providence Board of Trade Journal* 23 (June 1911): 285. One young woman of twenty-two, Lucy Evans, Boarder, was listed as a "Wool Sorter": no women were ever trained as wool sorters; Census of 1910, household 54.

43. Telephone conversation with Walter Hickey, Archivist, National Archives, Waltham, Mass.; Census of 1910, household 49.

44. Feldman and Baldwin, *Emigration and the British State,* 145–46.

45. Moya regarded community institutions as smoothing the immigrants' way into the new society. Strikes are not listed in the index, but the politics of anarchism caused some conflicts between immigrants; *Cousins and Strangers,* 400.

46. The Benn Company never revealed even its total workforce to the *Davidson's Blue Book* directory, much less the breakdown of employees in each department. Rhode Island state officials did not press industries to reveal the composition of their workforces. For background to this labor unrest among English immigrants, see Paul Buhle, "The Knights of Labor in Rhode Island," *Radical History Review* 17 (Spring 1978): 39–73.

47. *PJ,* Nov. 23, 1912. Also see CIS, *Twentieth Annual Report* (Providence, 1907), 11. In the Census of 1910, three women were listed as "minder" [mender], "burler," and "stitcher," see households 8, 31, and 79.

48. *BO,* Jan. 1, 1907.

49. Ibid., Feb. 19, 1907.

50. *YFT,* Feb. 22, 1907. The letter writer used both "Bradferd" and "Bradford." Dialect, a verbal medium, is seldom written down except in poetry or fiction or dictionaries.

51. CIS, *Twenty-second Annual Report* (1908), 604–5; CIS, *Twenty-fourth Annual Report* (1911), 272, 277–79, 286. In 1911 the Greystone mill officially employed 1,400 "hands" (the Yorkshire term for mill worker), *Providence Board of Trade Journal* 23 (June 1911): 285.

52. Census of 1910, households 153 and 163.

53. *Bulletin of the National Association of Wool Manufacturers* 40 (1910): 252–54. On Benn's lobbying activities, *Wool and Cotton Reporter,* Oct. 12, 1911, 21, and Nov. 9, 1911, 9. Also see obituaries of Harrison Benn, *Bulletin of the National Association of Wool Manufacturers* 51 (1921): 469, and *Wool and Cotton Reporter,* July 28, 1921, 39.

54. Herbert G. Gutman, *Work, Culture and Society in Industrializing America: Essay in American Working-Class and Social History* (New York: Vintage, 1977), 25 n. 19; Herbert Gutman with Ira Berlin, "Class Composition and the Development of the American Working Class, 1840–1890," in Herbert G. Gutman, *Power and Culture: Essays on the American Working Class,* ed. Ira Berlin (New York: New Press, 1987), 380–94. On Gutman see Blewett, *Constant Turmoil,* 5–8.

55. Blewett, *Constant Turmoil*; Laslett, *Colliers Across the Sea*; David Brundage, "Irish Land and American Workers' Class and Ethnicity in Denver, Colorado," in *"Struggle a Hard Battle": Essays on Working-Class Immigrants*, ed. Dirk Hoerder (DeKalb: Northern Illinois University Press, 1996), 46–67; Horst Rössler, "English Labor, Working-Class Culture and Migration" in *Labor Migration in the Atlantic Economies*, ed. Hoerder, 59–84, esp. 78.

56. David Jeremy and Charlotte Erickson argued that most British immigrants to the United States were technically obsolete hand weavers, David J. Jeremy, *Transatlantic Industrial Revolution: The Diffusion of Textile Technologies Between Britain and America, 1790–1830* (Cambridge: MIT Press, 1981), and Erickson, *Invisible Immigrants*. Jeremy did give credit both to skilled English immigrants who arrived even before Samuel Slater (see 15–18). Primarily interested in the issue of technology transfer, Jeremy insisted that most English immigrants from Lancashire did not fit well into American-style mills and, even worse, they had brought unsuitable political ideas with them, such as trades unions (169–75).

57. On pre–Civil War emigration, see Berthoff, *British Immigrants in Industrial America*, 30–31.

58. Caroline F. Ware, *Early New England Cotton Manufacture* (New York: Russell and Russell, 1966), 203–9; Philip Scranton, *Proprietary Capitalism: The Textile Manufacture at Philadelphia, 1800–1885* (Philadelphia: Temple University Press, 1983), 93–95, 142; Cynthia Shelton, *The Mills of Manayunk: Industrialization and Social Conflict in the Philadelphia Region, 1787–1837* (Baltimore: Johns Hopkins University Press, 1986); Berthoff, *British Immigrants in Industrial America*, 31, 37–41, 45.

59. David Zonderman, "Foreign Pioneers: Immigrants and the Mechanized Factory System in Antebellum New England," in *Work, Recreation, and Culture: Essays in American Labor History*, ed. Martin H. Blatt and Martha K. Norkunas (New York: Garland, 1996), 163–81; Blewett, *Constant Turmoil*, chap. 3; Ray Boston, *British Chartists in America, 1839–1900* (Totowa, N.J.: Rowman and Littlefield, 1971), appendix A, 88–97; H. I. Dutton and J. E. King, *Ten Percent and No Surrender: The Preston Strike, 1853–54* (Cambridge: Cambridge University Press, 1981), 67.

60. Charlotte Erickson, "The Encouragement of Emigration by British Trade Unions, 1850–1900," *Population Studies* 3 (1949): 248–73; "Lowell Loom," *American Workman*, June 26, 1869.

61. *London Times*, May 5, 1869, as quoted in *PJ*, May 14, 1869; Rössler, "English Labor, Working-Class Culture and Migration," 73–78. The legal word "willfully" was inserted at the last minute into the legislation and finally struck from the act in 1879; Blewett, *Constant Turmoil*, 133–34, 248–49.

62. *Lawrence Journal*, June 11, 1874.

63. *Fall River News*, Feb. 19, 1875. This agitation included a long-term struggle between the mule spinners and the weavers over strategy and tactics, Blewett, *Constant Turmoil*, chaps. 6–9.

64. Berthoff, *British Immigrants in Industrial America*, 38–39.

65. On the American Woolen Company in Rhode Island, *Fibre and Fabric,* Dec. 10 and 23, 1905, 9 and 8 respectively. Also see *Providence Board of Trade Journal* 23 (June 1911): 285–92.

66. CIS, *Twenty-first Annual Report* (1907), 3, 12.

67. Joseph Sullivan, "'Every Shout a Cannon Ball': The IWW and Urban Disorders in Providence, 1912–1914," *Rhode Island History* 54 (1996): 51–64; Beckart, "Migration, Ethnicity," 369–73.

68. Herbert J. Lahne, *The Cotton Textile Worker* (New York: Farr and Rinehart, 1944), 195; Melvin Dubofsky, *We Shall Be All: A History of the Industrial Workers of the World* (Chicago: Quadrangle Books, 1969), 235–36, 24, 260; Cameron, *Radicals of the Worst Sort,* 158–59, 167. Bramhall was a carpenter; David J. Goldberg, *A Tale of Three Cities: Labor Organization and Protest in Paterson, Passaic, and Lawrence, 1916–1921* (New Brunswick, N.J.: Rutgers University Press, 1989), 86, 101–3, 141. On the 1919 Lawrence strike as primarily led by Italian syndicalists, see Michael Miller Topp, *Those Without a Country: The Political Culture of Italian American Syndicalists* (Minneapolis: University of Minnesota Press, 2001), 206–18.

69. On the defeat in Paterson and its aftermath, Margrave, *Emigration of Silk Workers,* 340–42; Dubofsky, *We Shall Be All,* chap. 11; Goldberg, *Tale of Three Cities,* 24–25, 32–33.

70. *PJ,* Nov. 23, 1912; *Providence Tribune,* Dec. 5, 1912; *LA,* Dec. 15, 1912. On the Yorkshire style, *PJ,* Nov. 23 and Dec. 15, 1912. Also, CIS, *Twenty-seventh Annual Report* (1914), 89–96, esp. 89.

71. Jowitt, "Retardation of Trade Unionism," and Busfield, "Skill and the Sexual Division of Labour," 84–106, 153–70.

72. Some evidence on the sexual division of labor in the weaving and spinning operations appears in the CIS annual reports on strike activity.

73. Census of 1910, household 146, 5.

74. *PJ,* Dec. 1, 7, 14, 15, 17, and 19, 1912. Union mule spinners led by immigrant Robert Howard were most influential in the early formation of the UTW; Blewett, *Constant Turmoil,* chaps. 8–10. On Golden's role in the Lawrence strike, Topp, *Those Without a Country,* 103.

75. CIS, *Twenty-sixth Annual Report* (1913), 101–2; *PJ,* Dec. 14, 1912, and Jan. 12, 1913; CIS, *Twenty-seventh Annual Report* (1914), 90–92; *LA,* Jan. 5, 1913. For events in January–February, 1913, CIS, *Twenty-seventh Annual Report,* 92–96. Also see Sullivan, "Every Shout a Cannon Ball," 54–55.

76. *PJ,* Nov. 23, 24, 1912; *LA,* Jan. 12 and May 18, 1913; Paul T. Cherington, "After-War Problems," *Bulletin of the National Association of Wool Manufacturers* 59 (1919): 59, 79–81. The proposed changes in the Underwood tariff bill significantly reduced protection; *Bradford Telegraph,* May 2, 1913.

77. Paul Buhle, "Italian-American Radicals and Labor in Rhode Island, 1905–1930," *Radical History Review* 17 (Spring 1978): 135–46.

78. Topp, *Those Without a Country,* 92–34. On the extreme racialization of Italian

immigrants, Barrett and Roediger, "Inbetween Peoples," 22; Cameron, *Radicals of the Worst Sort*, 130–31; and Topp, *Those Without a Country*, 94–96.

79. For the quote, Barrett and Roediger, "Inbetween Peoples," 24, 28–29, 32. Eric Arnesen, "Whiteness and the Historians' Imagination," *International Labor and Working Class History*, no. 60 (Fall 2001): 3–32, 81–92.

80. *Providence Bulletin*, Jan. 11 and 13, 1913; *LA*, Jan. 12 and 19, and Feb. 23, 1913; *PJ*, Jan. 12, 1913; CIS, *Twenty-seventh Annual Report* (1914), 92–93. Paul Buhle rated the 1913 Esmond strike as "the prime site of state IWW activity" but estimated that the Esmond workforce was "mostly Italian and disproportionately female"; see Buhle, "Italian-American Radicals," 133.

81. *PJ*, Jan. 11, 12, 14, 16, and 27, and Feb. 7, 17, 28, 1913. On the Esmond settlement, *PJ*, Feb. 7 and 18, 1913 and CIS, *Twenty-seventh Annual Report* (1914), 92–96.

82. *LA*, Jan. 19 and 26, Feb. 23, 1913; *PJ*, Jan. 12 and Feb. 17, 1913. Ardis Cameron's work on the significance of female networks during the Lawrence strike is convincing: *Radicals of the Worst Sort*, 117–69. See also Donna Gabaccia and Franca Iacovetta's edited collection, *Women, Gender, and Transnational Lives: Italian Workers of the World* (Toronto: University of Toronto Press, 2002), on the heritage and militancy of Italian migrant women workers on a global basis.

83. *LA*, Feb. 23, 1913 (for the quote) March 23, 1913; *PJ*, Feb. 19, 1913; and CIS, *Twenty-seventh Annual Report* (1914), 92–96.

84. CIS, *Twenty-seventh Annual Report* (1914), 93–96; *PJ*, Jan. 21, 24, 28, and 30, and Feb. 17, 18, and 28, 1913.

85. *LA*, March 30, 1913. Fred Greenwood (possible relative of John Greenwood, Esmond activist) was also identified as one of the leaders of the striking Esmond weavers; *PJ*, Jan. 25, 1913.

86. *PJ*, April 4, 5, 6, 7, and 15, 1913; CIS, *Twenty-seventh Annual Report* (1914), 108, 110; *LA*, March 30 and April 20, 1913, and Jan. 23, 1914.

87. *LA*, March 23 and 30, June 22 and 29, and July 6 and 20, 1913; *PJ*, April 5 and 6, 1913. On the defeat in Paterson and its aftermath, Margrave, *Emigration of Silk Workers*, 340–42; Dubofsky, *We Shall Be All*, chap. 11. For a discussion of labor radicalism in Rhode Island after 1913, Buhle, "Italian-American Radicals," 135–46.

88. Donna Gabaccia, *Militants and Migrants: Rural Sicilians Become American Workers* (New Brunswick, N.J.: Rutgers University Press, 1988). Rudolph Vecoli's *contadini* in Chicago did not work in heavy or light industry, but instead did manual labor or railroad work: "Contadini in Chicago: A Critique of *The Uprooted*," *Journal of American History* 51 (December 1964) 410–11.

89. "We Want Integrity: An Interview with Al Sisti," ed. and trans. Paul Buhle, *Radical History Review* 17 (1978): 181–90, esp. 181–83. On English immigrant support for transcultural strikes in Connecticut, 1915–1925, see Cecelia Bucki, *Bridgeport's Socialist New Deal, 1915–36* (Urbana: University of Illinois Press, 2001), 36, 104, 110–12, 116, 209.

90. Duncan Smith, email to author, Jan. 3, 2006; "Minnie Kettlewell's Husband," in *More Yankee Yorkshiremen*, 13–29, esp. 15–16.

91. Smith "The Millmaster," 394–95; Paul Buhle, email to author, Sept. 18, 2000; John A. Salmond, *The General Textile Strike of 1934: From Maine to Alabama* (Columbia: University of Missouri Press, 2002), 83–102.

92. Hoerder, *Cultures in Contact,* 439–41; "The Wise Child," in *More Yankee Yorkshiremen,* 59–63, 66; *Yankee Yorkshirewomen,* 31–33, 52–53. Intensifying nationalism among Yorkshire migrants to Briardale became the major theme of "The Lion and the Eagle"; see chap. 4.

93. Goldberg, *Tale of Three Cities,* 13–14; Topp, *Those Without a Country,* 108–12.

94. Smith, "Yankee Yorkshire Days," 5, 9.

95. Smith, "The Mill Folk," 21–22.

96. Cohen, *Global Diasporas,* ix–xii and chap. 6; Smith "Yankee Yorkshire Yesterdays," 1, 4.

97. Smith, "The Mill Folk," 23.

98. Ibid., 23–25. *Knur:* a wooden ball; *spell:* a thin bat or piece of wood; *Transactions of the Yorkshire Dialect Society,* pt. 91, vol. 17 (1991): 27, 31, courtesy of Stanley Bradbury; Portia Thompson, email to author, Sept. 26, 2000.

99. Interest in variations of the broad Yorkshire dialect abounds in contemporary Yorkshire; see Arnold Kennett's columns in *Dalesman* (Bradford), October and November 1997, 47 and 54 respectively, courtesy Portia Thompson.

100. Phyllis Bentley, letters to Hedley Smith, Oct. 10, 1974, and Dec. 10, 1970, courtesy Portia Thompson.

101. Smith, "The Wise Child," 60; Frederic G. Cassidy, ed., *Dictionary of American Regional English* (Cambridge: Belknap Press of Harvard University Press, 1996), 3:128–29; Smith, "The Mill Folk," 113; Smith, "Miriam Ainsworth," 21.

102. Smith, "The Lion and the Eagle," 147–49.

103. For the quotes see ibid., 62, 148, 178–80.

104. On West Riding paternalism, see Jowitt, ed., *Model Communities in Mid-Nineteenth Century Yorkshire,* passim. For Smith's version, see his character, George Curtis, the first Briardale mill superintendent in "King George's Idea," in *More Yankee Yorkshiremen,* 81–82, and in "The Millmaster."

105. Elizabeth Roberts, *A Woman's Place: An Oral History of Working-Class Women 1890–1940* (Oxford: Basil Blackwell, 1984), 183–87.

106. Smith, "The Lion and the Eagle," 125–26.

107. Smith, "Introduction," and "Uprooted," both in *The Yankee Yorkshireman,* 8 and 55–70 respectively.

108. Smith, "Uprooted," 68.

109. Handlin, *The Uprooted,* 235–40.

110. Gabaccia, *From the Other Side,* 72–74, and "Introduction," in *Women, Gender, and Transnational Lives,* ed. Gabaccia and Iacovetta, 30–33; Gabaccia, "Immigrant Women," 68–71; Hoerder, "International Labor Markets and Community Building," 107.

111. Smith, "The Mill Folk," 27.

112. Smith, "The Wise Child," 58, 74; Smith, "Miriam Ainsworth," 27–28, 33, 35, 6.

113. For the calculating and prudish, see Smith, "The Lion and the Eagle," 92–94, 109–10, 114.

114. Portia Thompson, email to author, Sept. 26, 2000. For a discussion of Hedley Smith's marriage, see chap. 3.

115. Smith, "The Mill Folk," 28–37, and "The Millmaster," 23, 33–38. For the dismissal of "book nonsense," see the characters of Joth Booth in "The Conscience of Mr. King," 20, and Ruth Binns in "Squire Widdop's Wooing," 37–38 (both in *The Yankee Yorkshireman*) and David Greaves in "The Wise Child," 56, 63–64 (in *More Yankee Yorkshiremen*). For condemnation of "wedding" out of class, see Aunt Sarah Jane Denby in "Wedding Dress," 112 (in *The Yankee Yorkshireman*).

116. "Squire Widdop's Wooing," 37–38, 42–48. For Karl Ittmann's study of declining fertility in Bradford based on data between 1851 and 1881, see *Work, Gender and Family*, 230–33. On the use of more dangerous abortificients in Lancashire and Yorkshire, see Jeffrey Weeks, *Sex, Politics and Society: The Regulation of Sexuality Since 1800* (London: Longman, 1981), 69–72; Knight, "Women and Abortion in Victorian and Edwardian England," 62–63.

117. Smith, "The Mill Folk," 17–18. The "safe period" in the female fertility cycle was misunderstood and useless for birth control; Knight, "Women and Abortion," 59.

118. Laurence J. Sasso, book review of *More Yankee Yorkshiremen* in *Scituate Observer*, Nov. 29, 1974; Duncan Smith, email to author, Sept. 2, 2005.

119. Cherington, "After-War Problems," 82; Goldberg, *Tale of Three Cities*, 6–13, 111–13.

120. Richard Ivan Jobs and Patrick McDevitt emphasize choice and agency and ongoing negotiation in creating social life, "Introduction: Where the Hell Are the People?" *Journal of Social History* 39 (Winter 2005): 309–14, esp. 310.

121. Duncan Smith, emails to author, Jan. 26, 2005, and Jan. 18, 2006; Elaine Chaika, "Speaking Rhode Island: A Guide to Understanding and Speaking Rhode Island English," pamphlet, 1982, Rhode Island Historical Society, Providence.

122. The descendents of the Benn family continued to hold shares in the Greystone operations until 1972. *American Cotton and Wool Reporter*, July 28, 1921, 39; *Bradford Daily Telegraph*, July 25, 1921; *Yorkshire Post*, Aug. 23, 1939; William Benn of Harrogate, North Yorkshire, worsted manufacturers, papers for the trust under his will 1939–1972 10D76/3/73, Bradford Archives.

123. The monument titled Greystone Honor Roll, 1917–1919, is located on Route 104, Farnum Pike, Greystone Village, North Providence.

124. Smith, "The Tongue-Tied Town," 1–2.

125. Duncan Smith, email to author, Dec. 15, 2005.

126. Hedley Smith to Lindsay, c. late August 1983.

127. On Yankee domination of the village of Centredale, Frank C. Angell, *Looking Backward Four Score Years, 1845–1925* (Centredale, R.I.: Centredale Press, 1925), 98–104, 140–42, 158–78.

128. Smith, "Treacle and Brimstone," 49–56.

129. Smith, "The Tongue-Tied Town," 93–94, 107–11, 119–21.

130. Smith, "Miriam Ainsworth," 21–22, 30–32.

131. Smith, "The Tongue-Tied Town," 123–24.

132. Ibid., 229–34.

133. Smith, "Miriam Ainsworth," 40–43.

134. "Greedy Guts," no. 5 under "Outward Show" Yankee Yorkshire Comedy, c. July 31, 1986, unpaginated. Also Sam Shackleton in Smith, "The Tongue-Tied Town," 239.

Chapter 3. Working, Writing, Loving, Enduring

1. Douglas M. Reynolds, "Legacies of Deindustrialization and the Blackstone River Valley National Heritage Corridor," *New England Journal of Public Policy* 8 (Fall/Winter 1992): 37–50.

2. Patrick J. Hearden, *Independence and Empire: The New South's Cotton Mill Campaign, 1865–1901* (DeKalb: Northern Illinois University Press, 1982), 53–68, 125–44.

3. John Gaventa and Barbara Ellen Smith, "The Deindustrialization of the Textile South: A Case Study," in *Hanging by a Thread: Social Change in Southern Textiles,* ed. Jeffrey Leiter et al. (Ithaca, N.Y.: Cornell University Press, 1991), 182.

4. Timothy Minchin, *Hiring the Black Worker: The Racial Integration of the Southern Textile Industry, 1960–1980* (Chapel Hill: University of North Carolina Press, 1999), 265–71.

5. Mary Blewett, "Textile Workers in the American Northeast and South: Shifting Landscapes of Class, Culture, Gender, Race, and Protest," in *The Ashgate Companion to the History of Textile Workers,* ed. Lex Heerma van Voss et al. (Aldershot: Ashgate Publishing, forthcoming).

6. Sterne, *Ballots and Bibles,* 1–5, 38–39, 195–252.

7. On British immigrant letters to family, kin, and friends in the early nineteenth century, see David A. Gerber, "Acts of Deceiving and Withholding in Immigrant Letters: Personal Identity and Self-Presentation in Personal Correspondence," *Journal of Social History* 39 (Winter 2005): 315–31.

8. Smith destroyed all the manuscripts mentioned in the correspondence. Horace and Tom often asked for more information about his life and job.

9. Jonathan Rose, *The Intellectual Life of the British Working Classes* (New Haven: Yale University Press, 2001).

10. Hedley Smith, letter to Lindsay, undated, c. Jan. 25, 1975.

11. 1997 interview; Duncan Smith, email to author, Sept. 3, 2005. These books remain in the family.

12. Portia Thompson, email to author, June 15, 2007.

13. Smith, *Family Connections,* 35, 40–44, 47–48, 50.

14. Hedley Smith, letter to Lindsay, Aug. 7, 1979.

15. Smith had carried no proof of citizenship; Duncan Smith, email to author, June 14, 2007.

16. Duncan Smith, email to author, Dec. 15, 2005; see chap. 2.

17. Interview, *Scituate Observer,* June 21, 1973.

18. Smith, "The Lion and the Eagle," 54–55.

19. The reasons for Donald Fowler's abrupt departures remain a matter of conjecture: circumstantial evidence suggests binge drinking or womanizing.

20. Portia Thompson, email to author, Feb. 3 and March 24, 2006.

21. Smith, "The Lion and the Eagle," 126–27.

22. Ibid., 133.

23. For the quotes, ibid., 128–29, 135–37.

24. Salmond, *The General Textile Strike of 1934,* 83–102.

25. Duncan Smith, email to author, Jan. 3, 2006.

26. Later Carmen announced to her children that she had cured him of drinking scotch; Duncan Smith, email to author, Sept. 2, 2005. Hedley confirmed the story to an old friend in the presence of Duncan; Duncan Smith, email to author, Feb. 20, 2006.

27. Duncan Smith, email to author, March 31, 2006.

28. Ibid., April 3, 2007. Duncan Smith indicates that for whatever reasons his mother successfully exiled Alice Smith through silence.

29. Portia Thompson, email to author, Feb. 9, 2006.

30. Ibid., Nov. 12, 2005.

31. Ibid., Feb. 7, 2006; Duncan Smith, email to author, Feb. 7, 2006.

32. Smith, *Family Connections,* chaps. 2, 3.

33. Portia Thompson, email to author, Jan. 26, 2006.

34. Email, copy of Duncan Smith to Portia Thompson, email to author, Sept. 23, 2006.

35. Portia Thompson, email to author, Feb. 2, 2006.

36. Duncan Smith, email to author, Jan. 31, 2006.

37. Ibid.; Portia Thompson, emails to author, Feb. 2 and 3, 2006.

38. Smith, "The Lion and The Eagle," 87.

39. Smith, "Hussy in the Well," 17.

40. Duncan Smith, email to author, Jan. 19, 2005.

41. Duncan Smith, emails to author, Jan. 19, 2005, and July 27, 2008; Portia Thompson, emails to author, April 20 and May 6, 2005.

42. Donna R. Gabaccia, *We Are What We Eat: Ethnic Food and the Making of Americans* (Cambridge: Harvard University Press, 1998).

43. Duncan Smith, emails to author, July 7, 2005, and April 13, 2007.

44. Sterne, *Ballots and Bibles,* 230–35, 248.

45. Portia Thompson, emails to author, Nov. 12 and 14, 2005; Duncan Smith, email to author, March 16, 2006.

46. Duncan Smith, emails to author, July 8, 2005, March 22, 2006, and April 13, 2007.

47. Portia Thompson, email to author, March 26, 2006; Duncan Smith, email to author, March 22, 2006.

48. Duncan Smith, email to author, March 21, 2006.

49. Ibid., July 20, 2002; Portia Thompson, email to author, June 26, 2007.

50. Jones, *Accent on Privilege,* discussed the ways in which English immigrants used their backgrounds as cultural capital in an Anglophilic society 13, 61–107.

51. Duncan Smith, emails to author, Dec. 24, 2005, and Jan. 29, 2006.

52. Undated typescripts: "Stubborn Sinner," "Checkmate in Providence," "Mr. Verein's Women" (sent to Richard Curtis Associates, New York, returned, n.d.), Smith Collection.

53. Scott Meredith, letter to Hedley Smith, July 14, 1966, courtesy Portia Thompson.

54. Clipping, *Brown Daily Herald,* April 29, 1971, courtesy Portia Thompson.

55. Duncan Smith, attachment to email sent to author, Jan. 29, 2006.

56. Duncan Smith, email to author, Jan. 30, 2006.

57. Obituary, *Providence Bulletin,* March 4, 1985.

58. Many of the Polish works cited by Karen Majewski in *Traitors and True Poles* were published by Harlo Press.

59. Hedley Smith, *There was a Cat in Bethlehem . . .,* illustrated by Laura Furlong (North Scituate, R.I.: Hedley Smith Associates, 1979).

60. Sherwood Broome, letter to Hedley Smith, May 20, 1976.

61. See the Hedley Smith Canon, 1986, Smith Collection.

62. Duncan Smith, email to author, May 14 and 16, 2007.

63. Hedley Smith, letter to Lindsay, May 9, 1976.

64. Smith, *The Yankee Yorkshireman,* 7.

65. Hedley Smith, letter to Phyllis Bentley, copy, c. 1970.

66. Clipping, Bradford *Telegraph and Argus,* Feb. 12, 1979, courtesy, Portia Thompson.

67. The Smith-Balderson Letters, 1979–1984, courtesy Portia Thompson.

68. *Providence Sunday Journal,* Nov. 14, 1976, courtesy Portia Thompson; Portia Thompson, email to author, Feb. 14, 2006. Many of his activities during the years 1971–85 can be reconstructed from his correspondence with Bruce Lindsay; Hedley Smith, letter to Lindsay, Dec. 6, 1981; D. Urnov, note to author, February 2006; Duncan Smith, email to author, Jan. 3, 2006.

69. Duncan Smith, email to author, March 16, 2006.

70. Hedley Smith, letter to Brian Bicart, c. 1989, quoted in email from Portia Thompson, Jan. 28, 2007.

71. Duncan Smith, email to author, March 21, 2006; 1997 interview.

72. Sidney Goldsmith and Calvin Goldscheider, *Jewish Americans: Three Generations in a Jewish Community* (Englewood Cliffs, N.J.: Prentice-Hall, 1968), 234–39. Goldsmith and Goldscheider analyzed residence patterns, social mobility, demographics, patterns of religious change, educational achievements, occupational distribution, fertility rates, marital assimilation, and family structural changes between 1880 and 1963.

73. Robert A. Orsi, "The Fault of Memory: 'Southern Italy' in the Imagination of Immigrants and the Lives of Their Children in Italian Harlem, 1920–1945," *Journal of Family History* 15 (April 1990): 133–47.

74. Duncan Smith, email to author, Jan. 9, 2007.

75. Portia and Leslie Thompson had two sons and two daughters. Duncan Smith also had four children. A later marriage produced two more, a son and a daughter, born after Hedley Smith died. Portia Thompson, email to author, Sept. 2, 2006.

76. Rubén Rumbaut, "Studying the 'Second Generation': New Concepts, New Findings," *Immigration and Ethnic History Newsletter* 38 (November 2006): 1, 8–9.

77. Nancy Foner and Richard Alba, "The Second Generation from the Last Great Wave of Immigration: Setting the Record Straight," *Migration Information Source,* October 1, 2006, 6.

78. Melania Mazzucco, *Vita* (New York: Farrar, Straus and Giroux, 2005).

79. Foner and Alba, "The Second Generation," 6.

80. Duncan Smith, email to author, Feb. 7, 2006.

81. Hans-Joachim Bernhard and Duncan Smith, eds., *Remembering Rostock, 1972–1990* (New York: University Press of America, 1991), 1–3, 141–50.

82. Duncan Smith, email to author, Oct. 11, 2006. These posts included associate dean of the college and director of the Foreign Study Office, 1983; associate dean of the faculty and director of the Office of International Programs, 1985–89; and full professor, 1988; curriculum vitae, Duncan Smith, 2003.

83. This correspondence was not offered to me.

84. Duncan Smith, email to author, Sept. 3, 2006. After he retired, Duncan Smith published at least two pieces of fiction, *Kriemhild's Revenge* (Xlibris, 2000) and *The Unexploded Shell or The Perils of Masculinity* (West Warwick, R.I.: Cheap Suit Press, 2000).

85. Generational file by Portia Thompson, undated, in hands of author; Portia Thompson, emails to author, April 24 and July 20, 2006.

86. Portia Thompson, email to author, May 14, 2006.

87. Marcus Lee Hansen, "Law of Third Generation Return," is discussed by Kazal, "Revisiting Assimilation," 440.

88. He was in charge of a "clean-up" of the Boott hydropower complex next to the Lowell National Historical Park Museum and inspected the mills and canals system; John A. Thompson, email to author, Aug. 3, 2006.

89. Only one of Duncan Smith's four children answered the generational linkage questions (July 11, 2006).

90. Although encouraged by their parents, only three of the eight grandchildren of Hedley Smith responded to an admittedly complex set of questions in my generational linkage analysis, Smith Collection.

91. Andrew Leslie Thompson, email to author, July 24, 2006.

Chapter 4. Transatlantic Perspectives, Strong Women, and Sexual Politics in Fiction

1. Green and Weil, eds., *Citizenship and Those Who Leave,* 1–2.

2. Portia Thompson, email to author, Jan. 10, 2006.

3. Majewski, *Traitors and True Poles,* 1.

4. Hedley Smith, "Mill Village," 7–8; Smith, "Yankee Yorkshire Yesterdays," 9–10.

5. Front blurb on book jacket for *The Yankee Yorkshireman.*

6. Copy of story from *Providence Journal,* 1942, courtesy Portia Thompson.

7. Smith, "The Lion and the Eagle," 18–19.

8. Ibid., 77–82.

9. Duncan Smith, email to author, Jan. 3, 2006.

10. Smith, "The Lion and the Eagle," 146–47.

11. Ibid., 140.

12. Mary Blewett, "The Dynamics of Labor Migration and Raw Materials Acquisition in the Transatlantic Worsted Trade, 1830–1930," paper given at the conference, Connecting Atlantic, Indian Ocean, China Seas and Pacific Migrations, 1830–1930, German Historical Institute, Washington, D.C., December 2007, in *Connecting Seas and Connected Ocean Rims* (forthcoming).

13. Smith, "The Lion and the Eagle," 95–96, 101–3, 192–93.

14. Ibid., 164–66.

15. Ibid., 147–49.

16. Ibid., 106–8.

17. Ibid., 176–82.

18. Quotes respectively, ibid., 198–200, 205–8, 224–27.

19. The *Lusitania* was sunk off the coast of England in May 1915 with great loss of civilian life by German submarines. This controversial incident created a long-term crisis that resulted in the severing of diplomatic relations and war between the United States and Germany.

20. Duncan Smith, email to author, May 14, 2007.

21. Patrick MacGill, *The Great Push: An Episode of the Great War* (London: Herbert Jenkins, 1916).

22. Duncan Smith, email to author, May 17, 2007; Patrick MacGill, *The Rat-Pit* (1913; reprint, Kerry: Brandon Publishers, 1983); Patrick MacGill, *Children of the Dead End: The Autobiography of a Navvy* (1914; reprint, London: Caliban, 1985).

23. Smith, "The Mill Folk," 81–84.

24. Smith, *Yankee Yorkshirewomen,* 20–21.

25. Smith, "King George's Idea," 89.

26. Ibid., 104–6.

27. Smith, "The Spinster of Paradise View," unpublished novella, courtesy Portia Thompson. Doubtless, Smith was aware of the investment activities of Royal Little, a Yankee capitalist who purchased going textile concerns, closed them, and used the

tax losses; Royal Little, *How to Lose Ten Million Dollars and Other Valuable Advice* (Boston: Little, Brown, 1979).

28. Smith, "The Wise Child," 53–80, esp. 67, 75.

29. Smith, *Yankee Yorkshirewomen,* 38–39.

30. Ibid., 91–94

31. Ibid., 42–45.

32. Ibid., 37–41.

33. The term "Miss Nancy" in this sense means a pretentious, uppity girl. "Squire Widdop's Wooing," 31–37, esp. 31.

34. Ibid., 46–53.

35. Duncan Smith, email to author, Jan. 31, 2006.

36. Ibid., Feb. 7, 2006.

37. Kevin Kenny, "Diaspora and Comparison: The Global Irish as a Test Case," *Journal of American History* 90 (June 2003): 134–62. Kenny acknowledges the difficulties of locating evidence for comparative history.

38. Blewett, "Yorkshire Lasses and Their Lads," 325–28; Pessar and Mahler, "Transnational Migration," 815–18.

39. Most recently, Sinke, *Dutch Immigrant Women,* 4.

40. Smith, "The Mill Folk," 72–5.

41. My thanks to Felicity Harrison for this insight.

42. Smith, "The Mill Folk," 74.

43. Priestley, *Margin Released,* 10–14.

44. Ibid., 59–60.

45. Ibid., 60–61.

46. Memo of personal conversation with Bart De Wilde, participant in Global Textile Workers conference, Amsterdam, November 2004. See his *Witte boorden, blauke kielen: patroons en arbeiders in de belgische textielnijverheid in de 19e en 20e eeuw* ([Belgium]: Ludion: AMSAB: Profortex, 1997).

47. Euripides, *The Bacchae.* According to his son, Hedley Smith especially admired Euripides.

48. Smith, "The Mill Folk," 75.

49. Pessar and Mahler, "Transnational Migration," 816, 818.

50. Duncan Smith, email to author, Feb. 20, 2006.

51. Most recently analyzed in James Nagel, *The Contemporary American Short Story Cycle: The Ethnic Resonance of Genre* (Baton Rouge: Louisiana University Press, 2001).

52. Rocio G. Davis, "Identity in Community in Ethnic Short Story Cycles: Amy Tan's *The Joy Luck Club,* Louise Erdrich's *Love Medicine,* Gloria Naylor's *Women of Brewster Place,*" in *Ethnicity and the American Short Story,* ed. Julie Brown (New York: Garland, 1997), 3–24, esp. 7. Some novels were originally published in parts that were later combined; see Julia Álvarez, *How the Garcia Girls Lost Their Accents* (New York: Plume, 1992).

53. Davis, "Identity in Community," 5.

54. For example, Sandra Cisneros, Maxine Hong Kingston, Ramzi Salti, and Amy Tan.

55. In between these two books, Smith wrote the bicentennial history of Scituate.

56. Abraham Cahan, *The Rise of David Levinsky* (1917; New York: Harper and Brothers, 1960); Henry Roth, *Call It Sleep* (New York: Farrar, Straus and Giroux, 1934; New York: Avon Library, 1964); Mary Antin, *The Promised Land* (Cambridge, Mass.: Riverside Press, 1912; reprint, Boston: Houghton Mifflin, 1969), foreword by Oscar Handlin.

57. Also see "Squire Widdop's Wooing," "The Conscience of Mr. King," and "The Wedding Dress."

58. Smith, "The Black Sheep," *The Yankee Yorkshireman*, 75.

59. "Introduction," *More Yankee Yorkshiremen*, 7–8.

60. Smith, "The Wise Child," 57–58, 63.

61. Smith, "King George's Idea," 81–107.

62. Smith, "The Partnership," in *More Yankee Yorkshiremen*, 31–52, esp. 43.

63. Ibid., 51.

64. My thanks to Portia Thompson, email, June 24, 2006.

65. Jhumpa Lahiri, *Interpreter of Maladies: Stories* (Boston: Houghton Mifflin, 1999) especially uses the theme of tastes and smells of Indian cookery to evoke homeland longings.

66. Introduction by Cheryl Temple Kerr to her comparative study, *Critical Regionalism and Cultural Studies: From Ireland to the American Midwest* (Gainesville: University of Florida Press, 1996); "Introduction: Regionalism Revisited," in *A Sense of Place: Re-Evaluating Regionalism in Canadian and American Writing*, ed. Christian Riegel et al. (Edmonton: University of Alberta Press, 1997), ix–xiv; David Jordan, "Introduction," in *Regionalism Reconsidered: New Approaches to the Field*, ed. Jordan (New York: Garland Publishing, 1994), ix–xix.

67. J. P. Marquand examined the vexing connections between class and ethnicity in the Boston area in *The Late George Apley* (1936; reprint, New York: Pocket Books, 1944). Also see Mary Doyle Curran, *The Parish and the Hill* (1948; reprint, New York: Feminist Press, 1986).

68. Francesco Loriggio argues in "Regionalism and Theory," in *Regionalism Reconsidered*, ed. Jordan, 3–4, that the politics of ethnicity and the cityscape should be integral to regionalist considerations of the concept of space. On Smith's acquaintance with New England regionalists and American realists, see "The Lion and the Eagle," 87.

69. Donna M. Campbell discusses the tensions yet interconnections between feminine local colorists and masculinist writers of naturalism writers in *Resisting Regionalism: Gender and Naturalism in American Fiction, 1885–1915* (Athens: Ohio University Press, 1997).

70. For Marjorie Pryse, "nondominant men" are generally men of color, "Writing Out of the Gap: Regionalism, Resistance, and Relational Reading," in *A Sense of Place*, ed. Riegel et al., 19–34.

71. "Introduction," in *A Sense of Place,* ed. Riegel et al., xiii.
72. Pryse, "Writing Out of the Gap," 19, 24, 32.

Conclusion

1. Charlotte Erickson, Dudley Baines, and Brinley Thomas have done the most distinguished work of this kind on British emigration. On state policy, Feldman and Baldwin, "Emigration and the British State," 135–55.
2. Moya, *Cousins and Strangers,* 332, 404–7, 388–91.
3. "Mary Ann Wodrow Archbald: Longing for Her 'Little Isle' from a Farm in Central New York," in Gerber, *Authors of Their Lives,* 281–308. Also see "Catherine Grayston Bond: Letter-Writing as the Practice of Existential Accounting," 257–80, in *Authors of Their Own Lives.*
4. Hoerder, *Creating Societies,* 111–14.
5. Hoerder, "Historians and Their Data," 89.
6. Interview, *Scituate Observer,* June 21, 1973.
7. Duncan Smith, email to author, Dec. 24, 2005.
8. Scott Meredith, New York agent, letter to Hedley Smith, July 14, 1966.
9. Thomas Hardy, "Preface," in *Far from the Madding Crowd* (New York: Harper and Brothers, 1918), ix, cited in Smith, "Yankee Yorkshire Yesterdays," 9.
10. Bodnar, *The Transplanted,* 207.
11. Marta Bolognani, "The Myth of Return: Dismissal, Survival or Revival? A Bradford Example of Transnationalism as a Political Instrument," *Journal of Ethnic and Migration Studies* 33 (January 2007): 59–77.

Hedley Smith's Published and Unpublished Works

Published Works

Gift of Armor: A Romance of Warwick. 1968. New York: Vantage Press.
The Yankee Yorkshireman. 1970. Detroit: Harlo Press.
More Yankee Yorkshiremen. 1974. Detroit: Harlo Press.
The History of Scituate, R.I. 1976. Scituate: Bicentennial Committee of the Town.
Yankee Yorkshirewomen. 1978. Illustrated by Portia S. Thompson. Detroit: Harlo Press.
There was a Cat in Bethlehem . . . 1979. Illustrated by Laura Furlong. North Scituate, R.I.: Hedley Smith Associates.

Unpublished Works

NOVELS

Briardale Trilogy: Part 1, "The Millmaster"; Part 2, "The Lion and the Eagle"; Part 3, "The Tongue-Tied Town"
"Fable in Fustian," variation of "The Mill Folk"
"Hussy in the Well"
"Left-Handed Jack"
"Lively Experiment"
"The Mill Folk"
"Mr. Verein's Women"
"One Escaped," formerly "Checkmate in Providence"
"Sinners Corner"
"Stubborn Saint"

NOVELLAS

"Clever Clogs"
"Greedy Guts"
"Miriam Ainsworth"
"Peas All Hot!" (listed by Smith in his 1986 canon but not found)
"The Spinster of Paradise Row"
"The Woman at the Coop"

SHORT STORIES

"Yankee Yorkshire Yesterdays," projected short-story collection, also titled "Mill Village" and "Yorkshire Through and Through . . ." with introduction "About Briardale and Briardale Women."
"The Backslider"
"Juliet of Mill Row"
"Love and Lodgings"
"Treacle and Brimstone"
Source: Based on Hedley Smith's handwritten list of "The official canon of his literary work," July 31, 1986, courtesy Portia Thompson.

Index

Note: Italicized page numbers indicate maps and figures. Hedley Smith's works are listed by title in the index rather than under his name.

abortion, as birth control, 35, 36, 90, 142

accommodation and acculturation, 13. *See also* assimilation

Alba, Richard, 10–11

American Civil War: impact on Yorkshire industry, 31, 55

American Federation of Labor (AFL), 73, 80. *See also* United Textile Workers (UTW, AFL affiliate)

American Woolen Company (Lawrence), 55, 73, 175n11

American Workman (newspaper), 72

Anderson, Benedict, 13

Andros, Edmund, 11

Anglophilia, 115, 185n50

Anglo-Saxon and Anglo-American heritage: critique of, 11–13

anthrax regulations, 69

Antin, Mary, 147

Archbald, Mary Ann Wodrow, 7, 154

Argentina: Spanish immigrants in, 4–5

Arlington mills (Lawrence), 58, 74

Arnesen, Eric, 78

Asbury Methodist Church (Warwick), 102–3, 106–7

assimilation: assumptions about, 6–7; cen-

trality of, 3–4; complexities of, 155; critique of, 10–14; education in process of, 49–50; human capital key in, 6; rejection of, 9, 10–16; resistance to, 7–8, 14, 95–96, 152, 153–56; of second and third generations, 120–25; transplantation vs., 147–48

Australia: English migration to, 41, 43; fleece from, 19; Italian immigrants in, 4

Bainbridge, Amy Collins, 24, 34

Baines, Dudley, 41–42, 190n1

Baldassar, Loretta, 4, 10

Balderson, Alfred, 118

Balzac, Honoré de, 119, 127

Barkan, Elliott, 13

Barrett, James, 78

Bateman, Jeannie, 74

Behrens, Jacob, 28–29

Belgium: labor migration from, 26; sexual rituals in cotton industry of, 145; U.S. textile industry investments of, 53–54; worsted workforce from, 52

Benn, Harrison: brothers of (Alfred, Arthur, and Joseph), 29–30; death of, 82–83, 91–92; education of, 29; Greystone Mill and Village development and, 30, 53–54, 58–59; Greystone Social Club and, 63; motivations of, 65; protectionism of, 70; response to work stoppage, 76–77

Benn, Joseph, Jr., 29–30, 39–40

Benn, William Henry: Greystone Mill and

Village development and, 30, 58–59, 60, 70, 91; Greystone Mill sold by, 92; motivations of, 65; Yorkshire worsted and spinning operations of, 29–30

Benn Company: beginning of, 29–30; competition of, 68–69; fictional depiction of, 83–84, 86, 92; Greystone investment and assets of, 53–54, 58–59, 60, 70, 91, 147–48, 182n122; hoax propagated by, 69–70; niche of, 55; operations closed by, 175n20; operations of, 29–30, 40; as transnational player, 5; weavers of, 76; workforce records of, 177n46; WWI-era value of, 90–91; WWI monument costs paid by, 92. *See also* Benn, Harrison; Great Horton (Yorkshire); Greystone Mill (R.I.); Greystone Village (R.I.)

Bentley, Phyllis: on class conflicts, 22, 32–33; HS's correspondence with, 118; HS's homage to, 33; HS's reading of, 31–32; on HS's writings, 85, 139; as model, 127–28; on West Riding production, 19; works: *Inheritance*, 22, 32; *A Man of His Time*, 32; *O Dreams, O Destinations*, 32–33; *The Rise of Henry Morcar*, 32

Berthoff, Rowland T., 7, 42

birds of passage, 27, 41. *See also* labor migration

birth control, 35, 36, 90, 142, 182nn116–17

Black Dyke Mills (Bradford), 31, 37

"The Black Sheep" (short story, HS), 148–49

Blackstone River Valley mills, 55, 64, 97

Blewett, Peter, xii

Bodnar, John, 2, 12, 15, 159, 161n3

Boer War, 137

Book of Common Prayer, 120, 142

Bornat, Joanna, 35

Boston (Mass.): class and ethnicity in, 189n67; mainstream culture of, 12

Botany and Forstmann and Huffmann Companies, 175n11. *See also* Passaic (N.J.)

Bowers, Robert, 57–58. *See also Lawrence Journal* (newspaper)

Bradford (Yorkshire): contemporary picture of, 160; diversification of, 37; fertility decline in, 35–36, 182n116; gender antagonisms in, 33–36; Greystone Village compared with, 60, 61–62; Greystone workers pitted against, 77; HS baptized in, 102, 142; HS's books in, 118; indus-

trial workforce of, 23–25, 28–29, 31; links maintained to, 8; longing for, 13; Luddites in, 22; maps of, *19*, *30*; migration to and from, 26–29; Pakistani immigrants in, 160; plain worsted trade in, 20; population growth of, 20, 26; power source of, 18; social class in, 29–33; townships of, 169n30; university of, 123, 125. *See also* worsted industry, British

Bradford Chamber of Commerce, 29

Bradford Observer, 31

Bradford Technical Institute (Yorkshire), 46, 48–49

Bramhall, Samuel, 74

Bread and Roses Strike (Lawrence, 1912), 57, 75, 78

Briardale (fictional): autobiographical components of, 99; basis for, 2, 4–5, 8, 30, 54–55, 66; courtship in, 105–6; cultural contacts and conflicts in, 127–28; cultural identity and community in, 15, 148–52; cultural isolation of, 9–10, 86, 157–58; decline of, 118; domineering male characters in, 138–39; empirical data compared with, 52; family and social dynamics of, 8–9; German immigrants in, 131–33; imagining of, 82–90; landscape of, 4, 105–6, 176n22; names in, 21; outsiders in, 77–78, 94–95, 104–5, 106, 131–32; publication of tales, 116; Puritan-dominated surroundings of, 11; religious organizations in, 65; sexual customs in, 35, 142–46; as symbol of ties, 2; time of, 82, 83; transatlantic politics in, 127–39, 147–49, 152; window into, 156–57; women's strength and independence in, 139–42; WWI and aftermath in, 90–96; WWI memorial in, 92, 137, 157, 182n123. *See also* "The Lion and the Eagle" (Briardale Trilogy, Part 2, HS); "The Millmaster" (Briardale Trilogy, Part 1, HS); *More Yankee Yorkshiremen* (collection, HS); "The Tongue-Tied Town" (Briardale Trilogy, Part 3, HS); West Yorkshire dialect; *The Yankee Yorkshireman* (collection, HS); *Yankee Yorkshirewomen* (novella, HS)

Bridgeport (Conn.): Titus Salt operations in, 37, 51; Yorkshire immigrants in, 39, 40

Bristol (R.I.): mill strike in, 74

Britain. *See* Great Britain

British immigrants. *See* English immigrants

British roots in American culture, 11–13

Brontë, Charlotte, 31, 105, 119

Brontë, Emily, 29, 31, 105, 119

Broome Agency, 117

Brown Daily Herald (newspaper), 115–16

Brown University: Rostock Program of, 122–23; Smith father and son at, 113–16

Bryant Stratton Business School, 101

Buhle, Paul, 77, 81–82, 180n80

Bullough, Rebecca Grimshaw, 176n34

Burlak, Ann, 81–82

Byles, William, 31

Cameron, Ardis, 180n82

Campbell, Donna M., 189n69

Canada: English migration to, 41, 155; return migrants from, 43. *See also* English Canadian immigrants; French Canadian immigrants

castration fears, 146. *See also* "sunning" ritual

Catholicism, 26, 81, 98–99

Centredale (R.I.): Episcopal church of, 65, 102, 142; ethnic groups of, 66; IWW local in, 76, 79; labor rally in, 80; railroad spur to, 59; shopping for workers of, 64; Smith's family in, 99; stories told in, 83; strike threatened in, 79–80; textile mills investment and assets in, 58

Centredale Worsted Company, 79–80

Chartist movement, 23, 33, 72

children: HS's relatives as, 24; in industrial workforce, 23–25, 26; legislation on working, 24, 31; limiting number of, 35, 36. *See also* education; families

citizenship, 48, 53, 68, 126. *See also* naturalization

Clapham, J. H., 18

class conflicts: Bentley's descriptions of, 22, 32–33; cultural antagonism juxtaposed to, 86–87; transregional culture linked to transcultural, 5–6; as underlying political loyalties, 134; in Yorkshire, 20–21. *See also* cultural conflicts; social class

Clayton (Yorkshire): location of, 30

coal and coal mining, 18–19, 22

Cohen, Robin, 6, 8

Cole, Donald, 57

Collins family: migration patterns of, 43–44, 46

Collins, Alice. *See* Smith, Alice Collins (HS's mother)

Collins, Amy (later Bainbridge, HS's aunt), 24, 34

Collins, Arthur (HS's brother-in-law), 43, 49, 110

Collins, Dracup (HS's grandfather), 27, 46

Collins, Jane Holdsworth (HS's grandmother), 24

Collins, Mary Parkinson (HS's step-grandmother), 24

community organizations. *See* social organizations

Connecticut: Titus Salt operations in, 37, 51; Yorkshire immigrants in, 39, 40

contract labor: avoiding laws on, 60–61; Foran Act on, 174n109; immigration legislation on, 48, 73, 173–74n106; impact on Smith family's emigration, 47–48

cookery and baking: at Christmas time, 64; in fiction, 149–51, 189n65; of HS, 111–12

cooperative stores, 58, 61, 64

Cote, Joseph, 66

cotton textile industry, American: automation in, 61; decline of, 92, 97–98; English expertise in, 71; Lancashire immigrants and activists in, 55, 61, 71, 72–73; southern factory practices in, 97–98

cotton textile industry, British: disrupted by war, 31; innovations in, 21; sexual division of labor in, 23–24; workers of, 7, 38

Cromwell, Tom (HS's friend), 44, 100, 102, 119

cultural conflicts: dialect as foil for, 127–28; fictional depiction of, 86–87; marriage as metaphor for bridging, 149–51; as underlying political loyalties, 134. *See also* class conflicts

cultures: assumptions about mainstream, 11–12; class action linked to transregional, 5–6; literature as bridge across, 122–23; marriage across, 81, 106, 108–9, 128–29, 149–51; transcultural ties across, 74–80; translocal perspective and, 80–81; of work, 102. *See also* Yankee culture; Yorkshire culture

Cumbler, John T., 71

Dalesman (Yorkshire periodical), 181n99

Davis, Rocío G., 147

Delius, Frederick, 29

Dewsbury (Yorkshire): textile industry of, 30

dialect, 177n50. *See also* West Yorkshire dialect
diaspora: of labor, 6, 83–84; of merchants, 28–29. *See also* labor migration
Dickens, Charles, 115, 125
Diner, Hasia, 46
domestic servants, 66
Dracup, Daniel, 21, 25
Dracup, John, 25
Dracup, Nathan, 25
Dracup, Samuel, 36
Dubofsky, Melvin, 74
East Germany (GDR): Brown University's program in, 122–23
economic context: Atlantic, components of, 5, 19; depression periods as, 15, 39, 51, 73, 98, 100–101; migration peak periods in, 41–43; of Smith family's migration, 46, 50; Yorkshire agrarian, 19–20. *See also* tariffs
education: assimilation in, 49–50; in Greystone, 64; Smith's view of, 101, 102; Yankee vs. Yorkshire views on, 124
e/im-migration concept, 156
emigration: approach to, 1–2, 153–54; cultural effects of, 120–21, 156–58; downward mobility in, 99–100, 101–2, 154; emotional context of, 153–54; grief and loss due to, 1, 99, 154–56, 158–60; patterns of, 5; resistance to assimilation and, 7–8, 14, 95–96, 152, 153–56; unexpressed rage and, 154, 159. *See also* labor migration
emotional context: alienated self in, 1–2; conflicts in, 34–35; hidden feelings in, 99; of immigration, 153–54; of mother-in-law/daughter-in-law relations, 108–10; political loyalties in, 133–34; self-control in, 114; sexual rituals and female power in, 126–27; of Smith family's migration, 46, 48–49; translocal as highlighting, 4; unexpressed rage in, 154; Yorkshire dialect and, 84–85. *See also* grief and loss
English Canadian immigrants: assumptions about, 13; destinations of, 41; in Greystone Village, 67; political context, 137; resistance to assimilation, 7–8, 155
English immigrants: Anglophilia utilized by, 115, 185n50; assumptions about, 6–7, 13; characteristics of, 15–16; in Greystone Village, 66–68, 67; identities of, 9–10, 11, 14; invisibility of, 6–10, 13, 57; labor activism of, 70–74; patterns of, 40–44, 46, 61; quota system for, 47, 173n101; resistance to assimilation, 14; as skilled textile workers, 56, 57, 60–61, 175n13; social organizations of, 58; sources on, 42; Spanish immigrants compared with, 65; transcultural labor politics of, 74–80; U.S. industrial system rejected by, 12, 68–70; WWI service of, 92, 182n123. *See also* Lancashire immigrants; Yorkshire immigrants
Englishness, 15, 81
Episcopalian faith, 65, 102, 120, 142
Erickson, Charlotte, 7, 41, 42, 178n56, 190n1
Esmond (R.I.): cooperative store of, 64; IWW local in, 76, 78, 79; location of, 54; strikes in, 78–79, 80, 180n80, 180n85
ethics of work, 42. *See also* work traditions, Yorkshire
ethnic fiction: concept of, 126–27; nondominant male writers of regionalist fiction and, 152, 189n70; regionalist focus in, 151–52; sexual politics in, 142–46; themes of, 147–51; transatlantic perspectives in, 127–39; women's strength and independence in, 139–42. *See also* fiction and fictional world; literature
ethnicity: as both lived and imagined, 9–10; dilemmas and complexities of, 9, 147, 157–58; as foe of assimilation, 14–16; group consciousness of, 7–8; organizations based in, 7, 12; regionalist fiction and, 151–52; of worsted workers in U.S., 56–57, 60–61, 66–68, 67, 157–58. *See also* ethnic fiction
ethnoculture concept, 13
Factory Acts (Britain, 1874), 24, 31
factory system. *See* industrial system, American; industrial system, British
fairness concept in work culture, 68–70
Fall River (Mass.): Lancashire immigrants and labor activists in, 71, 72–73
families: assumptions about data on, 110; breakup of, 108–10, 154, 159; "culture of work" and, 102; economic support of, 99–100; limiting size of, 35, 36; research on, 167n3; unexpressed rage in, 154, 159; as weavers, 76; WWI's effects on, 134–35. *See also* households
fiction and fictional world: autobiographical components of, 99; domineering male

characters in, 138–39; forced migration in, 6; on immigration decision, 62; landscape or locale of, 4, 54–55, 105–6, 176n22; lived and imagined blurred in, 9–10, 15–16, 52; opening into, 156–57; regionalist focus in, 151–52, 189n68; on second-generation immigrants, 121–22; sexual antagonisms in, 34–35; time encompassed by, 82, 83; transatlantic perspectives in, 127–39; women's strength and independence in, 33, 36. *See also* Briardale (fictional); ethnic fiction; literature; West Yorkshire dialect

Fischer, David, 11

Fitzgerald, Keith, 173n99

Foran Act (1885), 174n109

Foster, John (of Black Dyke mills), 31, 37

fowk: use of term, 6, 81, 85

Fowler, Carmen. *See* Smith, Carmen Fowler (HS's wife)

Fowler, Donald (Carmen's father), 103–4, 111

Fowler, Ethel (Carmen's mother), 103–4, *107*, 110–11

Fowler, Marshall (Carmen's brother), 102–3

France: all-wool manufacture in, 20, 36; commercial treaty with Britain, 28–29; U.S. textile industry investments of, 53; worsted workforce of, 52

Franco-Belgian immigrants to Woonsocket, 78

Franco-Prussian war (1870), 28, 31

French Canadian immigrants, 40, 56, 57, 66, *67*, 70

French immigrants, 56, 92, 182n123

Gabaccia, Donna: on emotional ties, 46; on Italian migrants, 180n82; on Sambucesi migrants, 81; on sexuality, 8, 88; transnational perspective of, 4, 163n19

Gath, J., 39–40

gender: labor migration and, 75–76; of textile workers in Britain, 23–25; in working-class life, 33–36; of worsted workers in U.S., 56–57, 66–68, *67. See also* sexual division of labor; sexuality and sexual relationships

Georgiaville (R.I.): IWW local in, 76; location of, *54*

Gerber, David A., 7, 9, 12, 100, 154

German immigrants: as Bradford merchants, 28–29; in Briardale fiction, 131–33;

English compared with, 41; in U.S. worsted industry, 56, 57

Germany: tariffs of, 37; U.S. textile industry investments of, 53, 55; worsted trade learned in, 29

Giaconnelli, P., 78

The Gift of Armor (novel, HS), 113–14

Gjerde, Jon, 15–16

global migration: analytical approach to, 3; post-WWI, 50, 158; regional fiction and, 151–52

Goff, Darius, 113

Goldberg, David, 74, 75

Golden, John, 76

Goldscheider, Calvin, 185n72

Goldsmith, Sidney, 185n72

Gordon, Milton, 10

Gorki Institute of World Literature, 123

Gorton, Samuel, 114

Graniteville (R.I.): cooperative store of, 64; location of, *54*; as sanctuary for strikers, 79

Graves, Robert, 136

Great Britain: commercial treaty with France, 28–29; cultural changes and divisions in, 11; military service in, 91; organic materials law in, 69; Pakistani immigrants in, 160; politics of, 31, 117; return migrants to, 40, 43, 95, 136, 161–62n6; textile workers' strike in, 22–23; U.S. compared with, 129; WWI as metaphor for decline of, 137–38. *See also* English Canadian immigrants; English immigrants; Irish immigrants; Scottish immigrants; *specific areas and towns*

Great Horton (Yorkshire): control of mill in, 58; diversification of, 37; location of, 30; references to, 61. *See also* Benn Company

"Greedy Guts" (novella, HS), 95–96

Greenway, Berneice (later Smith), *107*, 109

Greenwood, Fred, 180n85

Greenwood, John, 79

Greystone Cooperative, 64

Greystone Fanciers' Associations, 64

Greystone Honor Roll (WWI monument), 92, 137, 157, 182n123. *See also* "The Tongue-Tied Town" (Briardale Trilogy, Part 3, HS)

Greystone Methodist Church, 65. *See also* Singleton, John; Whitsuntide

Greystone Mill (R.I.), *60*; census statistics on, 66–67, 91; closure of, 175n20; development of, 58–59; dyers in, 104, 132; ethnicity of workers in, 60–61, 66–68, *67*, 157–58; fictional depiction of, 83–84, 86, 92; IWW local in, 76–78; labor unrest in, 68–70, 74; mill lads of, *143*; number employed in, 177n51; opening of, 59–60; ownership of, 58, 182n122; strikes in, 57, 69, 75, 76–77, 80; tops of mixed wool for, 40; as Yorkshire business in Yorkshire-style village, 147–49

Greystone Primitive Methodist Chapel, 63, 65

Greystone Social Club, 63, 64, 85, 102, 157

Greystone Textile Local, 76

Greystone Village (R.I.), *60*; Bradford compared with, 60, 61–62; buildings remaining in, 176n33; census statistics on, 66–68, *67*; community buildings of, 63–64; complexities of migration in, 52; context of, 57; cultural activities in, 58, 64–65; cultural flexibility in labor support of, 74; development of, 30, 53–54, 59; governance of, 176n35; housing in, 62, 76; location of, *54*; refusal to assimilate in, 14; religious organizations in, 63, 65; social circles in, 102–3; stores and businesses of, 61, 64; surroundings of, 63; WWI and aftermath in, 82–83, 90–96; WWI monument of, 92, 137, 157, 182n123; Yankees in, 61, 66, *67*, 104–5, 106. *See also* Briardale (fictional)

grief and loss: centrality of, 1, 99, 155–56; as fuel for creativity, 154; reflections on, 158–60; in translocal perspective, 4

Grimshaw, Rebecca, 176n34

Guerin, Joseph, 53

Gutman, Herbert G., 70–71

Halifax (Yorkshire): location of, *30*; migration from, 28; power source of, 18–19; textile industry of, 20, 30

Handlin, Oscar, 2, 12, 71, 88, 161n3

Hansen, Marcus Lee, 40, 124

Hardy, Thomas, 83, 109, 119, 128, 159

Harlo Press, 116, 185n58

Harrison, Felicity, 2

Harrisville (R.I.): textile strike in, 74

Hartley, John, 24

Henson, Dayton "Doc," 115

Herder, Johann Gottfried, 122

Hinchcliffe, Richard, 58

The History of Scituate, R.I. (HS), 116, 118, 189n55

Hobsbawn, Eric, 13

Hoerder, Dirk: e/im-migration concept of, 156; on English immigrants in Canada, 8; on English migrants, 41, 155; on global migration, 3; on kin concept, 8; on resistance strategies, 82; on sexuality, 88

Hoglund, A. William, 164n37

Holdsworth, Jane (later Collins, HS's grandmother), 24

holiday celebrations (Greystone), 64–65, 148

Holliday, Thomas, 74

Holmes, Fred (HS's uncle), 92, 93

Holmes, George (HS's great-uncle), 27

Holmes, Horace (HS's uncle), 92–93, 103, 137–38

Holmes, John (HS's great-grandfather), 26–27

Holmes, Mary (later Smith, HS's grandmother), 24, 25, 26, 27, 46, 47

households: census statistics on, 66–68, *67*; mid-twentieth-century economic struggles of, 97–99; woolcombing in, 22; worsted production in, 20–21. *See also* families

Howard, Robert, 179n74

HS. *See* Smith, Hedley (HS)

HS collection, University of Rhode Island, Kingston, 113, 124

Huddersfield (Yorkshire): power source of, 18–19; textile industry of, 30

Hull (Yorkshire): location of, *19*; seaport of, 17

"Hussy in the Well" (novel, HS), 112

Iacovetta, Franca, 180n82

immigrants: categories of, 1; characteristics of, 40–43; comparative approach to, 8–9, 142; correspondence with non-immigrants, 7, 100, 102; cultural effects of migration on, 120–21; disappointments of, 49–50; downward mobility of, 99–100, 101–2, 154; emotional context of, 153–54; identity and integration paradox for, 4–5; "new and old," 53; second generation of, 121–24; third generation of, 124–25. *See also* migrants; *specific immigrant groups*

immigration: U.S. restrictions on, 46–50; use of term, 153

Immigration Acts (U.S.), 47, 48, 173–74n106, 173n99
Immigration Commission, 56–57
incorporation (cultural concept), 13
industrial system, American: English immigrants' moves to counter, 70–74; English immigrants' rejection of, 12, 68–70; mid-twentieth-century changes in, 97–99; profits vs. political loyalties in, 130–31; racialized workers in, 77–78; rural deindustrialization concomitant with, 21; transatlantic investment in, 52–55; Yankee capitalist's use of, 187–88n27. *See also* tariffs
industrial system, British: Bradford class society and, 29–33; labor migration in, 26–29; shift to, 20–23; workforce for, 23–25
Industrial Workers of the World (IWW): government's ban of, 80; ideals continued, 80–82; transcultural politics of, 74–80
"The Invention of Ethnicity" (Conzen et al.), 12–13
Ireland: labor migration from, 23, 26, 27–28
Irish immigrants: autobiographical novels on, 136–37; in construction industry, 57; dismissal of, 107; English compared with, 40; English harassed by, 48, 50; in Greystone Village, 67; in U.S. worsted industry, 56
Isaac, Julius, xii
Italian immigrants: anti-IWW cards signed by, 80; comparative perspective on, 8–9; dismissal of, 107; in Greystone Village, 66, 67, 70; intercultural marriage of, 149; later immigrants compared with, 121–22; occupational challenges of, 101–2; racialization of, 77–81; Smith on, 81; tailoring business of, 61; transcultural ties forged in organizing of, 77–79; in U.S. worsted industry, 56, 57, 175n14; as working women, 180n80, 180n82; WWI service of, 92, 182n123
Ittmann, Karl, 23, 36
Jacobson, Matthew Frye, 5
James, Henry, 133
James II (king of England), 11
Jeremy, David J., 178n56
Jewett, Sarah Orne, 151
Jewish immigrants: comparative perspective on, 8–9; later immigrants compared with, 121; occupational challenges of, 101–2; second- and third-generation, 120; in U.S. worsted industry, 56. *See also* Smith, Judith E.
Jewish people: as migrant merchants, 28–29
jickey: as ethnic slur, 8, 77, 85
Jobs, Richard Ivan, 182n120
Johnston (R.I.): Greystone residents' move to, 91; location of, 54; Smith's family in, 99
Jones, Katherine W., 14. *See also* Anglophilia
Jones, Maldwyn, 40–41
Joseph Benn Ltd. *See* Benn Company
Jowett, F. W., 26
Keighley (Yorkshire): location of, 19; power source of, 18–19; textile industry of, 20, 30
Kennett, Arnold, 181n99
Kenny, Kevin, 142
Keralake, George, 59, 68
Kershaw, Squire, 68
kin concept, 8, 99, 101–2
"King George's Idea" (short story, HS), 93, 137–38, 149
King James Bible, 120
Kings' Royal Rifles Regiment, 92, 103
Labor Advocate (Providence Socialist newspaper), 80
labor diaspora concept, 6, 83–84
labor migration: ambivalence about, 95–96; as apolitical, 7; Bradford as example of, 26–29; choices in, 91, 182n120; conditions fostering, 23–25, 38–39; consequences of, in fiction, 88; as diaspora, 6, 83–84; medley of peoples in, 52; patterns of, 18, 40–43; transatlantic investment and, 52–55
labor movement: British textile workers in, 70–74; class-based agendas in, 7–8; male domination of, 33–36; mule spinners vs. weavers in, 178n63; multicultural nature of, 6; press of, 72–73. *See also* Industrial Workers of the World (IWW)
labor unrest: female networks in, 180n82; in Great Britain, 22–23, 38–39, 72; identity and community organizations linked to, 68–70; key sites in, 180n80; leadership in, 74, 81; political implications of, 107; repressive state actions against, 98; Smith's ambivalence about, 81–82, 86–87; transcultural ties in, 74–80; in U.S., 57, 69, 70, 74–75, 76–77, 78–80, 90–91, 180n80,

180n85; wages issues in, 73–74, 75; in WWI, 90–91. *See also* strikes

Lahiri, Jhumpa, 189n65

Lancashire: emigration from, 28, 42; return migrants of, 40, 73; spinning mills of, 20; strike in, 72; working women of, 35. *See also* cotton textile industry, British

Lancashire immigrants: labor activism of, 72–74. *See also* cotton textile industry, American

Lawrence, D. H., 90

Lawrence (Mass.): cooperative store in, 58; English visitor to, 51; ethnicity and gender of textile workers in, 56–57; female networks in, 180n82; IWW local in, 74; strikes in, 57, 75, 78, 90–91; transcultural ties in, 78, 79; wage rates in, 55; Yorkshire immigrants and labor activists in, 57–58, 71, 72–74. *See also* American Woolen Company (Lawrence)

Lawrence Journal (newspaper), 57–58, 72–73

Lawrence Worsted Mills, 57

Leeds (Yorkshire): foundry labor in, 26–27; location of, *19*; migration from, 28; power source of, 18–19; textile industry of, 18, 20, 30

legislation (U.S.): on contract labor, 60–61, 174n109; on immigration, 47, 48, 173–74n106, 173n99; on ten hours, 58, 72–73, 79–80

letters and letter writing, 7, 100, 102, 154

Lincolnshire: migration from, 28

Linden, Marcel van der, 5

Lindsay, Bruce, 116, 117–18, 119

"The Lion and the Eagle" (Briardale Trilogy, Part 2, HS): Anglo-phobic characters of, 12; autobiographical components of, 99; character prototypes for, 103; courtship in, 105–6; cultural contacts and conflicts in, 127–28; description of, 128–31; dialect use in, 85–86, 127–28; female power in, 127; German immigrants in, 131, 170n40; inspiration for, 32; intercultural marriage in, 151; nationalism in, 181n92; transatlantic politics in, 129–36; women's antagonism in, 139; on Yankee cooking, 111; on Yankee-Yorkshire tensions, 104–5

Lister, Samuel C., 37, 38, 39

literacy test, 46–47

literature: as cultural bridge, 122–23; natu-

ralism in, 189n69; regional, 151–52; short-story cycles in, 147–48; specificity of context of, 159–60; Victorian sentimental, 140–41; wage and chattel slavery critique in, 58; on WWI, 136–37. *See also* ethnic fiction; fiction and fictional world

Little, Royal, 187–88n27

Loriggio, Francesco, 189n68

Lowell (Mass.): Greystone residents' move to, 91; Lancashire immigrants in, 71, 72, 125

Lowell National Historical Park Museum, 186n88

Lowell Textile School, 48

Loyal Greystone Lodge of the Odd Fellows, Manchester, England United and auxiliary, 64

Luddites, 22, 32

Lusitania (ship), 136, 187n19

MacGill, Patrick, 136–37

Mahler, Sarah, 142, 146

Maine: as background of Fowler family, 103–4

Majestic (ship), 51

Majewski, Karen, 14–15, 127, 185n58

Manningham (Yorkshire): diversification of, 37; location of, *30*; textile strike in, 38–39

Margrave, David, 74–75

Marquand, J. P., 189n67

marriage: intercultural, 81, 106, 108–9, 128–29, 149–51; labor migration and, 87–88

masculinity: dismissal of, 88–89; fictional depiction of, 93; model of, 103; reclaiming of, 87–88

Massachusetts: class and ethnicity in, 189n67; Lancashire immigrants and labor activists in, 71, 72–73; mainstream culture of, 12; regional fiction of, 151; ten-hour day legislation in, 58, 72–73; textile production in, 47–48, 55–56. *See also* Lawrence (Mass.); Lowell (Mass.)

Mazziallo, Giullo, 78

Mazzucco, Melania, 121

McCarthy, Patrick J., 98

McDevitt, Patrick, 182n120

McKeown, Adam, 48

McKinley, William, 37–38, 39, 51–52. *See also* tariffs

McKusick, Marshall (father-in-law of Carmen's mother), 103, 110

men and boys: deference and accommodation of, 33–34; in industrial workforce,
23–25; as labor migrants, 41; "nondominant," 152, 189n70; "sunning" of, 142–46.
See also masculinity; *specific immigrant
groups*
merchant diaspora (Jewish), 28–29
Meredith, Scott, 115, 117
Methodism: English followers of, 25, 27;
in Greystone, 63, 65; HS's link to, 102–3,
106–7
microhistory concept, 3
middle class: in Bradford, 31–32; dialect as
persistent in, 85–86
migrants: baggage of, 17; comparative perspective on, 8–9; definition of, 154; refugees compared with, 3, 5–6. *See also* immigrants; labor migration
migration: approach to, 3; author's experience of, xi–xiii; global type of, 3, 50,
151–52, 158; industrialization linked to,
18; transnational and translocal in, 3–6.
See also emigration; immigration; labor
migration
military service, xii–xiii, 92, 103, 182n123
"The Mill Folk" (novel, HS): agent's rejection of, 117; domineering male character in, 138–39; housing in, 62; independence and adjustment in, 96; locale of,
20; sexual antagonisms in, 34–35, 139;
storytelling in, 83–84; sunning in, 142–46;
women's sexuality in, 88–89; on WWI
patriotism, 137
"The Millmaster" (Briardale Trilogy, Part 1,
HS): agent's rejection of, 117; domineering
male character in, 138; German immigrants in, 131; immigration problems in,
48; inspiration for, 32; labor protest in, 81
mill owners and managers: cost-cutting of,
38; diversification of, 37; investment and
assets of, 30, 43, 51–55, 58–59, 60, 70, 91,
147–48, 182n122; mill reorganization of,
39; on tariffs, 76–77. *See also* Benn Company; transatlantic capital investment
"Minnie Kettlewell's Husband" (short story,
HS), 81, 149
"Miriam Ainsworth" (novella, HS), 85, 89, 94
mobility: downward cycle of, 99–100, 101–2,
154; in England, 167n3; industrialization
linked to, 18

Moch, Leslie Page, 168n14
Moore, George, 119
More Yankee Yorkshiremen (collection, HS):
dedication of, 33; publication of, 2, 116;
stories of, 137; themes of, 147, 149–52;
women's strength and independence in,
139
Moser, Jacob, 28
Moya, Jose, 4–5, 65, 68, 153, 177n45
"Mr. Verein's Women" (novel. HS), 117
musical activities: in Bradford, 28, 29; in
Smith home, 119; of third generation, 125;
WWI patriotism and, 137
NAFTA (North American Free Trade
Agreement), 98
National Industrial Union of Textile Work-
ers (IWW), 78
nationalism in wartime, 82, 181n92. *See also*
World War I
National Jewelers Board of Trade (Provi-
dence), 99, 100
National Woolsorters Union (Bradford), 69
nation and nation-states: limits of, 6; pro-
tectionist policies of, 37–38, 51–52, 55;
stepping outside category of, 4–5. *See
also* nationalism in wartime; patriotism;
tariffs
naturalization, 67–68, 69, 100, 155. *See also*
citizenship
Naturalization and Immigration Service, 68
Nee, Victor, 10–11
New England: regionalist fiction of, 151–52.
See also specific towns and states
New Jersey: worsted industry in (Passaic),
53, 55, 56. *See also* Paterson (N.J.); transatlantic capital investment
New York: Yorkshire immigrants in, 27
New York, New Haven and Hartford Railroad, 59, 60
New Zealand: English migration to, 41, 43
North American Free Trade Agreement
(NAFTA), 98
North Carolina: textile industry of, 98
North Chelmsford (Mass.): woolcombing
operation in, 47–48
North Providence (R.I.): Benn operation in,
5; ethnicity and gender of textile work-
ers in, 56, 66–68, 67; labor organizing in,
74–82; map of, 54; real estate development
in, 9; Smith family in, 83; stories told in,

8; strikes in, 57, 69, 70; tax exemptions in, 58; transatlantic politics in, 156–57; West Riding as translocal match to, 4; WWI population changes in, 91. *See also* Greystone Mill (R.I.); Greystone Village (R.I.)

North Scituate (R.I.): HS's history of, 116, 118, 189n55; location of, *54*; Smiths' home in, 114–16

Norwich (East Anglia): labor migration from, 23; worsted industry of, 17, 18

Nugent, Walter, 41

Oak Mills (Benn spinning operation), 29–30

Olneyville (R.I.): IWW local in, 78; transcultural alliances in, 79–80

"One Escaped" (novel, HS), 117

"Outward Show" (collection, HS), 95–96

Pakistani immigrants (in Bradford), 160

Parkinson, Mary (later Collins, HS's stepgrandmother), 24

"The Partnership" (short story, HS), 149–50

Passaic (N.J.): worsted industry in, 53, 55, 56. *See also* transatlantic capital investment

Pastore, John O., 113

paternalist ideology (Yorkshire), 33–36

Paterson (N.J.): cross-cultural ties in, 77; labor organizing and strike in, 74–75, 77, 80; silk textile industry in, 53. *See also* transatlantic capital investment

patriarchy: in labor movement, 33–36; women's sexual customs as challenge to, 142–46

patriotism: anti-English colonial, 11; in Briardale, 134–35, 137–38

Peace Dale (R.I.): strike at, 80, 84

Pell, Claiborne, 123

Pennsylvania: textile production in, 55–56. *See also* Philadelphia (Pa.)

Pessar, Patricia, 142, 146

Philadelphia (Pa.): English visitor to, 51; ethnicity and gender of textile workers in, 56; Lancashire immigrants in, 71; Yorkshire immigrants in, 38–39, 73

Polish immigrants: political writings of, 127, 185n58; in U.S. worsted industry, 56

political context: ambivalence about, 127, 156–57; apolitical migration and, 7; emotions and loyalties juxtaposed to, 133–34; immigrant issues and depression in, 107; political party shifts in (R.I.), 98–99, 113;

of son's career, 122–23; wartime patriotism in, 134–35, 137–38

Poor Law (British), 26

Portes, Alejandro, 7

Preston (Lancashire): strike in, 72

Priestley, J. B., 27, 28, 144–45. *See also* "sunning" ritual

Providence (R.I.): Anglo-phobia in, 12; first foreign-born mayor of, 98; German immigrants in, 131; high school in, 112, 122, 139; industrial development of, 97; location of, *54*; Smiths' arrival in, 48–50; textile technology and investment in, 55; West Riding as translocal match to, 4. *See also* North Providence (R.I.)

Pryse, Marjorie, 152

Queensbury (Yorkshire): location of, *30*

Quota Act (1924), 47

rape in Belgium cotton mills, 145

raw wool market, 39, 132

rayon mills, 98. *See also* transatlantic capital investment

refugees as migrants, 3, 5–6

regionalist fiction, 151–52, 189n68

religious context, 107–8. *See also* Catholicism; Episcopalian faith; Methodism

resistance: to assimilation, 7–8, 14, 95–96, 152, 153–56; to paternalism, 34–35; strategies in, 82. *See also* labor unrest; strikes

Rhode Island: changing economic and political climate of, 97–99; colonial period in, 11; ethnic groups in, 164n37; historical novels about, 113–14, 115; hours agitation and law in, 73, 79–80; industrial development of, 52–55; IWW locals in, 76, 78, 79; labor movement in, 5, 74; map of, *54*; regional fiction of, 151–52; worsted worker discontent in, 73–74; WWI population changes in, 91; Yorkshire immigrants in, 8, 38. *See also* Centredale (R.I.); Greystone Village (R.I.); North Providence (R.I.); North Scituate (R.I.); Providence (R.I.); Warwick (R.I.)

Rhode Island Company (trolley), 59

Rhode Island Department of State Library Services, 118

Rhode Island Heritage Commission, 7

Rhode Island Normal School, 104

Richard Curtis Agency, 117

Riding: use of term, 167–68n5. *See also* West Riding (Yorkshire)

Roberts, Elizabeth, 86

Rochdale plan, 58. *See also* cooperative stores

Roediger, David, 78

Roosevelt, Franklin D., 107

Rössler, Horst, 71

Rostock University (GDR), 122–23

Ruerat, Albert P., 107, *107*, 108, 113

Rumbaut, Rubén G., 7, 121

Russian Jewish immigrants as worsted workers, 56–57, 101–2. *See also* Smith, Judith E.

Salt, Titus, 31, 34, 37, 39. *See also* Titus Salt and Sons (Yorkshire)

Saltaire (Yorkshire): location of, *30*. *See also* Salt, Titus; Titus Salt and Sons (Yorkshire)

Scottish immigrants to U.S. textile industries, 56, 57, 67, 154

sexual division of labor: antagonisms in, 33–36; industrialization and changes in, 23–24; labor migration and, 75–76; sunning ritual and, 142–46

sexuality and sexual relationships: anxieties about, 106; effects of WWI on, 135–36; of female migrants, 8, 88–90; frankness about, 87, 138, 148; sunning ritual and women's power in, 142–46; women's experimentation in, 35, 106; WWI celebrations and, 137; Yorkshire expectations about, 89–90

Shann, Bill, 47–48

Sharp, Horace (HS's friend), 44, 100, 102

Sheldon, Frank P., 58, 60

Shepperton, Wilbur S., 161–62n6

Shipley (Yorkshire): location of, *30*

short-story cycles, 147–48, 151–52

"Th' Short Timer" (Hartley), 24

Sigsworth, E. M., 52–53

silk textile industry, American, 53, 74–75, 80, 92. *See also* Paterson (N.J.)

silk textile industry, British, *30*, 37–39

Singleton, John, 65, 91

"Sinners Corner" (novel, HS), 11, 117, 159

Sisti, Al, 81

Slater, Samuel, 178n56

slavery, 58

Smith, Alice Collins (HS's mother), *45, 107*; background of, 43–44; daughter-in-law's relationship with, 108–9, 184n28; death of, 109; disappointments of, 154; family relations of, 110; literacy and knowledge of, 101; marriage of, 35, 43; migration of, 39, 46; naturalization of, 100; as weaver, 25, 33, 36, 59, 102, 124; work in U.S., 48, 99

Smith, Berneice Greenway, *107*, 109

Smith, Carmen Fowler (HS's wife), *107*; background of, 103–4; characteristics of, 110–11; courtship and marriage of, 89, 103, 105, *107*, 107–8, 113, 114, 115, 118, 128; death of, 119, 159; education of, 104; family relations of, 110, 159; HS's manuscripts read by, 112; marital tensions of, 113, 114, 115, 116; mother-in-law's relationship with, 108–9, 184n28

Smith, Duncan (HS's son): assistance of, xiii–xiv, 81; author's interview of, 2; birth of, 108; career of, 115–16, 122, 186n82; children of, 186n75; education of, 112–13; on father, 114, 115, 120, 136, 158–59; father's writing shared with, 117; on grandparents, 101, 109, 184n28; on literary criticism, 147; on mother, 110, 111, 159, 173n88; religious interests of, 142; Rostock Program of, 122–23; as second and third generation, 121, 122–23; tenure fight of, 113–16; visits to Yorkshire, 118, 119, 122–23, 124; on women, 146; writing of, 123, 186n84

Smith, Duncan A. (Duncan's son), 125

Smith, Ernest S. (HS's father), *45, 107*; appearance of, 44; apprenticeship of, 43; birth of, 27; death of, 109; disappointments of, 154, 156; family relations of, 110, 159; grandchildren and, 108, 109, 124; literacy and knowledge of, 101, 117; marriage of, 35, 43; migration of, 5–6, 39, 46; naturalization of, 100; occupation and job skills of, 25, 47–49, 50, 124; work in U.S., 99; WWI and, 126, 136

Smith, Hedley (HS), *iii, 45, 107*; ambivalences of, 81–82, 86–87, 95–96, 127, 137–38, 156–57; author's reflections on, 119–20; background of, 5–6, 156–57; British Labour Party and, 117; characteristics of, 1–2; childhood in Bradford, 44, 46; children of, 111–12; circle of, 100, 102–3,

106–7; courtship and marriage of, 89, 103, 105, *107*, 107–8, 113, 114, 115, 118, 128; death of, 119; economic and political context of, 97–99; education of, 49–50, 101, 102, 113; ethnicity of, 147, 157–58, 158; forbears of, 21, 23, 24–25, 26–27; grief and loss of, 158–60; as "involuntary exile" and "separated man," 2, 10, 118, 121, 154–57; literary interests of, 22, 31–32, 33, 44, 46, 100, 105, 109, 115, 117–18, 119, 125, 127, 136–37, 145, 146, 159; migration of, 46, 47, 82; naturalization of, 100; older years of, 118–19; privacy of, 9, 16; religious interests of, 65, 102, 120, 142; satisfactions of, 118–19; self-identification of, 77–78; sexual rituals and female power as interests of, 126–27, 146; significance of, 13; sources on, 2–3; work life of, 99–102, 107, 108, 113–16; writings: autobiography, 117–18; goals of, 84, 90, 127, 148; habits of, 100, 112, 115, 116–17, 154; HS on, 83, 87, 133; list of, 2, 191–92; regional aspects of, 151–52; shared with son, 117. *See also* Briardale (fictional); fiction and fictional world; HS collection, University of Rhode Island, Kingston; *specific works*

Smith, Judith E., 8, 99, 101–2, 109. *See also* Italian immigrants; Russian Jewish immigrants as worsted workers

Smith, Mary Holmes (HS's grandmother), 24, 25, 26, 27, 46, 47

Smith, Portia. *See* Thompson, Portia Smith (HS's daughter)

Smith, Sam (HS's brother), *107*; apprenticeship of, 5, 49; birth of, 35; career of, 49, 101; childhood of, 25; childlessness of, 121; circle of, 100, 102–3; death of, 119; disappointments of, 154; education of, 46, 48–49; family relations of, 110, 124, 159; marriage of, 109; migration of, 46; naturalization of, 100, 155; visit to England, 101

Smith, Sam (HS's grandfather), 25, 27, 43, 156

Smith family: breakup of, 108–10, 154, 159; cats of, 116, 119; cultural effects of migration on, 120–21, 156–57; homage to strong women of, 139, 142; immigration restrictions and, 46–50; library of, 101; migration patterns of, 43–44, 46

social class: in Bradford, 29–33; cooperation in interests of, 77–78; dialect as highlighting, 85–86; labor agendas based in, 7–8; labor unrest and organizations linked to, 68–70. *See also* middle class; working class

Socialist Party, 80

social organizations: ethnicity-based, 7, 12, 58, 63–64, 85, 102, 157; identity and labor unrest linked to, 68–70; role in immigrant lives, 177n45

Sollors, Werner, 14–15

Soviet Union (USSR): son's visiting professorship in, 123; "Uprooted" published in, 118

Spanish immigrants to Argentina, 4–5, 65, 153

Spickard, Paul, 7

Spielhagen, Frederich, 119

spinning: production changes in worsted, 20–22, 23–24; specialization in, 29–30

"The Spinster of Paradise Row" (novella, HS), 118, 150–51

"Squire Widdop's Wooing" (short story, HS), 141–42, 188n31

St. Alban's Anglican Church (Bradford), 102, 142

steam power, 21

storytelling, 83–84. *See also* fiction and fictional world

Stott, Richard, 42

strikes: Bradford (1824–25), 22–23; Bradford (1913), 77; Bristol (1910s), 74; Britain general (1926), 32–33; Centredale (1913), 79–80; Esmond (1913), 78–79, 80, 180n80, 180n85; Greystone (1906), 69; Greystone (1907), 69, 70; Greystone (1910), 57, 70; Greystone (1912), 75, 76; Greystone (1913), 80; Harrisville (1910s), 74; Lawrence (1912), 57, 75, 78; Lawrence (1919), 90–91; Manningham (1890–91), 38–39; Paterson (1913), 74–75, 77, 80; Peace Dale (1913), 80; Peace Dale (1910s), 74; Preston (1853–54), 72; textile industry (1934), 81–82, 98. *See also* labor unrest

Strikwerda, Carl, 37, 50

"Stubborn Saint" (novel, HS), 115

"sunning" ritual, 142–46. *See also* Priestley, J. B.

Swaledale (Yorkshire): sublocal economy of, 18

Swearer, Howard, 123

Tariff Commission, 39–40

The University of Illinois Press
is a founding member of the
Association of American University Presses.

———————————————————————

Composed in 10.5/13 Adobe Minion Pro
with Meta display
by Jim Proefrock
at the University of Illinois Press
Manufactured by Cushing-Malloy, Inc.

University of Illinois Press
1325 South Oak Street
Champaign, IL 61820-6903
www.press.uillinois.edu

STUDIES OF WORLD MIGRATIONS

The Immigrant Threat: The Integration of Old and New Migrants
in Western Europe Since 1850   *Leo Lucassen*
Citizenship and Those Who Leave: The Politics of Emigration
and Expatriation   *Edited by Nancy L. Green and François Weil*
Migration, Class, and Transnational Identities: Croatians in
Australia and America   *Val Colic-Peisker*
The Yankee Yorkshireman: Migration Lived and Imagined
Mary H. Blewett

MARY BLEWETT has written articles and books on the labor and social history of New England industry, including the prize-winning *Men, Women and Work* (1988), *The Last Generation* (1990), and *Constant Turmoil: The Politics of Industrial Life in Nineteenth-Century New England* (2000). The use of ethnic fiction in *The Yankee Yorkshireman* explores the interconnections between imagined experience and empirical data. Her future research interests include nineteenth-century labor migration and material culture, specifically the production, transport, installation, and design of granite stones in the streets of many American cities on the East Coast.

74; labor activism of, 68–70, 72–74; links with past maintained by, 8; newspaper of, 57–58; as refusing to settle-in, 14–16; single mother as, 139–40; transcultural labor politics of, 77–82; WWI relocations of, 91; Yankees' tensions with, 137–38. *See also* Briardale (fictional); Greystone Village (R.I.); Smith, Hedley (HS); Yankee Yorkshiremen and Yorkshirewomen

Young Women's Christian Association (YWCA, Providence), 64

tions after, 50, 158; Greystone participants in, 91–92; literature on, 136–37; memorial of, 92, 137, 157, 182n123; as metaphor for England's decline, 137–38; as metaphor of identity, 126; outbreak of, 77; transatlantic effects of, 127–39; transcultural ties disrupted by, 82; U.S. nativism in, 47. *See also* "The Lion and the Eagle" (Briardale Trilogy, Part 2, HS); "The Tongue-Tied Town" (Briardale Trilogy, Part 3, HS)

World War II, 102, 128. *See also* Warwick (R.I.)

worsted industry, American: decline of, 97; English visitor's evaluation of, 51; ethnicity and gender of workers in, 56–57, 66–68, *67*; imported supplies for, 59–60; occupations listed on census, 68, 177n42; skilled English workers in (Lawrence), 60–61; transatlantic ties in, 52–55, 127–39, 147–49, 152, 156–57; as transnational player, 5; in WWI, 90–96, 158. *See also* Greystone Mill (R.I.); transatlantic capital investment; *specific locations*

worsted industry, British: decline of, 52–53; diversification in, 37; industrial development of, 17, 18–20; locale of, 17, *30*; materials for, 19, 39, 40, 69; McKinley and Dingley tariffs and, 37–40, 51–53; production changes in, 20–21, 20–23; slow unionization in, 75. *See also* Bradford (Yorkshire)

Worstedopolis: use of term, 20

worsted trade, British: Bradford businesses in, 28–29; disruption in, 31; exports to U.S., 51, 52–53; market protectionism in, 37–40, 51–52, 55; types of, 20, 40; U.S. branch operations of, 37, 51

Writers' Union of the USSR, 118

Yankee culture: defiance of, 2; disdain for, 7, 9, 14, 77–78; pride in, 104; WWI and politics in, 131–32. *See also* Smith, Alice Collins (HS's mother); Smith, Carmen Fowler (HS's wife)

Yankeeland: use of term, 158

Yankees: cooking of, 111; disdain for bodies of, 89; dislike and avoidance of, 85; ethnicity of, 151; as fictional characters, 94–95, 147; in Greystone Village, 61, 66, *67*, 104–5, 106; use of term, 7–8; Yorkshire migrants' tensions with, 137–38; Yorkshire workers' relationship with, 57

The Yankee Yorkshireman (collection, HS): on decline of mill villages, 118; publication of, 2, 115; Smith's description of, 87; themes of, 147, 148–49

Yankee Yorkshiremen and Yorkshirewomen: basis for, 8; as doubled identity, 147, 158; in ethnic fiction, 147–52; use of term, 1, 157–58. *See also* Yorkshire immigrants

Yankee Yorkshirewomen (novella, HS): ambivalence about war in, 137–38; daughter's role in, 124; publication of, 2, 116; skills highlighted in, 33; themes of, 147; women's strength and independence in, 139, 140–41; Yorkshire response to, 118

"Yankee Yorkshire Yesterdays" (projected short story collection, HS), 176n22

Yates, William, 74

Yorkshire: as capital of worsted trade, 17; cooking of, 111–12; emigration from, 42; exports from, 37, 51–53; ideal of female beauty in, 89, 138; industrial decline in, 36–40; labor migration in, 23–25; map of, *19*; pregnancy and marriage in, 35–36; strikes in, 22–23, 38–39, 39–40, 77; women's strength and independence in, 139–42; worsted industrialization in, 18–20; worsted production changes in, 20–23. *See also* Yankee Yorkshiremen and Yorkshirewomen; Yorkshire culture; *specific areas and towns*

Yorkshire culture: affirmation and defense of, 2, 9, 14; community events based in, 64–65; disdain for, 104; emotions repressed in, 153–54; loyalty to, 15; "right" women in, 146; teas (regular and knife and fork) in, 63, 151; work traditions in, 68, 70–71, *72*, 75

Yorkshire Factory Times (Bradford, Yorkshire, periodical), 39, 70

Yorkshire immigrants: as abstaining from whiteness, 78; ambivalence about WWI, 137–38; assimilation rejected by, 10–14; comparative perspective on, 8–9; definition of, 14; downward mobility of, 99–100; endurance of, 53, 99; ethnic slur for, 8, 77, 85; homesickness and perseverance of, 83–84, 109; HS's perspective on, 156–57; intercultural marriages of, 81, 106, 108–9, 128–29, 149–51; as IWW leaders,

United Textile Workers of the World (IWW), 76, 179n74
University of Bradford (Yorkshire), 123, 125
University of Rhode Island, 113, 124
uprooted, the, 2, 161n3. *See also* Handlin, Oscar
"Uprooted" (short story, HS), 87, 88, 118
Urnov, Dmitri, 118
U.S. Department of Labor, 47
U.S. Immigration Service, 48, 50
U.S. Information Agency, 123
UTW (United Textile Workers, AFL affiliate), 74, 76, 79
Vantage Press, 114
Van Vugt, William, 7
Vecoli, Rudolph J., 9–10, 11–12, 71, 180n88
Velva bread, 149–51. *See also* cookery and baking; "The Partnership" (short story, HS)
Victoria (queen of England), 29
Vinsun, Dennis, xii–xiii
wages: cutting of, 38; regional standards in U.S., 55, 73–74; strikes due to, 75, 78–80; wartime inflation and, 90–91
Warwick (R.I.): bakery near, 112; English sister city of, 128; Episcopal church in, 142; high school in, 112; historical novel about, 113–14; HS's employment in, 107, 108; location of, *54*; mayoral election in, 107; Methodist church in, 102–3, 106–7; Native American remnants in, 125; political changes in, 113; Smiths' homes in, 100, 108; social circle in, 102–3, 106–7
weavers: changing demographics of, 75–76; grievances of, 69; as industrial workforce, 23–25; production changes for, 20–22; strike of, 22–23
Wensleydale (Yorkshire): sublocal economy of, 18
Wesley, John, 25, 27
West Riding (Yorkshire): map of, *19*; McKinley and Dingley tariffs and, 37–40, 51–53; migration to and from, 26–29; Providence as translocal match to, 4; spinning mills in, 21; worsted industrialization in, 18–20; worsted production changes in, 20–23. *See also* Bradford (Yorkshire)
West Yorkshire dialect: Benn company hoax

in, 70; examples of, 6, 81, 84; as foil for cultural contacts and conflicts, 127–28; poetry in, 24; preservation of, 84–85, 159–60; social class and, 31, 85–86; usage of, 164n30; variations in, 181n99
Whitehall Building (Greystone), 63, *64*. *See also* Greystone Social Club
Whitehouse, Herbert, 78, 79
whiteness, 78, 81
Whitsuntide, 65, 148
Widdis, R. W., 7–8
Wilde, Bart De, 188n46
Williams, Roger, 115
Wilsden (Yorkshire): location of, *30*; as weaving village, 20. *See also* "The Mill Folk" (novel, HS)
Winifredian (ship), 99, 128
"The Wise Child" (short story, HS), 139–40, 149
women and girls: female networks of, 86–87, 180n82; ideal Yorkshire type of, 89, 138; independence and adjustment of, 96; labor migration of, 26–28, 41; in Manningham strike, 38–39; pregnancy and marriage in Yorkshire, 35–36; resistance to paternalism, 34–35; "sense of place" of, 86–87; strength and independence of, 139–42; "sunning" ritual of, 142–46; WWI work of, 135; as Yorkshire weavers, 23, 25, 33, 36, 59, 102, 124. *See also* sexual division of labor; sexuality and sexual relationships
woolcombers: displacement of, 23–24, 26–27; HS's forbear as, 26; strike of (1825), 22–23; tasks of, 21, 22; U.S. employment of, 47–48
wool sorters, 69, 177n42. *See also* strikes
Woonsocket (R.I.): Franco-Belgian immigrants to, 78; worsted industry in, 53, 55. *See also* transatlantic capital investment
working class: burden of cost-cutting on, 38; dialect as distinguishing, 85–86; gender antagonism and, 33–36
Working Men's Club (Greystone), 64
work traditions, Yorkshire: demand for maintaining, 70–71; fairness in, 68; labor protest in, 72; slow unionization in, 75
World War I: data and fiction on, compared, 90–96; "Englishness" in, 15; global migra-

tariffs: elimination of, 98; German protectionism and, 37; hearings on, 39–40; of McKinley and Dingley, 37–40, 51–53; mill owner's response to, 76–77; shifting views of Benn on, 70; U.S. protectionism and, 55, 70; working-class attitudes toward, 83
ten-hour legislation, 58, 72–73, 79–80
textile industry, American: adaptation to U.S. system in, 70–71; decline of, 97–98, 117; economic downturns in, 15; investment in, 51–55; profits vs. political loyalties in, 130–31; in silk, 53, 74–75, 80, 92; value of, by states, 55–56. *See also* cotton textile industry, American; textile workers, American; worsted industry, American; *specific locations*
textile industry, British: Bradford class society and, 29–33; decline of, 117; mule spinning frames in, 36; in silk, *30*, 37–39. *See also* cotton textile industry, British; textile workers, British; worsted industry, British; *specific locations*
Textile Manufacturer (Manchester, England, periodical), 38
textile workers, American: alliances among, 74; boys' beginning as, 143–46; British labor activists among, 70–74; defense of women as, 141–42; native-born workers as, 71–74; organizations of, 72–73; southern conditions for, 97–98; WWI shortage of, 90–91; young group of, *143*. *See also* labor unrest; strikes; wages
textile workers, British: characteristics of, 23–25, 55; compulsory overtime for, 37–38; forced migration of, 6; gender antagonisms among, 33–36; migration to and from Bradford, 26–29; strikes of, 22–23, 32–33, 38–39, 77. *See also* Lancashire immigrants; spinning; weavers; woolcombers; wool sorters; Yorkshire immigrants
There WAS a Cat in Bethlehem (HS and granddaughter), 116
Thistlewaite, Frank, 5
Thomas, Brinley, 42–43, 47, 61, 190n1
Thompson, Andrew Leslie (Portia and Leslie's son), 124, 125
Thompson, John A. (Portia and Leslie's son), 124–25, 186n88
Thompson, Leslie (Portia's husband), 113, 114, 124, 186n75

Thompson, Portia Smith (HS's daughter): assistance of, xiii–xiv, 169n32; author's interview of, 2; birth of, 108; children of, 186n75; education of, 112, 124; family relations of, 159; on father, 89, 114; gift for, 119; on grandparents, 101, 109; marriage and home of, 113, 114; on mother, 89, 110, 111; as second and third generation, 121, 123–24; visits to Yorkshire, 119, 124; writing of, 116
Tichenor, Daniel J., 173n99
Titus Salt and Sons (Yorkshire), 20, *30*, 37, 39, 51. *See also* Salt, Titus
"The Tongue-Tied Town" (Briardale Trilogy, Part 3, HS): German immigrants in, 170n40; inspiration for, 32; outsiders in, 106; WWI in, 92, 93–94, 137; WWI memorial and, 92, 137, 157, 182n123
Topp, Michael, 82
transatlantic capital investment: by Benn Company (of Yorkshire), 53–54, 58–59, 60, 70, 91, 147–48, 182n122; labor migration and, 52–55; in U.S. worsted industry, 127–39, 147–49, 152, 156–57. *See also* silk textile industry, American
transatlantic ties: in Briardale fiction, 127–39, 147–49, 152; effects on individuals, 156–57; political and cultural dimensions of, 126–27; sunning ritual in context of, 144–46; textile investments as, 52–55, 98
translocal perspective: components of, 3–6; HS's fiction in, 152; transcultural ties as reinforcing, 80–81
transnational perspective: components of, 3–6; wartime strengthening of, 82
transplanted, the, 1, 161n3. *See also* Bodnar, John
Truman, Harry, 113
Turgenev, Ivan, 119, 127
Underwood Act, 70, 77. *See also* Benn, Harrison
United States: British investments in, 30, 43, 52–55; England compared with, 129; English migration to, 41, 43; immigration restrictions of, 46–50; return migrants from, 43. *See also* assimilation; legislation (U.S.); tariffs
United Textile Workers (UTW, AFL affiliate), 74, 76, 79